HUMANITARIAN INTERVENTION

NOMOS
XLVII

NOMOS

Harvard University Press
I   *Authority* 1958, reissued in 1982 by Greenwood Press

The Liberal Arts Press
II   *Community* 1959
III   *Responsibility* 1960

Atherton Press
IV   *Liberty* 1962
V   *The Public Interest* 1962
VI   *Justice* 1963, reissued in 1974
VII   *Rational Decision* 1964
VIII   *Revolution* 1966
IX   *Equality* 1967
X   *Representation* 1968
XI   *Voluntary Associations* 1969
XII   *Political and Legal Obligation* 1970
XIII   *Privacy* 1971

Aldine-Atherton Press
XIV   *Coercion* 1972

Lieber-Atherton Press
XV   *The Limits of Law* 1974
XVI   *Participation in Politics* 1975

New York University Press
XVII   *Human Nature in Politics* 1977
XVIII   *Due Process* 1977
XIX   *Anarchism* 1978
XX   *Constitutionalism* 1979
XXI   *Compromise in Ethics, Law, and Politics* 1979
XXII   *Property* 1980
XXIII   *Human Rights* 1981
XXIV   *Ethics, Economics, and the Law* 1982
XXVI   *Marxism* 1983
XXVII   *Criminal Justice* 1985

NOMOS XLVII
Yearbook of the American Society for Political and Legal Philosophy

HUMANITARIAN INTERVENTION

Edited by

Terry Nardin
and
Melissa S. Williams

NEW YORK UNIVERSITY PRESS • *New York and London*

NEW YORK UNIVERSITY PRESS
New York and London
www.nyupress.org

Library of Congress Cataloging-in-Publication Data
Humanitarian intervention / edited by Terry Nardin and
Melissa S. Williams.
p.   cm. — (Nomos ; 47)
"Emerged from the papers and commentaries presented at the
Annual Meeting of the American Society for Political and Legal
Philosophy (ASPLP), held in conjunction with the American Political
Science Association meetings in Boston in September 2002"—Pref.
Includes bibliographical references and index.
ISBN-13: 978-0-8147-5831-1 (cloth : alk. paper)
ISBN-10: 0-8147-5831-2 (cloth : alk. paper)
1. Humanitarian intervention—Congresses.   I. Nardin, Terry, 1942–
II. Williams, Melissa S., 1960– III. American Society for Political and
Legal Philosophy. Meeting (2002 : Boston, Mass.) IV. Series.
KZ6369.H858 2005
341.5'84—dc22   2005015601

New York University Press books are printed on acid-free paper,
and their binding materials are chosen for strength and durability.

Manufactured in the United States of America
10 9 8 7 6 5 4 3 2 1

CONTENTS

PREFACE

This forty-seventh volume of NOMOS emerged from the papers and commentaries presented at the annual meeting of the American Society for Political and Legal Philosophy (ASPLP), held in conjunction with the American Political Science Association meetings in Boston in September 2002. The topic "Humanitarian Intervention" was selected by ballot by the membership of the Society.

I am deeply grateful to Terry Nardin for agreeing to join me in organizing the conference and editing this volume. He has dedicated a considerable portion of his ample talent and scarce time to bringing it together. Beyond the organization of the conference, he recruited excellent contributions to round out the volume and gave insightful critical feedback to each of our authors. In addition to writing the Introduction, he took the lead role in editing this collection. It has been a privilege to work with him.

Joseph Boyle, Thomas Franck, and Pratap Bhanu Mehta presented the three principal papers at the conference, each of which provided rich content for discussion. The discussion was further enriched by the thoughtful commentary offered by Stanley Hoffmann and Sohail Hashmi (on Boyle), Thomas Pogge and Catherine Lu (on Franck), and Anne-Marie Slaughter and Kok-Chor Tan (on Mehta). Terry and I extend our sincere thanks to all the conference participants (including ASPLP members who attended the sessions) for an exceptionally stimulating event. The original authors, together with the additional contributors to the volume, have tolerated the demands of production with admirable patience and good humor. We are delighted with the result, which we believe adds to previous debates on humanitarian intervention in novel and important ways.

We also wish to thank Rosemary Nagy for her superlative work as managing editor of the volume. She began this work while completing her doctorate in political science at the University of Toronto, and continued while also juggling the demands of becoming Assistant Professor in the Department of Law at Carleton University in Ottawa. We are tremendously grateful to her for staying on to see the volume through to completion.

The work of producing the volume has been shared by several people who also deserve our thanks. As she did for our previous volume, Catherine Connors has created a fine index. The editorial team at New York University Press, in particular Despina Papazoglou Gimbel and Salwa Jabado, have once again demonstrated their professionalism and high standards in supporting us through production. Since the publication of *Political Exclusion and Domination* (NOMOS XLVI, December 2004), Ilene Kalish has joined the Press as our editor. She has expressed a keen enthusiasm for the NOMOS series, and I very much look forward to working with her over the coming years.

Finally, a word of thanks to Jacob Levy, who serves as secretary-treasurer of the Society, for his conscientious management of the Society's affairs, for his participation in this and subsequent conferences, and for bringing the ASPLP into the twenty-first century by creating a Web site, available at http://www.political-theory.org/asplp.html.

MELISSA S. WILLIAMS

CONTRIBUTORS

CARLA BAGNOLI
Associate Professor of Philosophy, University of Wisconsin–Milwaukee

JOSEPH BOYLE
Professor of Philosophy, University of Toronto

ANTHONY COATES
Lecturer in Politics and International Relations, University of Reading

THOMAS FRANCK
Murray and Ida Becker Professor of Law Emeritus, New York University School of Law

BRIAN D. LEPARD
Professor of Law, University of Nebraska College of Law

CATHERINE LU
Assistant Professor of Political Science, McGill University

PRATAP BHANU MEHTA
President, Center for Policy Research, New Delhi, India

TERRY NARDIN
UWM Distinguished Professor of Political Science, University of Wisconsin–Milwaukee

THOMAS POGGE
Professional Fellow, Centre for Applied Philosophy and Public Ethics, Australian University; Professor of Philosophy, Columbia University, and (part-time) University of Oslo

KOK-CHOR TAN
  Assistant Professor of Philosophy, University of Pennsylvania

MELISSA S. WILLIAMS
  Associate Professor of Political Science, University of Toronto

INTRODUCTION

TERRY NARDIN

Intervention is the exercise of authority by one state within the jurisdiction of another state, but without its permission. We speak of armed intervention when that exercise involves the use of military force. An armed intervention is humanitarian when its aim is to protect innocent people who are not nationals of the intervening state from violence perpetrated or permitted by the government of the target state. Although humanitarian activists sometimes call their work of providing economic, medical, or other assistance humanitarian intervention, such assistance is normally provided with the permission of the local authorities and therefore raises questions different from those raised by armed intervention.

When, if ever, armed intervention is warranted is a substantive question that cannot be settled by a definition. But it may help to begin with some definitional criteria simply to delimit the scope of the inquiry. The criteria mentioned in the preceding paragraph have been contested, but taken together they identify a discourse of intervention that is as old as the international system itself—the system of legally independent ("sovereign") territorial states that emerged in Europe during the sixteenth and seventeenth centuries and now encompasses the world. This discourse is part of a larger discourse of just war, though it is more complex than conventional invocations of "the just war tradition" imply because, as Anthony Coates argues in his chapter, that tradition is in fact a plurality of traditions that frame the issues in different ways.[1] Nor is it easy to distinguish armed intervention from other kinds of warfare, or humanitarian interventions from other

1

interventions. Arguments for humanitarian intervention, though not under that name, can be found in the writings of Vitoria, Grotius, and other early modern European moralists, and these arguments draw upon ideas about the duty to defend the innocent that go back to Augustine and beyond. Analogous discussions can be found outside Europe.[2] For this reason, dating the origin of humanitarian intervention to the appearance in the middle of the nineteenth century of the word "humanitarian" (in the sense of advancing the welfare of humanity), or to the post-1945 human rights era, or to the theory and practice of collective intervention in the 1990s, misses the element of tradition in debates over the rights and responsibilities of states with respect to atrocities committed beyond their territories. Since the sixteenth century, the principle that states whose governments abuse their subjects (or fail to protect them from abuse) lose their immunity from coercion has been so often asserted and denied, so often defined, dissected, deduced, and deconstructed, that one must acknowledge that humanitarian intervention has long been a standard topic of international controversy.

International lawyers debate the legality of humanitarian intervention under the United Nations Charter and other treaties, and according to customary international law. They debate whether the Charter, which seems to forbid humanitarian intervention, should be amended to permit it, or whether (as Thomas Franck argues) it would be wiser to avoid tinkering with the law, "legitimizing" humanitarian intervention without formally "legalizing" it. Journalists and historians investigate particular cases of humanitarian intervention, as well as cases in which states arguably should have intervened but did not, revealing tensions between principles and practice. Moral and political philosophers (including, in this volume, Joseph Boyle and Carla Bagnoli) continue the age-old effort to identify the moral principles that determine proper and improper uses of coercion in human affairs, and to assemble these principles into a coherent theory of war in general and humanitarian intervention in particular. Public officials and political activists worry (with Thomas Pogge and Pratap Mehta in their chapters) about the politics of humanitarian intervention and the abuse of its principles, arguing that we must develop institutional alternatives to the remedial use of force by states.

And others explore the ethical premises and implications of these institutional alternatives (see, for example, the chapters by Catherine Lu, Brian Lepard, and Melissa Williams).

The essays in this volume of NOMOS can thus be read as contributions to an ongoing discussion. They draw upon the resources of this discussion and continue it in response to new contingencies. These include the failure of the international community to halt genocides in the Balkans and in Africa during the 1990s; the subsequent NATO action in Kosovo; the events of 9/11 followed by American-led wars in Afghanistan and Iraq and the invocation of humanitarian principles, among others, to justify those wars; and, more generally, the halfhearted embrace by the United States of humanitarian responsibilities acquired as a result of its central—some would say imperial—place in the current global order. The events are new but the questions are familiar: Is humanitarian intervention permitted by international law? If not, is it nevertheless morally permissible? Morally required? If there is a moral duty to protect victims of intrastate violence, does that duty trump the prohibitions of international law? If humanitarian intervention means using force to prevent genocide and other crimes against humanity, are states ever motivated by that intention? Can a state or its government even be said to have motives? Realistically, might not the main consequence of the humanitarian intervention principle be that powerful states will coerce weak ones for purposes of their own? The world will continue to generate occasions for asking these traditional questions.

This does not mean that we are bound by the traditional answers or barred from asking new questions. The current debate on humanitarian intervention is marked by two innovations in particular, which we explore in this volume. The first is a shift of emphasis from the permissibility of intervening to the responsibility to intervene. The second is an emerging conviction that the response to humanitarian crises needs to be collective, coordinated, and preemptive—in a word, institutionalized. These developments rest on a consensus that genocide, ethnic cleansing, and other atrocities are the world's business—as their inclusive name, "crimes against humanity," implies. If the international community has not only the right but also a duty to respond to such crimes, what should that communal response be? How can that community incorporate principles of humanitarian responsibility into international law without weakening already frail Charter constraints on the use of armed force by states? How can the international community strengthen its collective capacity to respond not only after genocides are under way but also in advance —to anticipate and prevent genocide and other crimes against humanity? And is it true, as Kok-Chor Tan and Carla Bagnoli in particular emphasize, that everyone has a duty to demand and support institutions able to intervene effectively when intervention is necessary?

In considering these questions, and especially for the purpose of entering the debates posed by the contributors to this volume, some basic distinctions need to be kept in mind. These are the distinctions between (1) morality and law, (2) intentions and motives, (3) rights and duties, (4) perfect and imperfect duties, (5) protection and enforcement, (6) antecedent and retrospective authorization, and (7) principles and institutions. Each captures an important dimension of debate about the ethics and politics of humanitarian intervention. The last—between principles and institutions—marks a tension that so thoroughly pervades the debate over humanitarian intervention at the beginning of the twenty-first century that we have used it to organize this volume, which begins with essays on the moral principles that define humanitarian intervention and ends with essays on the procedures by which collective decisions about intervention should be made. My aim in this introduction is to clarify the humanitarian intervention debate—within this volume and beyond it—by exploring these distinctions. I have tried to avoid the usual style of introductions, which is to summarize the various contributions. Instead, I highlight some areas in which the contributors engage one another's views, and I have not been shy about advancing my own.

1. MORALITY AND LAW

It is a commonplace of academic discourse on law to assert the dependence of legal ideas on moral beliefs, political practices, and the realities of interest and power that permeate common life. Law is influenced by moral ideas and political practices, and it in turn influences these ideas and practices. Several of our contributors offer versions of this claim. But to say that law is influenced by morality or expediency, or that there are tensions between legality and legitimacy, is already to acknowledge distinctions between them, and therefore to deny an inherent or conceptual connection that would make it impossible to distinguish legal from other modes of discourse or practice. Certainly the question of law's relationship to morality and politics is a complicated one, as long-running debates between legal positivism, natural law jurisprudence, and legal realism illustrate. But however complicated these relationships may appear when viewed through the lens of theory, in practical discourse it is both possible and necessary to distinguish between legal, moral, and prudential considerations.

It is, for example, important to distinguish between the rules of positive international law that govern the practice of humanitarian intervention, on the one hand, and the moral principles we use to judge particular interventions and to evaluate those legal rules, on the other. Whether there is a right of humanitarian intervention under the U.N. Charter or other parts of international law is a legal question. To discuss it one must know something about the relevant law and how to make a legal argument. Whether the law of humanitarian intervention is *morally* defensible, and whether there might be a moral duty to intervene even if intervention is unlawful, are moral rather than legal questions— questions that require one to apply the relevant moral principles. Moral disputes cannot be decided by appealing to positive law any more than legal disputes can be decided by appealing to morality.

The distinction between law and morality may seem obvious, but confusion arises when it is unclear whether an argument is supposed to have legal or moral force. For this reason, we should be careful not to confuse legal and moral claims, claims about what the law is with claims about what it should be or about what should be done, morally speaking, given the law as it is. We should be clear, in speaking of "the nonintervention rule" or other "norms" governing intervention, whether we are speaking of a positive legal rule, a rationally grounded moral principle, or a custom, practice, or widely shared opinion that is neither legally nor morally binding. Because law and morality share a vocabulary of rules, rights, and duties, it is easy to slide from one discourse to the other.

As an example of how failing to distinguish legal from moral concerns can confuse the discussion, consider the argument that humanitarian intervention is justified as an emergency measure. Most legal systems recognize a doctrine according to which the government can suspend certain laws to deal with threats to public order or national security. Thomas Franck articulates an international version of this doctrine when he suggests that genocide creates a situation of "exceptional humanitarian necessity"—an emergency in which the normal prohibition of armed intervention, found in the U.N. Charter and in other parts of international law, is suspended for the duration of the emergency. Because (Franck reasonably assumes) only the international community, as embodied in the Security Council and other U.N. organs, has the authority to suspend the prohibition, the question whether a given intervention is "legitimate" or not must be decided by these bodies. They constitute the jury that decides whether a given intervention meets this test. "Legitimate" here means that the intervention, though illegal, is acknowledged to be a morally permissible departure from the law that is in effect retrospectively legalized by this acknowledgment.[3] But exactly how it is legalized remains a mystery because "jurying" is, despite the legal analogy, a political practice, not a legal one.

The jury argument, Franck thinks, balances the need for strict limits on the use of force by states with the need for action in humanitarian emergencies. Here, the rules that are set aside are legal rules. One might also plead emergency to get around the nonintervention rule, understood not as a rule of positive international law but as a *moral* norm of international society.[4] The emergency argument works differently, however, when it is used to justify exceptions to moral rules. If there are moral objections to humanitarian intervention, to defend it as an emergency measure is to set these objections aside for the sake of other, presumably higher, values. But we cannot argue that an emergency justifies suspending *moral* obligations without bringing morality itself into question. For one thing, to speak in this way is to misuse the word "moral" and its cognates. On almost any theory of morality, a moral rule cannot be nullified by an act of will. But there is also a logical objection. If an action that is normally forbidden is permitted in exceptional situations, it makes no sense to say that the moral rule forbidding it in ordinary situations must be suspended. No properly stated moral rule must be voided to accommodate it, nor does the action need to be defended on extramoral grounds. To say that humanitarian intervention is morally justifiable is to acknowledge that, morally speaking, the nonintervention rule—understood as a moral rather than a legal rule—already allows for intervention to thwart grave human rights abuses. A government's moral right to exercise authority within its own territory is premised on its respecting the moral rights of its people. Humanitarian intervention is not an exception to the nonintervention principle but an integral part of it, for if the principle were fully and precisely stated it would be seen to allow interventions to end such abuses.

There is, in short, an important difference between actions that violate positive human laws and those that are immoral. It is one thing to argue that, in an emergency, a government may suspend enacted laws for the good of the community—that doing so is morally justified and should be permitted by the constitution of any well-regulated state or well-regulated international order. There are dangers in this argument, given the absence of a legal procedure for declaring law-trumping emergencies, but it is not an inherently incoherent one. But that a government may suspend acknowledged moral prohibitions for the common good is a different matter. No government has the authority to suspend morality; suspension here is a euphemism for violation.

If intervention were never morally permissible, no state could rightly engage in it. But that is not the case. Morally speaking, it is permissible for one state to violate the *legal* rights of another that is engaged in massacring innocents, for attacking the innocent is a moral crime and remains so even if some regime decides it is lawful. Morally speaking, a regime cannot assert its legal rights as cover for committing gross moral wrongs. But there is no need to invoke the idea of supreme emergency to rationalize violating *moral* rights because a state that perpetrates or permits crimes against humanity has already lost its moral right to freedom from foreign interference. To say that in a humanitarian emergency moral rules must be set aside is to misuse the idea of emergency, which has its proper home in the discourse of positive law—a misuse that, because it rationalizes immoral conduct, is politically dangerous as well as morally incoherent.

This does not mean that a narrowly legal concept of emergency is sound in the context of international law, however. The argument that a humanitarian emergency can make lawful wars that would otherwise violate international law must contend with several objections.

First, emergency powers presuppose an authority empowered to declare an official state of emergency—which is a state of exception to some but certainly not all laws—and we expect this authority to be accountable in some way. One might argue that the intervening state has that authority in a humanitarian crisis, and that subsequent review ("jurying") by the international community provides the accountability. But this, like much else in international law, simply acknowledges the primitive condition of that law, where the distinction between ruler and ruled is blurry. States, not the U.N., interpret the law and judge that interpretation. This is no surprise—it simply reiterates the fact that international law is, at bottom, a system of customary law.

Second, the situations that call for humanitarian intervention are not unpredictable events but evidence of a recurring problem. That the international community deals with this problem largely in an ad hoc way is a sign of collective myopia and moral failure, not brilliant improvisation. As several contributors to this volume argue, and probably all would affirm, governments have a moral duty to establish institutions to anticipate and prevent humanitarian crises.

Finally, it is worth bearing in mind that humanitarian intervention can be defended on legal grounds, making the appeal to supreme emergency superfluous. Thomas Pogge argues that U.N. intervention to prevent the Rwandan genocide would not have violated its Charter—the U.N. already had forces in Rwanda, and its failure to disarm those who were plotting genocide was the consequence of administrative timidity, not a scrupulous respect for legality.[5] One might even argue, as Pogge does, that international law can be read as *requiring* intervention when genocide occurs. An academic interpretation cannot settle the legal question, but that a plausible legal case for intervention can be made suggests the wisdom of looking for the spirit of the law in the letter rather than the exception.

2. INTENTIONS AND MOTIVES

I began by defining humanitarian intervention as the use of force by a state that aims to protect innocent people who are nationals of another state from harm inflicted or allowed by that state's government. It is sometimes said that because states are collective entities, they cannot intelligibly be said to have intentions or motives. A more frequent objection is that the definition is naive because rescuing foreigners is seldom the real reason states intervene. Moreover, good intentions are no guarantee that a humanitarian war will be justly conducted; as Joseph Boyle and Anthony Coates explain, traditional just war thinking has always emphasized the character of those who engage in war, as well as their goals or justifications, because how they are predisposed to act will influence what they do.

There are several threads to untangle here. First, collectivities *can* have intentions. It is sometimes said that to attribute intentions to a group is to commit the fallacy of personifying an aggregate—only individuals can think, choose, and act. But if a group is organized to make decisions, it is perfectly intelligible to say that it can choose, according to its procedures, among alternative actions. The end or purpose of the action it chooses is its intention with respect to that action, even if individual members of the group see things differently. Boyle makes this point when he suggests that making war is a "social act." Whatever the intentions of those who are involved in deciding to fight, or in actually fighting, this social act is "an accessible reality within the social world," a collective choice whose intentions "are manifest in that world." The intentions of individuals can be distinguished from and do not necessarily affect the justice of a government's actions: "The intention of the social act of undertaking war is revealed in the war aims sought and in the specific actions called for to achieve these aims."[6]

Second, intentions can be distinguished from motives, even though the words "intention" and "motive" are often used interchangeably. Just war theory is commonly said to include "right intention" among its criteria for the licit use of force, and this intention is often identified as the motive or spirit of an act; "right intention," so conceived, is contrasted with "just cause." But when one looks at discussions of these criteria, the line between them can be hard to see. The "cause" that makes a given action "just" is its end or purpose—defending the innocent from violence, for example. But that action can be unjust if the asserted purpose is a pretext and the real purpose is something else, like economic gain or winning an election. It is this "real intention" or "ulterior motive" that explains the action. But here the words "intention" and "motive" are misused because they fail to distinguish the goal aimed at from the desires or dispositions that lead people, individually or collectively, to choose that goal. It is these dispositions that Aquinas (following Augustine) had in mind in distinguishing right intention from just cause. But this traditional use of the word "intention" blurs the distinction between the end one wants to achieve and the desires that move one to pursue that end. One should distinguish a person's goals—what he or she aims at— from that person's dispositions and desires—why he or she is aiming at it. There are good reasons for keeping these two aspects of choice separate; calling the former an intention and the latter a motive is one way to do that. It would be less confusing if the just war lexicon were to use the expression "right motives" rather than "right intention."

We can, then, distinguish the grounds on which an act is judged right or wrong from the agent's motives. The agent's intention is what he chooses to do; his motive is the dispositions and desires that explain his choice. Here, "intention" is not a synonym for "motive" but, rather, a way of distinguishing one act from another. The intention of an act is the state of affairs it seeks to bring about. A motive, in contrast, is the frame of mind in which the agent acts —the desires and other passions that propel him. Motives are a necessary element in judgments of responsibility, of praise and blame, culpability and excuse, but are often incidental to judgments of the justification, the objective rightness or wrongness, of an act. Motives are nevertheless relevant in making moral judgments because we have moral duties to act from the proper motives.

How do these ideas apply to humanitarian intervention? A government can choose to rescue the victims of an atrocity, making this its intention and acting to bring it about, from a variety of motives. If the chief motive is concern with the injustice to the victims and compassion for their suffering, we may call its action "humanitarian." But suppose that its motive is to appear compassionate or to gain an advantage in the target state? Does this matter? Cynics maintain that there are no humanitarian interventions because states are never motivated by benevolence. India's intervention in East Pakistan in 1971 was not humanitarian, they argue, because although it ended a massacre, its real aim was to prevent refugees from entering India or, worse, to weaken Pakistan by creating Bangladesh. As Thomas Pogge puts it, "[T]here are no . . . humanitarian heroes out there."[7] But this is no reason why an intervention that is aimed at ending violence and is conducted in such a way as to realize this intention cannot be called "humanitarian," even if it is motivated by more self-interested considerations. A humanitarian act is defined by its intention, not by its motive.

3. Rights and Duties

The morality of humanitarian intervention is usually discussed as a question of rights or permissions. Is intervention ever permissible? Can one state ever have a right to act within the jurisdiction of another and, if so, when? The usual premise is that intervention is normally forbidden but that it might be justified as an exception to the nonintervention principle. Morally speaking, a state is a territorial community, legally constituted and regulated, within which persons can coexist and enjoy protected liberties. A state that successfully provides these benefits has a right to exist without interference from other states. Just as persons coexist within a state, so states must coexist within the international order. Just as persons must respect one another's autonomy and bodily integrity, states must respect one another's political sovereignty and territorial integrity. And this means that one state may not exercise its authority, and therefore may not use armed force, within the territory of another without its permission. Any such intervention is an act of aggression.

The reasoning behind this nonintervention principle also accounts for the commonly recognized exceptions to it. Because a state exists to protect the rights of its citizens, if it violates those rights it loses its moral rationale and therefore its immunity from foreign interference. Other states are justified in providing the protection it no longer provides. When the government of a state commits or permits violence against its own citizens, other states may be justified in coercively thwarting that violence, at least if certain conditions are met: the violence is extreme, the intervening states do not make their intervention a pretext for pursuing other aims, and so forth. The government of an unjust state cannot invoke its rights of political sovereignty or territorial integrity to abuse those it governs.

Once we acknowledge that there is a right of humanitarian intervention—that in crimes against humanity, outsiders may forcibly intervene—we can move on to a more complicated and controversial question: whether there is a *duty* to intervene in such situations. Surprisingly, this question has only recently become prominent in the literature on humanitarian intervention.

There is little warrant in positive international law for arguing that states have a duty to intervene for, at most, international law supports a right to intervene. But whether states have a moral duty to intervene is not so clear. If they do, it is hard to say exactly what that duty is. Most moral traditions recognize both negative and affirmative duties—duties to refrain from harming but also duties to assist and protect. These two principles—"law" and "love," as they are sometimes called—are combined in the major moral traditions, certainly in those of Christianity, Judaism, and Islam. They are combined in one way or another, most often and most plausibly by making beneficence ("love") a goal to be pursued within the constraints of respect for everyone's moral rights ("law"). Given the principle of beneficence, we have some responsibility to assist others. It is not enough to avoid harming them. We should help other people achieve their ends, when we reasonably can, and in that way promote their well-being. We have a duty to assist others when assistance is needed, and we can provide it without doing wrong and without undue cost. And the more pressing their need, the stronger our duty—for example, when they are victims of violence.

It is reasonable to argue, on these grounds, that the government of one country should respond when people in another are being massacred or driven from their homes, assuming it is able to end that oppression. There is a duty to intervene if the victims cannot be protected in any other way. Normally a government's duty to protect people's well-being is limited to those within its territory. But when there are catastrophes in other countries that the governments of those countries cannot handle, and especially when those governments themselves grossly threaten the well-being of their own citizens, the duties of other states no longer stop at their own borders. But such duties do not automatically translate into armed intervention. That requires a justification that providing humanitarian aid does not. And even when the case for armed intervention has been made, the duty to intervene may be overridden by other concerns—for example, by worries about the ability of the intervening state or states to fight within moral limits. But if one state can effectively prevent genocide in another, and other moral and prudential conditions can be met, armed intervention is not merely permissible but, as Boyle says, may be obligatory.[8] That is the formula, also, proposed in the influential report of the International Commission on Intervention and State Sovereignty (ICISS), *The Responsibility to Protect.*[9] The title of that report suggests a move from a right to intervene to a duty to intervene. But what, exactly, is the duty? And on whom does it fall?

Several of the contributors address these hard questions, and they do so in ways that go beyond the conventional analysis that I have just sketched. According to Carla Bagnoli, the duty to intervene when human rights are grossly violated rests not only on the principle of beneficence but more directly and compellingly on the principle of respect. Because every person has a duty to respect the basic moral rights of every other person, the duty to support remedial intervention is universal.[10] This, of course, raises the question of how that universal duty should be interpreted, and in particular how we get from a general duty to do *something* to the very specific duty to intervene militarily. Kok-Chor Tan explores this question, and his conclusion (with which Bagnoli concurs) is that the duty to protect must be institutionalized. The members of the international community must establish and support appropriate institutions to perform what would otherwise be a diffuse, uncertain, and, for most, unperformable duty to protect.

4. Perfect and Imperfect Duties

Those who think that humanitarian intervention is a duty are usually thinking of what is sometimes called an "imperfect" duty—not a specific obligation, such as one might have under a contract, but rather a general obligation to promote a goal, such as the well-being of others. But unlike the duty to avoid violating someone's rights, the duty to assist that person cannot be precisely specified. It is not a matter of clear prohibition but of reasonably achievable good. If humanitarian intervention is an imperfect duty, states are free to decide how to meet it. They must not simply watch while people are being slaughtered, but they can choose *when* and *how* to respond. And no *particular* state is obligated to act in a given case. In both these ways, intervention is optional.

The duty to intervene seems, then, to be a rather weak duty—not exactly an oxymoronic "optional duty" but a duty that leaves the bearer with many options. So it is reasonable to ask whether there can be a nonoptional duty to intervene—a duty people could, in principle, be required to perform. Tan thinks there is such a duty under certain conditions: if a state is specially related to those needing protection, for example, or if a state is capable of intervening effectively and other states are not. More generally, there is a nonoptional duty on the part of each state to support collective intervention and to establish or strengthen institutions for implementing the collective duty. This is one of the main conclusions of the ICISS report. In Tan's formulation, each state has a nonoptional or "perfect" duty to cooperate with others to perform their collective duty to protect the victims of violence. Bagnoli, in her chapter, shows how a specifically Kantian theory of moral obligation supports this conclusion.

Let us examine the perfect/imperfect distinction on which these arguments rest. Not surprisingly, we can interpret that distinction in different ways. Some of the trouble it gives comes from confusion about which interpretation we are using. The distinction belongs to the tradition of modern (Protestant) natural law, whose most famous theorists are Grotius, Pufendorf, and, for present purposes, Kant. At least three ways of making the distinction can be found in this tradition.

The first turns on the question of *whether the duty can be satisfied.* The duty to pay a debt is perfect because you can complete it by paying what you owe. That duty can be precisely specified and can, therefore, be fully discharged. Performing an imperfect duty grants the recipient a substantive benefit that is indeterminate in form or quantity. The duty to aid the poor is imperfect because what needs to be done cannot be precisely specified. Providing assistance performs the duty but does not complete it. Unlike a debt, the duty of charity is never completed by an action or finite series of actions. But this way of making the distinction runs into difficulties, for the duty *not* to violate another's rights cannot be completed, in the usual sense of that word, whereas a beneficent rescue can in fact be completed. More generally, no rule can ever determine the individual contingent actions (as opposed to types of actions) required to comply with it. Rules state considerations to be taken into account in choosing and acting, and whether a given action responds adequately or not to those considerations is always a matter of interpretation. There is, in short, an inherent indeterminacy in all rules, and therefore in all duties, not only imperfect duties.

The second way of making the distinction focuses on *who must perform the duty.* Perfect duties are duties of specified persons, such as the debtor. In the case of imperfect duties, no performer is specified. Duties of beneficence are imperfect in this sense: assistance should be provided (the passive voice works well here), but no one is designated to provide it. There is a duty to assist, but it is not clear *who* is required to perform this duty (Tan calls this "the agency problem"). Some moralists (Tan himself, for example, and some of the authors he mentions) argue that if the duty to protect is imperfect, it can be made perfect by assigning it to an organization such as the U.N. This makes it perfect in having a specified performer, even though what that performer must do remains indeterminate.[11]

The third interpretation is that the perfect/imperfect distinction has to do with *whether the duty is enforceable.* Perfect duties pertain to what Kant calls "justice"—that is, they are based on rules that prohibit one person from violating the rights of another, and therefore they must be performed no matter what the cost to oneself. Imperfect duties, in contrast, rest on the principle of beneficence, which demands that we provide advice, goods, or other assistance to those who need it, within the limits of reasonable cost. To violate an imperfect duty may be "inhumane," but it is not unjust.[12] Justice, then, implies coercion, in the sense that it cannot be wrong to enforce the rule against violence. The question of justice is not the general moral question of how people ought to treat one another but the specifically political question of how they should be *compelled* to treat one another.[13] Perfect duties (like the duty to pay a debt) can be legally enforced because people can be forcibly prevented from violating one another's moral rights. This follows from the moral right people or communities have to use force to defend themselves from violence if no legal procedure is available, as when a person is assaulted on the street or when a state goes to war to defend itself against aggression. Imperfect duties, in contrast, belong to the domain of what Kant calls "virtue," whose principle is the freely chosen promotion of morally good ends.

The thought here is that virtue is a matter of motives. Morality is a matter not only of external action but internal frame of mind. So even if an act you perform benefits others, you have not acted beneficently unless you intend to benefit them and are moved by feelings of compassion or benevolence. We can judge people's motives but we cannot dictate the motives. There is a moral duty of beneficence, then, but that duty is not enforceable because, according to Kant, we cannot be forced to act from benevolent motives. But we can be forced to respect people's rights, and this remains true even when it is not clear who should perform the duty or whether it can be discharged fully. In some cases, we may have discretion in the choice of means for fulfilling a duty; in others, the agent having the duty may be unclear. But it does not follow that we are free to ignore the duty, or (as Tan emphasizes) that indeterminacy with respect to agency means that nobody has a duty to act.

We are now in a position to understand the claim that humanitarian intervention is not merely a duty, but that it might become, in some situations, a perfect duty, where "perfect" means enforceable. So far, we have looked at humanitarian intervention from the perspective of the *victim*. The victim's suffering is the problem and the aim of intervention is beneficent: to end that suffering.

But what happens when we shift the focus from victim to *perpetrator*? Now, the ground for intervening is not beneficence. It is enforcement of the rule forbidding violence (unjustified coercion)—a basic rule that makes common life possible. The rationale of humanitarian intervention, from this perspective, is that it enforces the laws protecting the moral rights of every member of the community. The perpetrator of violence must be constrained in order to uphold those laws and vindicate those rights. Failure to resist those who commit crimes against humanity is unjust for the same reason that appeasing an international aggressor is unjust. It fails to uphold the laws that distinguish a civilized society from the rule of those committed to aggression, genocide, enslavement, and terror.

If our concern is with unilateral intervention—that is, with intervention by a state or states acting outside the framework of common institutions—this shift in perspective does not necessarily turn an imperfect duty to intervene into a perfect one. The duty of any particular state to intervene militarily, viewed apart from common institutions, remains imperfect in the sense that no individual state can rightly be compelled to intervene. But enforceable duties emerge as soon as institutions enter the picture.

First, even if individual states have no duty to intervene, they do have a duty to make intervention possible—for example, by working to establish institutions capable of thwarting crimes against humanity. When the violation of human rights is gross, the international community as a whole must act: as Bagnoli argues, if it fails to protect the victims of serious violence, it culpably fails to observe the Kantian principle of respect. Tan reaches a similar conclusion, arguing that the international community has a duty to adopt whatever measures are needed to insure that the duty to protect is discharged.

Second, if the international community chooses to fulfill this duty to protect human rights by establishing institutions empowered to deal with violations, these institutions acquire the duty to intervene when necessary. Such institutions can enforce international law, if they have been established and empowered for that purpose. Because its Charter confers some coercive powers of this kind, the U.N. can rightly use those powers. And because the U.N. has these powers, it can require states to cooperate in efforts to suppress crimes against humanity. The duty to comply with this requirement would be a perfect duty, again in the Kantian sense that the duty is enforceable. It would not be *wrong* to enforce that duty, whether or not enforcement is possible in a particular case.

5. PROTECTION AND ENFORCEMENT

Talk of enforcement in international affairs makes many people uneasy. Pratap Mehta, for example, thinks it is dangerous to regard armed humanitarian intervention as an enforcement mechanism. This judgment is based partly on skepticism about the objectivity of moral principles and partly on the fear that claims to enforce international law are almost always a cover for aggression by the powerful against the weak. But there is a deeper objection: that intervention cannot be a way of enforcing international law because enforcement implies action by an appropriate international institution, or, at least, states authorized by such an institution to use force on behalf of the international community. If individual states decide, on their own, to enforce international law, this requirement of proper authority is not met. The view that unilateral intervention can be an act of enforcement—a "legal sanction"—is, then, mistaken. Unilateral—that is, unauthorized —intervention is both unlawful and dangerous. It threatens the security of states, violates the rights of their citizens, harms the inevitable victims of humanitarian wars, and undermines the solidarity of the international community.

There are two lines of argument here, one focusing on the consequences of enforcement and the other on the concept itself. Taking the objection from consequences first, whether interventions are likely to do more harm than good is a question about which it is hard to say much in general. Certainly a lawful and effective system of international institutions for dealing with human rights abuses would be preferable to relying on unlawful, ad hoc, and self-serving unilateral interventions. But suppose the relevant institutions are politicized or ineffective. Suppose a contemplated intervention is badly needed and not self-serving. The question whether armed humanitarian intervention is morally justified cannot be avoided simply by imagining a situation in which institutions are just and effective and unilateral intervention is never required.

The conceptual objection to viewing humanitarian intervention as an exercise in law enforcement is only marginally more persuasive. As Joseph Boyle observes, a state has authority over its own citizens, not over the citizens or the governments of other states. But to rescue the victims of genocide is not, properly speaking, to exercise authority over foreigners. Since "defense" in the just war tradition means the defense of rights, a state may do more than defend itself from aggression; it may also defend other victims of aggression, including citizens of another state if their own government oppresses them. Morally, a state may act to thwart genocide and other atrocities wherever they occur, but it has no legal right, on its own, to enforce international law against the offending government. It certainly lacks legal authority to punish that government (though it is worth pointing out that under international law any state has the right to punish citizens and even officials of another state for war crimes and crimes against humanity). Boyle agrees, then, with Mehta, that the enforcement of international law by individual states lacks a proper legal rationale. But in that case it is also true that *thwarting* the injustice and *defending* its victims is something a state, acting on its own, is not legally authorized to do. One cannot ignore the criterion of proper authority at one stage in the argument and bring it in at another. If a state lacks authority to enforce international law, it also lacks authority to rescue or protect. If it has a right to intervene, that right is a moral right, not a legal one. And if a state is authorized by the U.N. to protect, it is authorized to enforce as well.

Carla Bagnoli brings out the moral relationship between protection and enforcement. She argues that the international community has a duty to act whenever human rights are gravely abused, and that this duty can be analyzed as comprising two complementary duties. One is the duty to protect the victims of violence. The other is the duty to thwart the violator, using force, if force is necessary. In protecting the victim, the intervening powers *at the same time* enforce the rule against violence. Protection and enforcement are two sides of the same coin. How the victims of violence should be protected and how the rules against violence should be enforced—by whom, on whose authority, and so forth—are legal and practical questions. How we answer those questions does not affect the inherent connection between protection and enforcement. Those who gravely abuse human rights or permit them to be abused lose their immunity from coercion. They must be coercively thwarted to protect the victims and to enforce the rule against violence, which is itself merely an expression of the fundamental principle of respect. That rule is enforced whether or not the international community authorizes the actions of those who uphold it. That authorization, or its denial, certainly affects the legality of the enforcement action. But it does not follow that we cannot speak of enforcement in a moral context. An intervention that lacks proper authority cannot be defended within the discourse of international law as enforcing that law. But that same act, if morally justified, can without contradiction be said to enforce respect for human rights as well as to protect those whose rights are violated. No disagreement over terminology can erase this conceptual link between protection and enforcement.

Enforcement is an indispensable element in protecting human rights in yet another way. When a state or coalition intervenes to halt a massacre, it faces not only a crime but also a criminal. Often that criminal is the regime that has allowed, encouraged, or carried out the massacre, and that regime has to be replaced if people are to be secure against further violence. Traditional just war theory does not adequately consider the rights and wrongs of using force once an enemy has been defeated. Or at least those who use its principles have paid more attention to the principles' implications for choosing and conducting war (*jus ad bellum* and *jus in bello*) than to their implications for ending war (*jus post bellum*). As Michael Walzer argues, "[H]umanitarian intervention radically shifts the argument about endings."[14] Humanitarian intervention must go beyond rescue to reform and reconstruction. A new regime must be established *and enforced* until it can sustain itself. How this can be done effectively and justly will depend on circumstances, but the larger principle that must guide the effort is clear enough: the responsibility to protect includes responsibility to help change the conditions that allowed crimes against humanity to be committed in the first place.

6. ANTECEDENT AND RETROSPECTIVE AUTHORIZATION

Both the U.N. Charter and other important treaties seem rather plainly to prohibit intervention. Those who want to make room for humanitarian intervention within the framework of international law have therefore had to resort to various expedients— arguing, for example, that if the Security Council does not condemn an action, it has in effect authorized it, or that there are other bodies besides the Security Council able to authorize the use of force by states. Thus it has been argued that NATO authorized the Kosovo bombing, which it then carried out. The question of whether humanitarian intervention is or is not lawful under the U.N. Charter and international law generally has been thoroughly canvassed, and I will not discuss it here.[15] But because it is treated by several of our contributors, I want to say something about the question of how authority is created in international law.

All authority is contested and therefore to a degree uncertain. It often seems as if the authority of international institutions is especially contested and uncertain, but we might reach a different conclusion were we to compare these institutions with the full range of states and not only with the most stable of them. Certainly the authority of the U.N. in the international system is more contested and uncertain than that of the United States government within the United States, but the authority of the governments of Somalia or Afghanistan is more contested than that of, say, the International Monetary Fund. There are many reasons for the uncertain authority of the U.N. beyond the fact that, like the League of Nations before it, it is at the mercy of its most powerful members. The U.N. Charter is a treaty, and a treaty is a terminable agreement among the states that are party to it. The organization's authority is limited to the powers specified in the Charter and, strictly speaking, does not extend over states that are not its members. Many Charter provisions are in evident tension with customary international law, and the procedures for adjudicating these tensions are weak and unreliable.

Such doubts are reasonable but overblown. Authority is not a given but a construction that rests ultimately on the beliefs and practices of a community. As Melissa Williams argues in her chapter, the activity of granting and exercising authority, even uncertain authority, is one in which a community is itself defined or constituted. People constitute a community by acting like the citizens of one, appointing authorities, granting them powers, and debating the proper exercise of those powers. In the same way, states constitute an international community by adopting common rules and institutions and by debating the meanings of those rules and the powers of those institutions. A community is maintained in the continuous enactment of its practices. The "jurying" of past actions by states within the U.N. framework therefore has a significance that goes beyond particular judgments regarding those actions. Retrospective judging is a communal practice that affirms the institution by using, altering, and, sometimes, expanding its procedures and powers.

But even if we grant these points, we have reason to be uneasy. One of the basic requirements of the rule of law is that those whose conduct is regulated by laws should know in advance what the laws are. Retrospective authorization of legally doubtful conduct, like retrospective legislation, violates this requirement. These points apply to international as well as to civil society. It is one thing to stand outside the international legal system and observe the creative, if often questionable, ways that its laws and institutions adapt to changing circumstances. We can argue about whether particular changes are bringing international law closer to an emerging moral consensus, whether they are strengthening international institutions, or are otherwise desirable. It is quite another thing to conclude, within the discourse of international law, that the failure to condemn a putatively illegal action is tantamount to authorizing it. This is why Thomas Franck speaks of retrospective judgments as tending to "excuse" legally questionable actions rather than to justify them. But like other international lawyers, Franck is often forced to excuse oddities of international law that inspire doubts about the rule of law at the international level because the alternative is to reject international law not only as ineffective but as failing to meet rule of law criteria.

Despite these reservations, authority in international law is in fact granted retrospectively as well as in advance. This is the paradox of customary international law: if enough states treat an illegal act as legal, it is legalized. We must therefore look at the authority for humanitarian interventions as something that may indeed emerge after the fact when, as often happens, a state acts before the U.N. has given it a green light—even, conceivably, when the U.N. has given it a red light. If the "jury" afterwards decides that an action meets the criteria for a "legitimate"—that is, morally defensible—intervention, even though it violated the relevant laws and procedures, those laws and procedures have in effect been modified. This is a process of law creation closer to that of customary law than to that of a system based on legislation. But this is in fact how international law worked for centuries before the creation of the U.N., and it is therefore not surprising that it continues to work this way. The U.N. is a hybrid institution: both an arena within which old ways of power politics, diplomacy, and customary law continue to be followed and a supranational authority with nascent legislative powers. Operating inside the institution's legally messy framework, lawyers and judges argue the fine points of law while diplomats and politicians exploit its complexities. Operating outside that framework, philosophers and historians seek to understand the magic by which authority is created where there was none before and the processes through which practices and institutions acquire and maintain legitimacy.

Whether jurying by international institutions can help to close the gap between legality and moral legitimacy depends on how those institutions are constituted and the procedures under with they operate. All of the contributors who discuss this topic agree that the jury process must be impartial, and that impartiality is undermined if powerful interests corrupt the process. But they differ over how this impartiality is best achieved, and how it can be made effective. Should we begin with the Security Council or with some other, more representative, body? Does a body in which the great powers have special rights violate the principle, implicit in the jury metaphor, of judgment by one's peers? If jurying is a judicial rather than a political function, perhaps it should not be located in the Security Council or any other political body. Might the jurisdiction of the International Court of Justice be extended so that humanitarian interventions can come more reliably within its purview? What, if anything, can be said of jurying by the international community as a whole, acting not through particular political or judicial bodies but in "the court of public opinion?"[16] What if we were to have taken that expression literally and established a tribunal to reach judgments not only about the legality but also about the moral propriety of interventions? But such a tribunal could not formally adjudicate the use of force by states on the basis of something other than international law. The point of law is to have a common body of norms, and this commonality is undermined if law is merely one of several normative systems relied on by that tribunal.

One might argue that this argument takes words like "jury," "court," and "adjudication" too literally. The idea of jurying humanitarian interventions is a metaphor, and what it stands for is not a legal process but a political one. Politics involves deliberation about what law should be, not about how existing law should be applied. It is a process of debate—ideally, like the procedure of a trial jury, involving what Brian Lepard calls "open-minded consultation." But, unlike a jury procedure, the outcome of this process is not particular rulings that bind the parties in a given case but laws. Politics is legislative, not judicial. Consensus in politics depends on wide participation in deliberation, so that different groups are "represented" by having a voice and being understood to have a voice. In forming a political consensus, the deliberative process need not be either secret or unanimous, as in a jury trial. On the contrary, as philosophers from Kant to Rawls have urged, there are moral and prudential reasons for thinking that political deliberation should be open or public. Our contributors disagree whether the Security Council or other existing international institutions meet the requirements of open, or open-minded, deliberation, and some of them offer suggestions for institutional reform, but none challenges the ideal.

7. PRINCIPLES AND INSTITUTIONS

We are used to discussing humanitarian intervention, like other uses of armed force, in relation to a standard list of just war principles—just cause, right intention, proper authority, proportionality, military necessity, and so on. A common objection to just war discourse (made here by Pratap Mehta and challenged by Kok-Chor Tan in his response to Mehta) is that these principles are imprecise, controversial, and routinely abused, and that their main use is to rationalize war, not to constrain it. But principles necessarily require interpretation and are therefore contested, uncertain, and abused. Morally speaking, abuse of a principle does not negate it. But, practically speaking, there might well be reasons for attempting to devise procedures for judging armed intervention by states that are more certain and less subject to abuse than moral principles, whose meaning is easily distorted because there is no authoritative interpreter. It is tempting to conclude that if judgments about intervention are to be sound, we need not principles but procedures.

The just war tradition already grants this point, for the criterion of proper authority is in effect a requirement that any decision to use force must be the outcome of an appropriate procedure. But unlike theories that would substitute procedures for principles, traditional just war theory insists that proper authorization, though necessary, is not a *sufficient* ground for using armed force. As Boyle explains, the choice to use force must *also* meet the criteria of just cause, right intention, and so forth. For the moral skeptic, there are no such independent principles. Moral principles have meaning only as they are interpreted and applied. But in that case one might ask why so much confidence is placed in institutional procedures, for procedures too can be uncertain or abused. A justified intervention is *normally* one that the U.N. Security Council has authorized. But there are exceptional cases, where the Council has not approved unilateral action but the moral case for intervention is compelling. Here, trusting entirely to institutions leads to a morally unacceptable result: the failure of states to perform their duty to protect the innocent from violence.

In short, both principles *and* institutions are contested, uncertain, and abused. One appeals to procedures when people cannot agree on principles, and to principles when institutions are unjust or ineffective. The case for communal interpretation is plain: there is no community if each state may decide on its own when to use force. There must be common procedures to check unilateral uses of force and unilateral interpretations of common principles. But the case for unilateral interpretation is also plain: there is a moral duty to act when institutions fail. That is the lesson of Rwanda. No institution can be counted on to make moral judgment unnecessary.

The tension between "principles" and "institutions" is a tension between morality and law, between the general duties of every human being and the specific duties of citizens and officials under the laws of the states, international organizations, and other legally constituted institutions to which they belong. Given this tension, the challenge for those who want to develop a coherent doctrine of humanitarian intervention is to reconcile the particular obligations of international law with the general duties of morality. From the standpoint of morality, the solution is that states must respect the authority of international institutions, unless these institutions are ineffective and unjust. One cannot say in general when international laws are sufficiently ineffective or unjust as to justify a state in defying them, to defend either itself or humanity. It should be obvious that if the rule of law is to exist in international affairs, those laws must be presumed to be authoritative. But that authority is not beyond question. And if the laws are defective, there is a moral duty to repair them. Working to reform and strengthen common institutions for controlling the use of force and for protecting the innocent is part of that duty.

When we began this project, the prevailing opinion was that 9/11 had effectively removed humanitarian intervention from the international agenda, except as a cover for American efforts to put imperial policy above international law. The implication was that our topic is no longer practically, perhaps not even theoretically, important. As we go to print, the world is debating what to do about civil war and genocide in the Darfur region of Sudan. And the issues we explore—including the duty to protect and the need for institutional reform—are, not surprisingly, at the center of that debate.

NOTES

1. It is difficult to get away from the narrative, typically progressivist, model that Coates criticizes. Scholarship that examines distinguishable

languages or traditions of political discourse avoids the ahistorical character of this model, as his chapter illustrates.

2. Sohail H. Hashmi, "Is There an Islamic Ethic of Humanitarian Intervention?" in Anthony F. Lang Jr., ed., *Just Intervention* (Washington, D.C.: Georgetown University Press, 2003), 62–83.

3. The word "legitimate" hovers uncertainly between two meanings in the humanitarian intervention debate: that the practice is morally justified and that it widely *believed* to be warranted regardless of whether it really is. As a result, it is sometimes unclear whether claims about the legitimacy of humanitarian intervention are ethical or sociological.

4. Nicholas J. Wheeler suggests that one criterion for judging an intervention is that it responds to a "supreme humanitarian emergency," which invokes the realist argument that security trumps morality. Here it is the security of an oppressed people rather than of a state that is at stake, but the logic of the argument is the same: in extremity, moral constraints must yield to necessity. *Saving Strangers: Humanitarian Intervention in International Society* (Oxford: Oxford University Press, 2000), 13, 50–51.

5. Thomas Pogge, "Moralizing Humanitarian Intervention: Why Jurying Fails and How Law Can Work," this volume, chap. 6.

6. Joseph Boyle, "Traditional Just War Theory and Humanitarian Intervention," this volume, chap. 1, 42.

7. Pogge, "Moralizing Humanitarian Intervention," 166.

8. Boyle, "Traditional Just War Theory," 44.

9. Ottawa: International Development Research Center, 2001.

10. Strictly speaking, beneficence is an aspect of respect, not a separate principle. We respect the humanity of others by assisting them as well as by not harming them.

11. The interpretation that Tan identifies as possibly Kantian—a distinction between duties owed to specifiable persons and those not owed specifically to anyone, which makes imperfect duties a matter of unspecified *claimants* rather than unspecified *agents* (Kok-Chor Tan, "The Duty to Protect," this volume, chap. 3)—seems to be a version of the first interpretation, for if the claimants are not specified, then the duty cannot be fully discharged.

12. The language is Pufendorf's, not Kant's. Samuel von Pufendorf, *The Law of Nature and of Nations*, I.i, 19–20. Catherine Lu explores the theme of humanity in "Whose Principles, Whose Institutions? Legitimacy Challenges for 'Humanitarian Intervention,'" this volume, chap. 7.

13. Arthur Ripstein, "Authority and Coercion," *Philosophy and Public Affairs* 32 (2004): 6.

14. Michael Walzer, *Arguing about War* (New Haven: Yale University Press, 2004), 19.

15. Oliver Ramsbotham and Tom Woodhouse review the legal issues, as they were framed in the first half century of the U.N., in *Humanitarian Intervention in Contemporary Conflict: A Reconceptualization* (Cambridge: Polity Press, 1996). For the period since the mid-1990s, see J. L. Holzgrefe and Robert O. Keohane, eds., *Humanitarian Intervention: Ethical, Legal, and Political Dilemmas* (Cambridge: Cambridge University Press, 2003).

16. See Lu, "Whose Principles? Whose Institutions?" 204.

PART I

PRINCIPLES

1

TRADITIONAL JUST WAR THEORY
AND HUMANITARIAN
INTERVENTION

JOSEPH BOYLE

1. INTRODUCTION

By "traditional just war theory," I mean the organized set of precepts and their rationale concerning the moral permissibility of engaging in warfare developed by medieval canonists and moral theologians chiefly from the work of St. Augustine. I do not call this medieval just war thinking because it has continued to develop in the modern period, not only in the work of sixteenth-century scholastics such as Vitoria but also in continuing Roman Catholic teaching, and in the reflections of neoscholastic philosophers and theologians. I do not call this Catholic just war thinking because it is not narrowly religious or theological and remains of interest to many non-Catholics.

By "warfare," I follow the older tradition in understanding it to be simply "contending with arms." So a violent conflict need not be formally declared nor need it be conducted by established polities to be a war: one can go to war with brigands or terrorists, although such wars, like others, can be wrong to undertake or to execute in some ways.

An important component of the idea of war in this older just war tradition is that it is a collective action—something individuals cannot do acting alone but only in concert with others, and

31

therefore with some coordination of individuals' contributing actions by social authority. This further implies as a condition for a war's permissibility that the authority coordinating the bellicose action be of the right kind.

The kind of war to be discussed is an intervention. I understand that interventions are not necessarily by force or its threat; it is only interventions that compel by force that I address, and they surely are morally a kind of warfare.[1]

Interventions are held to be to be similar to, if not instances of, the kind of aggressive war widely held to be impermissible, indeed criminal, insofar as it ordinarily involves border crossing and is not undertaken for the sake of legitimate self-defense. But an intervention can be understood to be distinct from aggression when this is defined as a crime, and to be possibly justifiable because its purposes do not include an ongoing occupation of the target's territory, or the removal of whatever political independence that nation may have. Thus, to take two of the three kinds of intervention that Michael Walzer identifies—a state's intervening to support the secession of a people from a larger polity or a state's intervening in a civil war to balance the interference of other states—are not, or at least not obviously, cases of aggression.[2]

The sort of intervention I will discuss is humanitarian in a narrow sense: namely, intervention undertaken for the sake of protecting or securing noncitizens' fundamental human rights when these rights either (1) are violated by their government's own action or by its refusal to prevent other agents from doing so, or (2) are in jeopardy because of an anarchic situation in which no government exists capable of securing those rights, typically the condition of a failed state. This defines roughly the third species of intervention identified by Walzer. One of Howard Adelman's definitions captures the idea nicely and is sufficient to specify the kind of human activity I will discuss: humanitarian intervention is "[t]he use of physical force within the sovereign territory of another state by other states or the United Nations for the purpose of either the protection of, or the provision of emergency aid to, the population within that territory."[3]

It is perhaps worth noting that this definition is of a kind of social act—of warfare undertaken for a certain purpose. Thus, it is not intended to be a definition of an action already evaluated as morally good. According to this relatively descriptive account of humanitarian intervention, a use of force can be wrong even after it is agreed to be a humanitarian intervention.[4]

Relating traditional just war theory and the moral issues raised by humanitarian intervention has more than merely historical interest. Because its focus and vocabulary differ somewhat from those of modern international law and powerful current formulations of just war theory like Walzer's, this theory offers a practically relevant alternative to those views.

The modern international law applicable to the legitimacy of going to war has initial and primary focus on the crime of aggression, on the presumptive impermissibility of border crossings, and on the fundamental importance of states' mutual respect for one another's sovereignty and political independence.[5] This same focus is central in current just war theory. For example, the casuistic method that arrives at and applies rules for justified warfare begins with widely accepted ideas about the relationships between members of a society and develops analogies to the relationships between states. Developing the relevant analogies plainly requires careful attention to the ways in which states and individuals within a society are different, but states are presumptively free, much as individual members of a society ordinarily should be, to carry on their business unimpeded by other relevant actors. So, political sovereignty and territorial integrity function in international society much as individual rights do within a polity. Walzer has formulated the general results of this "domestic analogy" as what he calls "the legalist paradigm": a set of norms and normatively interpreted facts that he plausibly holds to be the basis for the significant consensus underlying the legal status quo on the legitimacy of going to war.[6]

In contrast to the focus and vocabulary of international law and current just war theory, the older tradition focused on the common good of a polity, and therefore on the (conceptually consequential) question of the authority of those leading a state's bellicose action, and on the justice of the cause for fighting. So, aggression will be wrong not simply because it is a border crossing or a violation of sovereignty but either because it is substantively unjust if a just cause is lacking, or because it is *ultra vires* for a state's leaders to undertake, or because the bellicose actions are not strictly for the sake of the just cause and, more ultimately, for the sake of peace. This difference in focus and vocabulary suggests there may be important moral differences between older just war moralizing and the deliverances of current just war theory and practice. For two reasons I think the suggestion is correct.

First, traditional just war theory is an integral part of a larger view of moral and social life. Its casuistry is controlled by moral principle, and its reasoning and norms are integrated with other personal and social moral concerns. If modern just war conviction were equally imbedded in a rich moral framework, it could not have achieved the widespread positive establishment and the consensus surrounding its norms that it actually enjoys. So traditional just war theory has different and likely richer, if also more contentious, resources to bring to the questions raised about humanitarian intervention than do positive legal developments and such moral reasoning as is likely to be widely acceptable.

Posing the question about the permissibility of humanitarian intervention in terms of what is legally established or widely acceptable within what Walzer calls the common moral world seems unlikely to provide an unambiguous answer. Indeed, the accepted categories raise the question as especially problematic and exceptional. Similarly, seeking resources to answer this question from larger conceptions of international society, whether from those premised on the sovereign independence of states, or from those emphasizing their interdependence and mutual interests, moves one very quickly outside the areas in which there is normative consensus.

Second, the ideas that dominate traditional just war theorizing —notably the common good, political authority and its limits, and, to a real but lesser extent, justice—certainly appear to be both distinctive and theoretically important for reflection upon the responsibilities of various kinds of communities and of various persons within them. These ideas do not dominate modern discussions of justified war. And if ideas such as sovereignty and aggression now do the work these concepts once did, it is not clear that the results of reflection carried on in these different vocabularies will turn out to be identical. Even if the normative conclusions justified did turn out to be the same, the differences in the reasoning would likely remain significant.

2. THE TRADITIONAL CRITERIA FOR A
MORALLY JUSTIFIED WAR

Thomas Aquinas gathered the teachings of Augustine on the morality of war, by his day widely interpreted and incorporated into canon law, and in a short, clear statement provided what is probably the classic statement of the traditional just war theory. This treatment appears in Aquinas's best known and most mature work, the *Summa Theologiae*, in the second part of the second part, which deals with moral problems. The discussion falls within the sins against the virtue of charity because war is presumptively a sin against charity.[7]

Aquinas maintains that a war can be morally justified if and only if three conditions are met. Those conditions are proper authority, just cause, and right intent. His concern is plainly with conditions for what came to be called *jus ad bellum,* the moral permissibility of going to war. I believe that all the central norms usually associated with just war, although not their casuistic nuancing, are assumed by or implicit in what Aquinas says here. The *jus in bello* norms for the conduct of war that have been the center of just war concern about twentieth-century warfare were not explicit until Vitoria's work, but the normative direction is surely here as well.

It is reasonable to think that Aquinas assumes in this discussion that the absolute prohibition against murder—intentionally or wantonly killing innocents—applies in warfare just as robustly as the prohibition against lying, which is explicitly held (in article 3) to remain in force. For, as he makes plain in the discussion of killing, no one can be authorized to intentionally kill innocents.[8] But since the main issue at stake today is the moral permissibility of undertaking warfare to defend or secure human rights, Aquinas's focus on the conditions for going to war is more useful than concerns about how war is executed.

Proper Authority

The first of Aquinas's conditions is proper authority; that is, only the head of a polity (*princeps,* often translated as "sovereign") can properly command the waging of war. Two reasons are given: first, private persons have no business waging war, and public officials lacking the sovereign authority can appeal to higher authority to settle disputes and to remedy injustices; second, only a sovereign, as head of the community, is authorized to bring together the members of that community to fight.

What grounds the sovereign's authority, in both these relationships, is the fact that the care of the community is entrusted to the prince, who has the responsibility to look after its welfare. This responsibility includes authority to use force not only internally against domestic criminals but also against outsiders who harm the polity. It is perhaps relevant to our inquiry that one of the biblical proof texts Aquinas uses here is taken as addressing political leaders as follows: "Rescue the weak and the needy; save them from the clutches of the wicked."

So, war waged without public authority is not permissible. And not any kind of public authority qualifies. Only the authority of one who has the final say for the welfare of a political community may rightly take it to war; by implicit definition, a public official has "final say" when there is no higher authority capable of and authorized to deal with the harm to the polity. The idea seems to be that the welfare of a political community requires care and protection and that sometimes this requires using armed force. Those who are in charge of the community's welfare are the legitimate primary agents of this force. Those officials who can invoke higher authority within the community are not in this ultimate way in charge of its welfare.

Nothing in this analysis requires the sovereign to be a single individual; sovereign authority may be exercised by a constitutional group operating according to some fixed decision procedure, such as a parliament. Nor is there anything in it that prohibits the relevant official or body of officials from having worldwide jurisdiction.

Plainly, such worldwide authority as exists in the world today is not the authority of a great polity. Such worldwide authorities as exist, in the United Nations and in the wider U.N. system, do serve a genuine common good that has global reach, but that common good appears to be less than an all-encompassing common good that contains the proper goods of the states of the world as subordinate parts. Neither the treaties and customs that normatively bind peoples together nor the technology that allows their extensive interaction and cooperation have yet created the conditions for a superpolity that might allow worldwide officials to care for the welfare of each polity.

In other words, in terms neither of capacity nor of normative considerations are officials with some worldwide responsibility in charge of the common good of the whole world. In the older scholastic language: the community of states and any other communities that make up the world politically do not constitute a *societas perfecta*, capable of definitively settling all things pertaining to all human interactions and so capable of generating law and so being a general court of last resort.

My application of Thomistic categories to the normative sources of political authority in the world today cannot resolve the important questions raised by the fact that a state's or an alliance's unilateral intervention to protect human rights may be illegal by the terms of the U.N. Charter or by international law. The claim is only that in traditional just war theory the authority to undertake war lies in the sovereign, and that, in the world as it now is, a sovereign is the ruler of a sovereign state, and worldwide organizations are not sovereign states. This complex view is compatible with a very considerable limitation of a sovereign's authority to undertake war, primarily by way of treaties of the kind that have shaped the modern international system. Such treaty-based limitations might also be extended and reinforced by the normative force of widely held custom. If it were sensible today to think of a renewed *jus gentium*, it would plausibly contain the expectation that sovereign authorities of a state will not undertake warfare without the consent of international authorities except in conditions in which the common good of the state is imminently and gravely threatened.[9]

The grounds for some such normative expectation would likely include the developing awareness of the need for impartiality in relations between states, especially when those relations are bellicose. The sovereign of a state cannot be impartial between his state's interests and those of enemies. The sovereign's responsibility for the common good of his or her own polity is precisely the ground of the authority to undertake warfare. Nevertheless, the sovereign is bound to act only for a just cause in the service of peace, and justification within the framework of the U.N., and international law surely contributes to meeting these conditions.[10]

Just Cause

Aquinas's second necessary condition for the permissibility of a war is that there be a just cause. He gives little justification for what he rightly takes to be an obvious ethical condition; that any action should be done only for a good purpose is, for him, a fundamental requirement of moral life. Nor does he provide a list of just reasons for undertaking warfare; such a list shows up later in Vitoria. But Aquinas does provide something more than the obvious moral requirement. He specifies the just cause needed for a permissible war as arising only in the face of wrongdoing by outsiders and further specifies it as being essentially punitive. He thus goes beyond the self-evident ethical point that a just cause is necessary, and beyond the intuitive requirement that a just war responds to wrongdoing, and adds the punitive understanding of that response, bolstering his claim with a reference to Augustine's authority.

He says that those who are rightly attacked must deserve it on account of some wrong they have done. The Augustinian text he cites makes plain that this response to wrongdoing is understood to be punitive: "We usually describe a just war as one that avenges wrongs, that is, when a nation or state has to be punished either for refusing to make amends for outrages done by its subjects or to restore what has been seized injuriously."[11] It is important to note at the outset that the punishment Augustine has in mind is just, legal retribution, not an expression of revenge or hatred.

One of the major developments of just war thinking in the twentieth century is that many have come to question the legitimacy of this punitive conception of just cause. Recent Catholic thinking—both ecclesial and scholarly—has moved toward a more defensive conception, very much in line with the broader international tendency to treat aggression, even if it could be justified for just punitive reasons, as completely out of line. I will take a few moments to argue that this is a genuine development of the tradition.[12] This development marks one very clear aspect in which traditional just war theory is markedly different from contemporary just war theory of the sort Walzer expounds. The right to punish, once a war has been deemed just, is widely thought to be justified by the domestic analogy, and so is listed by Walzer among the norms defining the legalist paradigm.[13] By contrast, the defensive conception of just cause that now characterizes the Catholic interpretation of traditional just war theory does not allow that war is a proper instrument for imposing punitive sanctions within international society. Harms inflicted incidental to defense are justified and may be understood as punitive, but any further punitive measures are not justified.[14]

The decisive document that marks the Catholic endorsement of a strictly defensive conception of just cause is the Second Vatican Council's (1962–1965) Constitution on the Church and the Modern World (*Gaudium et Spes*). This document is well known for its condemnation of total war and indiscriminate bombing, but it also gave evidence to a wider suspicion by the bishops of modern warfare generally. These Catholic teachers may have been "just warriors" in their political philosophy, but they had recently lived through a war most of them found deeply problematic. So they called for "an evaluation of war with a totally new attitude."[15]

Part of that new attitude is the limitation of just cause to defense. The bishops say,

> As long as the danger of war remains and there is no competent and sufficiently powerful authority at the international level, governments cannot be denied the right to legitimate defense once every means of peaceful settlement has been exhausted. Therefore, government authorities and others who share public responsibility have the duty to protect the welfare of people entrusted to their care and to conduct such matters soberly.
>
> But it is one thing to undertake military action for the just defense of the people, and something else again to seek the subjugation of other nations.[16]

This restriction of just cause may seem to have no deep justification but simply to reflect the revulsion of the bishops at the council to the horrors of the Second World War and their desire to get Catholic teaching in line with emerging international law and the U.N. But I think that this restriction improves traditional just war doctrine by removing tensions in the doctrine and in the wider moral view of which it is part.

The restriction of just cause to defense presupposes a distinction between defense and punishment. Punishment can be a means to defense, insofar as its prospect deters some from actions for which punishments are prescribed or prevents the punished persons from continuing in their criminal activity. But the choice to defend and the choice to defend *by punishing* are plainly distinct. The negative effects on those against whom someone rightly defends can perhaps be understood as punishment, but those harms are unavoidable aspects of the defense, many of which the defender need not intend. And defense plainly is possible with no further punitive element than this. Just as a private self-defender may ward off an attack with no punitive authority and no such interest, so may a community.

The argument for limiting just cause to defense is that a community and its leaders have the right to defend themselves from aggressors but not the more robust right to punish them. Political officials have authority over their subjects and authority to punish malefactors. They also obviously have authority to order defensive measures against external threats to the polity.

There is no account, however, about how the officials of one polity get authority to punish another polity or its subjects. The relationship of officials to the common good of their own polity legitimizes their using force internally to stop and deter criminals. This reasonably includes the right to punish criminals as a means of restoring justice, which also enhances the deterrent and defensive resources of a society. Defending subjects from injuries inflicted by outsiders is also a public responsibility based on the common good. But those who are resisted in that defense do not thereby become subjects of the defending state, subject to the authority of its rulers, as citizens are.

Like legal punishment, that defense often has a deterrent effect and can have a deterrent intent. The capacity of a state to defend itself and perhaps others from unjust aggression deters potential aggressors, and this capacity may be developed for this purpose. But deterrence by justified defensive warfare does not provide a distinct just cause that might justify violence beyond the requirements of defense.

As already noted, attackers often justly suffer the effects of the violent exercise of the authority of the polity they injure. And when they attack wrongfully, there is more to the exercise of defending authority than its power. Just as any fair-minded observer could address the attacker in moral terms, so too can they who defend themselves or others from injury. This appeal to general standards of decent conduct—"You are out of line and we are within our rights"—appropriately expresses moral condemnation of unjust aggression, but this moral truth does not make the attacker part of the community in a way that justifies anything like legal punishment.

To sum up this line of reasoning: the defensive rather than punitive understanding of just cause that has developed in Catholic just war thinking in the twentieth century is a genuine development of traditional just war doctrine. Reflecting on this development makes clear that the grounds for undertaking warfare are very constrained and that, plainly, the exact shape of these limitations will be important for assessing the permissibility of humanitarian intervention.

There is further reason for limiting just cause to defense, namely, the connection to the sanctity of life theme within natural law and Catholic moralizing. Exploring that reason must await a consideration of the third of Aquinas's conditions for the permissibility of undertaking a war.

Right Intention

Aquinas argues that fighting can be wrong even if there is proper authority and just cause because one can fight with a perverse intention. The citations from Augustine make clear that the kind of bad motives Aquinas has in mind are hatred, revenge, a desire to dominate, and so on. Hence, the existence of a just cause is not sufficient; it must not be a pretext for fighting for other morally questionable purposes. Rather, the just cause must function as the practical principle of the bellicose action. This condition is reasonably understood as ruling out the practical influence of any other motives for undertaking warfare. Thus, even good motives that might justify international actions that are not bellicose do not justify violence or further violence, unless, of course, they are included within the set of reasons encompassed by the just cause.

The reason for my interpretation is as follows: the condition of right intention plainly serves to lock tightly together the just cause and the actions taken for that cause. For intention in Aquinas's view is a volition bearing on the end and making it not simply the object of a wish but a practical goal, by linking the goal to something one can do about it, the means one can choose for its sake. Consequently, a state will act with right intent only if it undertakes bellicose actions for the sake of the just cause and not for any other end. Since the violent activities of warfare would be wrong except when done for the sake of the just cause, doing them for any other purpose is wrong.

This assumes that the intention whose rectitude is a condition for undertaking war is the intention involved in the social act of making war and not in the private intentions of individual warriors. Obviously, the motives of revenge and anger, which are in the hearts of many who fight in a morally justified war, compromise their own involvement in that war. But surely the inevitable but essentially private sins of soldiers—unless sanctioned or overlooked—do not necessarily flaw an otherwise justified war. The social act of undertaking war, although related in complex ways to the often mixed and opaque intentions of individual warriors, is an accessible reality within the social world; its intentions are manifest in that world. The intention of the social act of undertaking war is revealed in the war aims sought and in the specific actions called for to achieve these aims.

If a state has a just cause for fighting and undertakes war by proper authority for the sake of that just cause, there will be a state of affairs in which the justice of the motivating just cause will be realized: for example, the victim of unjust attack will have been successfully defended by turning back the enemy. Such a state of affairs, even if it cannot be articulated except vaguely or disjunctively when undertaking the war, is the aim of that war. The bellicose actions planned to realize that aim should be strictly instrumental to it and not taken for the sake of other goals a state might have. The condition of right intention requires that any act of war that serves another or a further goal remains unjustified.

A further point is needed here to indicate what is sufficient to meet the condition of right intent: a just war aims at peace, as Aquinas, quoting Augustine, holds. This simple idea has two quite different implications. First, the goods that come from peace may be hoped for as a result of succeeding in achieving morally defensible war aims. Peace and its benefits are rightly intended by those who justly undertake war. But the peace we can hope for and intend is a further goal that war is never alone sufficient to achieve and that war cannot rightly advance, except by seeking to bring about the just state of affairs that will satisfy the just cause. Second, the pursuit of a just cause, even by actions strictly instrumental to it, can fail the condition of just cause if peace is not in sight as a further good. That can happen when a state refuses to take steps within its power to bring about peace—for example, to refrain from oppressing groups some of whose members engage in terrorism.

Returning now to the defensive limit on just cause: let us suppose that the intent of a morally justified war is simply to defend, to repel invasion, to stop ongoing violation of property and other rights, and other similar action to thwart international wrongdoing. Such a conception limits the steps that a state defending itself, an ally, or other people or states may take to punish enemies. It limits the kind of rectification of grievances one can seek by warfare. And it avoids a mysterious conception of political authority that allows the leaders of one community to punish outsiders.

But it also makes it easier to meet the condition of right intent, since the defensive intention does not allow punitive actions beyond what is immediately involved in defense; punitive acts are often difficult in practice to distinguish from acts of vengeance. Just punishment should not seek to injure the punished person, but all punishment imposes odious limitations on freedom and often intentional injuries besides. Punishing in this context seems to me incompatible with the further goal of international peace, particularly in the absence of clear authority to punish. Moreover, at the deepest level, aiming precisely to harm people, especially to kill them, is morally problematic. A defensive conception of war avoids that intention and can instead reasonably regard the harms inflicted in defensive action as side effects of that action, in a kind of strategic application of double effect to the social act of undertaking violent defense.

3. APPLYING THE JUST WAR CONDITIONS TO HUMANITARIAN INTERVENTION

Violation of Human Rights Constitutes a Just Cause

As such, defending and securing human rights is a good thing to do. Certainly, it would be praiseworthy for private persons to act to secure the threatened rights of others in the absence of effective social protections; and even violent activity to defend another person would be morally permissible when grave harm is, or is about to be, inflicted and other options for defense are not available. Securing others from serious injury is one form of helping others. Helping those in need is a positive (and so defeasible) but quite general responsibility of those who are in a position to help. It is an aspect of the general responsibility of neighborly assistance, which is an obvious and immediate implication of the Golden Rule and related principles, for example, the second commandment: love your neighbor as yourself.

The question, then, is whether the responsibility of neighborly assistance applies when (1) those to be helped are not fellow citizens and (2) the help includes bellicose actions by one's polity. I do not see how these circumstances change the praiseworthy character of trying to help. Of course, those to be protected or saved may be difficult to help and so one's ability to help may be very limited. Moreover, bellicose intervention requires more stringent justification than more pacific forms of aid, and the other great responsibilities of governments may trump the duty to help. But if a polity really can help the citizens of another polity by the use of force, and if the stringent conditions for using force are met, then, so far forth, it is a good thing—maybe an obligatory thing—to do.

The limitation in the developed form of traditional just war theory that force must be used defensively does not mean that a state is limited to defending itself or to defending its allies. In that theory it is human beings' welfare and interests, not simply the welfare and interests of a given polity's subjects or allies, that is rightly defended from injury. Any reasonable limitation of defense to *self*-defense must be based either on a limitation of proper authority or an inability to act with right intention and not on the justice of the cause.

There is precedent in traditional just war theory for thinking that humanitarian intervention responds to a just cause. Vitoria, writing in the 1530s, considered all the possible headings under which the Spaniards might have just cause for making war on the American aboriginals. One batch of such reasons is simply set aside as unjust titles for subduing the Amerindians; others are allowed as possible grounds for using force against the American aboriginals. Vitoria did not fully carry through the casuistry to the point of seeking to determine whether any of the possible conditions justifying war was in fact met. But it is plain that he was skeptical that such conditions generally obtained as he wrote.[17]

Vitoria did appear to think that one of the potentially just grounds for using force did have some application in the de facto situation in the New World. Some aboriginals were believed to practice cannibalism, and Vitoria held that it is morally permissible to stop the practice by force—and presumably by conquest if necessary. So, he held that a violation of the rights of innocents is a justifying cause for war. It is significant that what grounds his view is not blanket moralism—that aboriginal practices are contrary to the natural law—but the fact that innocent humans are being mistreated.[18] He states the view succinctly in a Thomistic commentary:

> The reply to this is that there are some sins against nature which are harmful to our neighbors, such as cannibalism or euthanasia of the old and senile, which is practiced in Terra Firma; and since the defense of our neighbors is the rightful concern of each of us, even for private persons and even if it involves shedding blood, it is beyond doubt that any Christian prince can compel them not to do these things. By this title alone the emperor is empowered to coerce the Caribbean Indians.[19]

It is clear that Vitoria's limited moralism in this line of reasoning is arguing not simply for the abstract righteousness of the intervention but also for the authority of the Spaniards to intervene. How *they* get this authority remains unclarified. We will return to this important issue below.

A State Can Engage in Humanitarian Intervention
with Right Intention

The condition of just cause, understood abstractly as Aquinas and Vitoria understood it, is the most straightforward match between the logic of just war theory and the demands of humanitarian intervention. Considering the matter independently of the question of whether a polity has any business using force in this context, and independently of whether a polity, its leaders, or its subjects are capable of acting precisely for such a purpose, the question about just cause is easily settled in the affirmative.

The condition of right intention can also be met in cases of humanitarian intervention, but not easily. Recall that this condition requires that the justifying cause not be a pretext for using force for other purposes, and that bellicose action can be undertaken only for its sake. As Walzer has noted, humanitarian intervention will seldom stand as the sole component of the reason justifying going to war.[20] Ordinarily, there is reasonable worry that anarchy or tyranny will spill over into international troubles. But the ethically and legally puzzling cases of humanitarian intervention arise when the humanitarian purpose prevails to the extent that other considerations would not alone justify any use of force beyond what the humanitarian requirements indicate.

How is a state to undertake the use of force to protect or secure human rights when *just this* purpose may rightly be in view? Surely, if the norms and sentiments that make humanitarian intervention seem to be a good, or even obligatory, undertaking were merely moralistic slogans or rules, the motivation to act just for these purposes would be lacking.

But helping those in need is not generally mere dutifulness; instead, it is based on some sense of solidarity, some possibility of future friendliness and community, and in many cases on ties that bind people together across international borders. So, solidarity provides intelligible reasons for the people of one polity to help those of another. The prospect of future peace and friendship, to be realized by securing the rights of the oppressed in another country, can be a real motive, one that does not add anything to the just cause but is instead what securing the just cause promises.

The more such interpersonal goods can unite those who suffer and those who come to their aid, the greater is the chance that the condition of right intent will be satisfied.

The motivational problem is, however, further complicated by the fact that states are not likely to accept losses of their soldiers when anything less than their vital interests are at stake. The moral-psychological story I have just been telling hardly seems sufficient to identify a foreign polity's vital interests with one's own. In this situation, it may be nearly impossible to resist the temptation to cut and run, to which the United States seemed to succumb in Somalia in 1993, or to use tactics that minimize casualties but at the price of putting noncombatants unreasonably at risk, as NATO's bombing in Yugoslavia in the mid-1990s seemed to do.

The variations on both possibilities seem to me to evince a failure of right intent. To waver in the face of casualties at a level inherent in military action, but not at a level so great as to signal likely defeat, indicates a lack of commitment to realizing the just state of affairs that is contained in the just cause. To avoid casualties at the price of putting innocent lives at stake may wantonly, even murderously, injure the very people one claims to be rescuing and inevitably makes peace more difficult.

Since undertaking warfare for humanitarian purposes without serious expectation of some concrete outcome to which the rescuing state is seriously committed is likely to further harm those who are to be rescued, to weaken international stability, and to impose considerable expense and probable loss of life on the rescuing state, it seems wrong to fail to face this motivational problem fully before intervening.

I am not suggesting that the condition of right intention cannot be met by a state undertaking humanitarian intervention. But the difficult questions this condition raises are not easily answered with the necessary confidence. This is an empirical point, not one of motivational theory. Those who are convinced that states either cannot or should not act except for their own narrow expedience or national self-interest are bound to think that defense of strangers is never what a state could or should do. But traditional just war theory is not based on Hobbesian psychology.

There Can Be Proper Authority to Wage War for Humanitarian Purposes

It seems clear that, for traditional just war theory, meeting the condition of proper authority is the main hurdle for humanitarian intervention. This is the theory's version of the problem that the modern emphasis on sovereignty and political independence poses for humanitarian intervention.

The problem is straightforward, and it arises, *mutatis mutandis*, for intervening states acting unilaterally, for regional alliances, and for actions organized on behalf of the U.N. To take the case of an intervening state: the officials of such a state have authority because they are responsible for the common good of their own society. Their authority to conduct war justly, to mobilize subjects and command them to kill, and to expose themselves to being killed—all these come from their responsibility to look after their community. Where the community and its needs come to an end, so too does their authority to wage war. And humanitarian intervention lacks that relationship to a polity's common good.

This problem has an outer-looking and an inner-looking aspect. Those outside the state that is undertaking humanitarian intervention have reason to ask by what right that state meddles in the affairs of others, and those within it have reason to ask by what right their rulers ask them to kill and be killed for a benefit outside the polity's common good.

The fundamental answer must be that in situations that call for humanitarian intervention, morality demands that we consider not only the good of a single polity but also the more embracing good of the human community. As I noted in the previous section, this moral demand is not an abstract moral imposition: the humanity of strangers is of interest to us since they are potential friends, neighbors, and trading partners. In at least some conditions, the morally compelling appeal of these goods requires that the leaders of a polity serve that universal common good directly, with the only authorization being that which comes from common human morality itself.[21]

This plausibly happens when a state or group of states can predict a murderous episode, such as the massacre of the Tutsis in Rwanda, and has the resources to prevent it from happening. It seems wrong to stand by and watch in such situations when one can save many lives. The only authority available is the plain demand of morality, but that is all that is required. In moral life generally, obedience to authority and its exercise within the limits of its justification are serious but defeasible obligations. When acting in accord with them plainly prevents the fulfillment of very serious responsibilities that one would have independently of any authority, then often the requirements of authority must give way. So, I believe that humanitarian intervention poses a kind of limit case for the exercise of authority.

This kind of morally justified overriding of the requirement of proper authority does not undercut the deep rationale for authority: it is the political leader who leads his or her community into war for a common interest, not, in this case, their specific interest as a unique political community but the common human interest of peoples' welfare. If there were a higher authority to whom the leader could appeal so as to solve the problem, he or she should do that; then the moral demand would be met. The role of enforcer of morality by protecting human rights for all cannot be a standing responsibility of any political leader, but when there is no option, it is right to act. Thus, the duty is exceptional and episodic.

Moreover, this responsibility is also limited in the actions it can authorize. The immediate defense of human rights and rescue of oppressed people—such things as stopping massacres and ethnic cleansings—are clear cases. They are the precise object of the moral imperative driving the intervention. On the other end of the spectrum are efforts to remake the social fabric of a failed state or to reconstruct the political life of a tyranny. It is difficult to see how an intervening state could undertake such actions simply within the mandate of universal moral norms. Even if the temptations to act for one's own interest and to colonize, while wrapped in the mantle of morality, are successfully resisted, it seems that much of the work involved in organizing a polity can be done only by its own citizens and that many steps in setting things right will involve the discretion that only a proper political authority can exercise. Interveners lack that specifically political authority and have only such authority as can be claimed under universal moral law. And that law cannot settle such matters.

There may not be a bright line separating these extremes. There is still work for casuists.

Similarly, although the leader of a polity has the authority to organize it for war, since the ground here is strictly moral, not the widely discretionary service to the common good that political leaders normally have, it seems that the polity can be rightly led into a humanitarian intervention only if there is duty for *this* polity to intervene. That duty will exist when the norm of neighborly assistance applies and when a given state or coalition can help more effectively than others. This is another stringent limitation on authority in this situation: the authority may command subjects rightly only if convinced that their state is morally obliged to rescue or take part in the rescue.

These are stringent conditions but they plainly could have been met if the U.N.—or, if not the U.N., a state or alliance—had been willing and ready to act in Rwanda. These conditions might also have been met in Somalia or in Yugoslavia had the United States and its allies been more resolutely committed to protecting human rights in those failed states.

My analysis suggests some objections. I will consider two of them.

The first is that much of what I have been arguing is too abstract in one particular way, namely, that the U.N. Charter, the subsequent development of international law, and many treaties make humanitarian intervention illegal. So, even if in the absence of these developments of positive law, my analysis might be interesting, it is completely null in the world today.

I am not in a position to dispute the claim that humanitarian intervention is illegal. *Arguendo*, I will suppose that it is.[22] According to most just war theorists, the U.N. Charter and other international treaties and covenants are important steps toward peace. They have the force of very serious promises about most important matters of life and death for many of the people in the world. It is morally obligatory to keep promises, except in rare circumstances. So, this objection is not legalistic niggling but a profound moral concern.

However, the law should track morality at least to the extent of allowing what serious people and groups think there is a grave obligation to do, and, therefore, if situations in which humanitarian intervention is called for continue to emerge, the law should be modified to establish procedures for dealing with such cases by U.N. action or agreed-upon actions by appropriate states or alliances.

Ideally, then, the U.N. or a similar worldwide authority should be authorized and made capable of executing this humanitarian function on behalf of humanity in an effective and timely way. That would resolve the legal problem caused by the provisions of the Charter. It would also go some way toward resolving the challenge that humanitarian intervention presents to political authority at all levels. The common goods of states do not ordinarily include the welfare of the subjects of other states, and the international community is a treaty-based alliance of states. However, an international body such as the U.N. does plausibly represent humanity in a way that any member state or regional alliance cannot. If the ground for intervention is the common good of humanity, expressed in common morality, the U.N. has claim to be the authoritative body. But the U.N.'s track record on such matters is not heartening, as the example of Rwanda indicates. So, then, the challenge returns: what is an alliance such as NATO to do when faced with ethnic cleansing and genocide in a place like Kosovo and no clear mandate from the U.N.?

Here, urgent moral demands can override at least the letter of positive law, and most legal systems allow some mechanism for such an override. Aristotle's "equity" is such a mechanism, in which reasonable appeal to the legislator's likely intent provides a legal ground for setting aside the letter of the law. Determining legislative intent in international law is surely complex and uncertain, but reasonable exceptions should perhaps be undertaken and then defended in court to test and build the case law.

Positive international law, whether based on customs, treaties, or judicial decisions, must, like all law, be accorded great moral respect. Like other law, international law often tracks and implements serious moral concerns, such as respecting individual and social rights that have moral standing prior to legal enforcement. International law also implements treaties, which, as noted above, are serious promises about grave matters. Nevertheless, not all provisions of international law are absolutely binding on rulers of states. As already noted, these rulers have grave responsibilities to the common goods of their states, and those responsibilities cannot be completely ceded to international officials who do not have these responsibilities. It follows that in cases of urgent threat that cannot be effectively addressed by internationally sanctioned action, rulers have a duty to act. Consequently, since acting to secure the rights of strangers can become a duty for a state uniquely capable of providing that assistance, such action cannot be simply ruled out by moral considerations, even in the face of apparently prohibitive international law.

A second objection is that there is no practical way to distinguish between limited rescue in the face of impending or ongoing atrocity and the kind of intervention that involves remaking a society or operates from an ideological conception of human rights. I have conceded that the line between what is legitimate and what is not is not a bright line and requires casuistry. But I think there is a clear principle for working out the shape of that line; in fact, there are two.

First, I have implicitly admitted that any violation of human rights can provide a just cause for warfare because that wrong, taken abstractly, can justify actions to remedy it, including, as a last resort, actions involving military force. But I have also argued that a state, whether acting on its own or as the authorized agent of the international community, cannot easily meet the condition of right intent. The use of military force in this context must be strictly limited; it must aim precisely and only at stopping or preventing a violation of the rights of subjects of another state whose government either violates the rights itself or cannot prevent their violation by others. Consequently, the intervening state may undertake to remedy a violation of rights only when ready to do this properly by committing itself to realizing a just state of affairs that includes a real improvement in the situation of those whose rights are in jeopardy.

The prospect of realizing this just state of affairs will not be obtained when the rights to be vindicated are not important enough or threatened enough to sustain shedding blood and accepting other sacrifices by the intervening state. So a fair-minded assessment of the difficulty of securing the rights of strangers, together with willingness to accept losses to do so, provides a practical limit to the kind of intervention a state may morally undertake. Thus, one realist objection to much moralism in international dealings is a factual premise in an old-fashioned moral argument. It is only when the violation is significant enough to demand and sustain the force of arms necessary to remedy it that it crosses the threshold into the category of grave and intolerable violations of rights.

The condition of proper authority is also difficult to meet. Except in the most extreme cases, a state's military response to the failures of another state's authorities to accept or live up to widely held ideals of human rights will almost inevitably involve a usurpation of the legitimate authority of the other state's leaders and of its citizens' ability to shape their own affairs.

As I have already argued, common morality can allow some actions outside established authority, but common morality cannot authorize an intervening state to do what it cannot do, and remaking a regime or, more radically, a constitution and political culture, appear to be among the things intervening powers cannot successfully carry out by warfare and so should not undertake to do. Similarly, when one goes beyond stopping atrocities, preventing ethnic cleansing, protecting refugees, and perhaps deposing a tyrant, what is needed to establish the rights under threat involves many steps and much decision making. This process cannot be carried out by appeal to the authority of the moral law alone but also requires the discretion and authority of local political leaders.

4. Conclusion

Traditional just war theory has the advantage of coming at current international conflicts in a vocabulary and conceptual scheme that are distinct from much international law and modern thinking about the justification of war, even though it forms part of the background of that thinking. The categories of proper authority, just cause, and right intention put into the forefront of the discussion the concepts of the common good and social authority and insist on war aims limited to the realization of the just cause by actions strictly proportioned to those aims.

The application of these concepts to the prospect of intervention for the sake of securing human rights surely does not provide a crisp, decisive answer to this difficult moral dilemma, but it does throw distinctive light on several of its aspects. Although the violation of rights that provokes humanitarian intervention grounds a just cause, it is the defense of these rights, not the punishment of those who violate them, that is the just cause. The condition of right intention is difficult to meet and likely is not met except in rare circumstances: the intervening state or states must use force only as needed to secure the just cause, and no more. They must also be seriously prepared to do what it takes to secure this just cause in accordance with other conditions limiting violence in warfare. Finally, the condition of proper authority is even more difficult to meet, both for individual states and for members of the international community acting in concert, primarily, but not entirely, because of the U.N. Charter and the state of international law. But even when the condition of proper authority is met —by agreement in the Security Council or unilaterally by states appealing in an urgent crisis to common human morality—the reality and importance of local political authority sets significant limits: the more intervention is limited to defending people and their rights, and the less it is extended to taking over the governing of the country whose government violates its people's rights or cannot secure them, the easier it is for interveners to meet the conditions of right intention and proper authority.

In short, traditional just war theory adds to the discussion of humanitarian intervention a sober general assessment that emphasizes the difficulty of justifying intervention, and a robust sense of the limitations of what intervening states can rightly seek to do to protect the human rights of outsiders even when morality and widespread revulsion at oppression call for intervention.

NOTES

1. For some useful reflections on definitional issues, see Jeff McMahan, "Intervention and Collective Self-Determination," *Ethics and International Affairs* 10 (1996): 1–4.

2. See Michael Walzer, *Just and Unjust Wars: A Moral Argument with Historical Illustrations* (New York: Basic Books, 1977), 90–100.

3. Howard Adelman, "Humanitarian Intervention: The Case of the

Kurds," *International Journal of Refugee Law* 4 (1992): 18, 38, cited in Pierre Laberge, "Humanitarian Intervention: Three Ethical Positions," *Ethics and International Affairs* 9 (1995): 15.

4. Contrast this with Nicholas Wheeler, *Saving Strangers: Humanitarian Intervention in International Society* (Oxford: Oxford University Press, 2000), 34ff. For Wheeler, a humanitarian intervention has four defining conditions: (1) just cause: a supreme emergency of some noncitizens; (2) last resort; (3) proportionality; (4) promotion of a positive humanitarian outcome. This defines a morally justified action. I prefer to begin more descriptively with an action defined only by its presumptively morally good purpose (roughly Wheeler's first condition), and then ask under what conditions it can be permissible to undertake and execute such an action. As the tradition would ask of any action correctly described as a war whether it is a morally permissible action, I am asking of a war further described as being undertaken for humanitarian purposes whether it is permissible.

5. This vocabulary and the ideas it represents are on or very near the surface of the U.N. Charter, especially in Article 2 (4): "All members shall refrain in their international relations from the threat or use of force against the territorial integrity or political independence of any state . . ." and 2 (7): "Nothing in the present Charter shall authorize the U.N. to intervene in matters that are essentially within the domestic jurisdiction of any state."

6. Walzer, *Just and Unjust Wars*, 58–64; see J. Bryan Heir, "Intervention: From Theories to Cases," *Ethics and International Affairs* 9 (1995): 1–13, for an account of the power and importance of the Westphalian agreement about the structure of international society and its resistance to interventions.

7. Thomas Aquinas, *Summa Theologiae*, 2-2 (second part of the second part), q. 40, a. 1. All editions and translations of Aquinas's work follow this form of citation. There are four articles in question 40: (1) whether some war is licit; (2) whether it is licit for clerics to fight in a war; (3) whether it is licit to lay traps (*uti insidiis*) in war; and (4) whether it is licit to fight on feast days. My focus is on article 1, but the set of concerns addressed is important for our subject. The interpretation of Aquinas developed here has been adapted into the interpretation in my "Just War Doctrine and the Military Response to Terrorism," *Journal of Political Philosophy* 11, no. 2 (2003): 1–18 at 5–13.

8. Aquinas, *Summa Theologiae*, 2-2, q. 64.

9. Some within the Catholic just war tradition believe that the limitation of the authority of the sovereign rulers of states can, and ideally should, go very far indeed. See Vatican Council II, Constitution on the

Church in the Modern World (*Gaudium et Spes*), paragraph 82: "It is our clear duty then to strain every muscle as we work for the time when all war can be completely outlawed by international agreement. This goal undoubtedly requires the establishment of some universal public authority acknowledged as such by all and endowed with effective power to safeguard on behalf of all, security, regard for justice and respect for rights." This bold project does not seem to include a hope for a worldwide polity in which sovereign authority would alone reside, but a global authority created by treaty.

10. Thomas Franck, "Legality and Legitimacy in Humanitarian Intervention," this volume, chap. 5, spells out the importance of what he calls the "jurying" function of the international community in making general norms reasonably applicable to interpretatively difficult situations. This function also serves to guarantee impartiality in situations in which involved parties are unlikely to achieve it. David Rodin, *War and Self-Defense* (Oxford: Oxford University Press, 2002), 173–88, argues that states lack the impartiality necessary to justify anything like the criminal punishment of other states and their citizens. I agree. If the authority to undertake warfare were strictly analogous to that involved in justly administering a criminal justice system, states could not rightly undertake warfare; as Rodin argues, only an international authority could do so. I believe that traditional just war theory holds that the common good of the state is the ground of the authority of its rulers to punish criminals and to defend from aggressors, but that defense against aggressors is not strictly an instance of the punishment involved in criminal justice.

11. *Quaest. in Heptateuch.*; *in Joseu 10, super Joseu 8*, 2. PL 34, 781.

12. John Finnis, "The Ethics of War and Peace in the Catholic Just War Tradition," in *The Ethics of War and Peace: Religious and Secular Perspectives*, ed. Terry Nardin (Princeton: Princeton University Press, 1996), 22–23, suggests that the older tradition might not have been as robustly punitive as some of the classical texts suggest.

13. Walzer, *Just and Unjust Wars*, 62–63.

14. Pratap Bhanu Mehta, "From State Sovereignty to Human Security (via Institutions?)," this volume, chap. 10, takes just war theory to be inherently punitive and then reports the puzzle that arises because of the absence of a superior neutral authority capable of characterizing acts of war as crimes. I think that the puzzle is insoluble but that defense as such is not imposing sanctions.

15. Second Vatican Council, Constitution of the Church and the Modern World, par. 80.

16. Ibid., par. 79. *The Catechism of the Catholic Church*, par. 2309, summarizes the current Catholic understanding of the just war doctrine,

including many conditions I have passed over in silence. The limitation to defense in this formulation is definitional. The kind of action to be evaluated by the moral conditions of just war doctrine is said to be "defense by military force."

17. See Francisco de Vitoria, *On the American Indians* (1539), in *Vitoria: Political Writings*, ed. John Pagden and Jeremy Lawrance (Cambridge: Cambridge University Press, 1991), 233–92, esp. 277–92. He concludes the *relectio* with a consideration of the objection that his position would remove the wealth and power of Spain in the New World.

18. Ibid., 287–88.

19. Vitoria, "On the Evangelization of Unbelievers" (1531–32), in Pagden and Lawrance, *Vitoria*, Appendix B, 347.

20. See Walzer, *Just and Unjust Wars*, 101–4.

21. Walzer, *Just and Unjust Wars*, 107, argues in the same spirit. More needs to be said, I think, than he says about extent of the authority of an appeal to "humanity as a whole." Similarly Terry Nardin, "The Moral Basis of Humanitarian Intervention," *Ethics and International Affairs* 16, no. 1 (2002): 57–70, argues much as I do that humanitarian intervention has its normative justification in common human morality. Again the extent of the authority of strictly moral imperatives on relationships structured by authority and more particular goods remains a concern.

22. Pierre Laberge, "Humanitarian Intervention," states well the difficulty a nonlawyer must have in sorting this out. He makes a telling case that all of the ethical approaches he considers (all close to the position emerging here) are more or less at odds with the U.N. Charter.

2

HUMANITARIAN INTERVENTION: A CONFLICT OF TRADITIONS

ANTHONY COATES

Except for terrorism, no issue is more prominent in contemporary ethical debate about war than humanitarian intervention. This is, in part, a reflection of its practical importance but also, in large measure, of its perceived theoretical incongruity. Like terrorism, humanitarian intervention appears to break the existing ethical and legal mold of war. In particular, the issue seems to defeat just war theory in what is presumed to be not only its prevalent but its definitive form. Many would agree with the judgment that "humanitarian intervention is not best understood as an action which fits into theories of just warfare."[1] This assessment owes much to a Westphalian interpretation of just war theory, which sees it as an essentially statist conception of war, too wedded to the twin principles of state sovereignty and nonintervention and to an aggressor-defender paradigm of war, to yield a satisfactory account of humanitarian intervention. This strand of just war thinking does exist (it may even be dominant), but it should not be regarded as definitive. Nor should it be assumed that the difficulties encountered in reconciling just war with humanitarian intervention are duplicated throughout the entire range of just war thinking.

Michael Walzer's immense influence on contemporary just war thinking is partly responsible for this narrow and unrepresentative reading of what is, in reality, a much more complex and varied tradition. Walzer's *Just and Unjust Wars* continues to be regarded as representative, especially by critics of just war theory.[2] David Rodin's powerful recent criticism of just war thinking, for example, relies heavily and openly on a Walzerian interpretation of the tradition. It is this that accounts for his conclusion that "the traditional just war categories of aggression and defense are failing us. They are mute or even obstructive over the problems of civil war and domestic oppression."[3] Rodin's judgment that humanitarian intervention "sits uncomfortably with [Walzer's] deeper theoretical commitments"[4] rings true but is not conclusive as far as the broader tradition is concerned. Many of the assumptions and principles that critics attribute (via Walzer) to the just war tradition are alien to that tradition in some of its other historical and contemporary expressions. The fact is that many just war theorists would agree with the criticisms directed at Walzer's version of just war theory.

1. THE INTERNAL VARIETY OF THE JUST WAR TRADITION

If the resources of just war thinking in relation to humanitarian intervention are to be adequately assessed and fully exploited, it seems essential that the tradition should be understood in a properly historical way. That means (among other things) that it should not be understood monolithically. "It belongs to the nature of a tradition," writes Oakeshott, "to tolerate and unite an internal variety, not insisting upon conformity to a single character."[5] The unity that is the just war tradition embraces many formulations that contend one with another and that defy uniform classification. The theoretical disjunctions that occur within it are at least as important in understanding the tradition (and its potential use) as its elements of continuity. Rather than reducing the tradition to a single voice, its internal arguments and controversies need to be brought to the fore.

It is equally unhistorical and unhelpful to think of the tradition in a fragmented or atomistic way, that is, without regard to its internal composition and structure. The just war tradition is not the simple aggregate that it is often portrayed to be. The random listing of individual thinkers (a common way of identifying the tradition) does little to reveal its dynamic internal structure and divisions. As a result, we are forced to rely on an abstract and uniform definition ("the standard theory offered by the Just War Tradition")[6] that may serve the purposes of philosophical argument but that seriously distorts and diminishes the tradition by suppressing its internal variety and complexity.

The internal structure of the just war tradition is a matter of conceptual contrasts and affinities, of variable patterns of association and dependence established among individual thinkers throughout its long history. These shifting patterns of association constitute a plurality of traditions, lending historical definition and coherence to the work of individual theorists and, by the same token, countering the tradition's monolithic image. These are traditions with different historical pedigrees, contrasting ethical concerns, and divergent implications. The location of individual thinkers within them uncovers matters of fundamental dispute that are often obscured in historical accounts that neglect the plurality and interplay of traditions.

Recognizing that the comprehensive "just war tradition" includes alternative strands that are often in radical disagreement with one another is essential if we are, as Walzer says, to "recapture the just war for political and moral theory"[7] in its fullness and complexity. That recognition often seems to be lacking. The reason why the internal variety of the tradition is overlooked may come from thinking of historical change as a process of substitution, according to which later theories supplant earlier ones. From this standpoint, the history of the tradition is one of linear progression. Differences are acknowledged but are seen to have been successively overcome or left behind, not to persist as alternative traditions with their own separate identities, reaching into the present and informing contemporary thinking. The plurality of traditions gives the lie to the assumption of linear progression.

2. Traditional and Modern Just War Theory

From this historical perspective, the claim that just war theory cannot accommodate humanitarian intervention appears too sweeping. It may apply to one (or some) of the traditions that make up the complex historical corpus of just war writing but not to all of them. In responding to the ethical challenge of humanitarian intervention, several authors have drawn attention to the internal diversity and varied resources of the just war tradition and, in particular, to the claims of an earlier but still enduring strand of that tradition. For these writers, the recovery of that alternative way of thinking is seen as an important step toward a more satisfactory understanding of the ethics of intervention.

Bryan Hehir, for example, has argued for a revised ethic of intervention that draws on a "medieval model" of just war thinking, as well as on the writings of Vitoria, Suarez, and Grotius, all of whom sought "to maintain the moral teachings of the Natural Law and its derivative, the Just War doctrine, in the face of the challenge posed by the secular, sovereign state."[8] Tony Coady's defense of humanitarian intervention also appeals to an earlier, premodern tradition of just war thinking focused on the recourse to war (*ius ad bellum*) in a much fuller and more critical way than current legal and moral theory.[9] Similarly, Terry Nardin's reexamination of the issue rests on a contrast between two traditions of thought: "One, embedded in modern international law and the UN Charter, sees intervention as inherently problematic. . . . The other, which belongs to the tradition of natural law or common morality, sees humanitarian intervention as an expression of the basic moral duty to protect the innocent from violence."[10] Finally, Joseph Boyle appeals to "traditional just war theory," a way of thinking about war that is medieval in origin but that reaches into the present, uniting "medieval canonists and moral theologians," "sixteenth-century scholastics," and contemporary "neoscholastic philosophers and theologians."[11]

As far as the moral aspect of humanitarian intervention is concerned, substantial rewards are to be had by drawing on this older (but still living) tradition of just war thinking. In the first place, grounded as it is in natural law, it brings to bear on the issue an ethical perspective of moral universalism that is lacking in what Joseph Boyle describes as "the positive just war doctrine." This is the doctrine critics have in mind when they berate just war theory for its preoccupation with state sovereignty and its consequent neglect of internal conflict and oppression. Thus, Rodin writes, "[B]ecause it concentrates exclusively on sovereignty and the rights of states, the national-defense paradigm [which Rodin sees as central to just war theory] fails to provide, and indeed obstructs, legal regulation of the recourse to internal military conflict."[12] Similarly, Janna Thompson argues (persuasively with respect to some strands of just war thinking) that just war theory "takes the entitlements of sovereignty for granted and closes off attempts to criticise these entitlements."[13] This understanding of just war theory as an essentially statist or realist doctrine is widespread, as is the association, if not assimilation, of just war theory with the work of Michael Walzer.[14] On this reading of the tradition, it is, at best, no more than an expression of the "morality of states" and, as such, quite incapable of any sustained defense of humanitarian intervention. For that we must look beyond the just war tradition to some more cosmopolitan tradition of thought that "gives greater recognition and protection to the rights of individuals as against states."[15]

In fact, the older, natural law form of just war thinking contradicts the "positive just war doctrine." In its older manifestation, the tradition seems well equipped to tackle the problem of internal conflict and intervention. By concentrating on issues of just recourse (*ius ad bellum*), it helps to articulate the problems of humanitarian intervention in a way that the modern legal positivist tradition (with its neglect of *ius ad bellum* and its overriding emphasis on *ius in bello*) does not. In particular, its critical understanding of legitimate authority, its insistence on the moral limitation of state sovereignty, and its broader and less restrictive understanding of just cause (along with its refusal to rule out offensive war) provide humanitarian intervention with a more coherent and defensible normative basis.

In its typically modern or legalistic form, the principle of *legitimate authority* is uncritical and undemanding. The prevailing emphasis is on *de facto* rather than *de iure* authority, with the result that most states pass the test with ease. The ability of a regime to maintain some minimal degree of order within the borders of a state is considered reason enough to warrant recognition of its sovereign authority. In this accommodating form, neither the origins of power nor the manner of its present use are objects of further moral scrutiny. From the natural law standpoint of traditional just war theory, things are seen very differently. The authority of the state is not taken for granted. Justice (as well as order) is a primary concern. The manner in which power is deployed internally is as important as the manner of its external use. Morally speaking, the internal constitution of the state is not a black box. The exercise of sovereignty, together with its corollary nonintervention, is always conditional, never absolute.

Similar considerations apply to the principle of *just cause*. As commonly understood, the principle does not lend itself to defending intervention. The problem is that humanitarian intervention appears to contradict the prevailing national security paradigm of war, which equates a just war with a war of self-defense and an unjust war with a war of aggression. That paradigm appears to exclude humanitarian intervention on principle. As an apparent act of aggression, intervention cannot be accommodated within the conventional moral and legal parameters of war. For those who are convinced by the moral case for intervention, this is a fundamental deficiency—hence Rodin's conclusion that "the traditional just war categories of aggression and defense are failing us."[16] However, there are strong grounds for thinking that it is not "traditional" just war thinking that is deficient in this regard but its "modern," attenuated, rival.

The traditional concept of *just cause* is broader and more critical than its modern counterpart. The simple equation, in much contemporary thinking, of the just war with a war of self-defense and the unjust war with a war of aggression reflects the dominance of the states-system with its twin principles of state sovereignty and nonintervention. From a traditional viewpoint, the equation begs too many of the fundamental moral questions about war. The aggressor-defender distinction is understood too literally, too physically, to be morally illuminating. In that restricted, nonmoral sense, it is of little use as a means of distinguishing just from unjust war. Without reference to some notion of justice, the distinction is ethically unproductive.

In the older tradition, the justice of a defensive war is not taken for granted. The internal constitution and practice of the defending state needs to be taken into account. Would a totalitarian or tyrannical state bent on annihilating a social class or ethnic minority enjoy a right of self-defense against external attack? Would its use of force be justified simply by virtue of its defensive mode? There is no right to defend morally indefensible policies of that kind. Similar considerations apply to the use of force in an offensive capacity. Such use is not, as such, unjust. It all depends on the moral status of those who use it and of those against whom it is used. Force can be used offensively without such use constituting an act of "aggression," as long as that word is understood in a critical and moral sense.

The aggressor-defender distinction is less important in the traditional view of the just war than it is in its modern counterpart because that earlier view has a broader moral horizon. The concepts of aggression and defense are present, but the context within which they are applied is a universal moral order that transcends the system of states. When viewed from the wider, universalist, moral perspective, what looks like an act of unjustified aggression in the state-centered context is defending the innocent, upholding justice, and vindicating the universal moral community to which all states belong and to which all are subject. The broader moral context is capable of accommodating humanitarian intervention with comparative ease.

Recognition of the internal variety of the just war tradition is, then, essential to any assessment of its potential contribution to understanding the ethics of intervention. The form of just war thinking that happens to be dominant at any one time must not be allowed to speak for the tradition as a whole. The idea that "traditional" conceptions of just war can clarify the issue of intervention in ways that "modern" versions cannot is part of the present argument, something that it shares with the approaches of the writers cited earlier. However, to achieve maximum effect, traditional conceptions require further scrutiny and discrimination. They are not all of one piece, and their impact on the issue of humanitarian intervention varies considerably.

3. The Variety of Traditional Just War Theory

Often the appeal to "traditional" just war theory masks differences among the writers comprised by that broad category, not just of detail but also of principle. Assumptions of continuity and internal coherence are common, yet such assumptions often appear questionable. Not only is there a radical discontinuity between the older natural law tradition and the modern tradition of international law, there are also cleavages and discontinuities of the most fundamental kind within the natural law tradition itself. The natural law tradition is not homogeneous but subsumes a number of rival traditions. As a result, any uniform appeal to it must give rise to serious ambiguity and misunderstanding. As far as humanitarian intervention is concerned, these divisions within traditional just war thinking are just as instructive as the division between traditional and modern just war thinking.

Consider the relationship between Vitoria and Grotius, two thinkers who figure prominently in any history of just war thought. Conventional accounts of the just war tradition portray Grotius as the heir of Vitoria.[17] Though differences are acknowledged, the prevailing emphasis is on the continuity of thought between the two thinkers, often expressed in terms of their common allegiance to natural law as the basis of just war reasoning and, more specifically and relevantly, their common acceptance of humanitarian intervention. Yet appearances are deceptive. As Richard Tuck demonstrates, the shared vocabulary of natural law and just war cannot conceal fundamental differences that undermine any assumption of continuity or linear progression. In Tuck's account, differences between the two thinkers reflect the different traditions to which they belong. Vitoria's scholasticism precludes the "fracturing of the Aristotelian notion of social life [that] was at the heart of Grotius's enterprise, and [that] was to remain characteristic of many of his followers [including Kant]."[18] Though both are classifiable as natural law thinkers, their conceptions of natural law are of radically different pedigree and import. One, in typical Thomist and Aristotelian fashion, upholds the political and social nature of man; the other, in an individualist mode that is Stoic and Epicurean in inspiration, denies it.[19]

Though Grotius's philosophy is not without some notion of human sociability, his conception of it falls far short of Vitoria's and of the Thomist tradition to which Vitoria belongs. Far from continuing or developing that tradition of thought, Grotius's thinking calls it seriously into question. As Nardin points out, "Grotius' understanding of sociality is only superficially like that of Aristotle and Aquinas, for it attributes to human beings no more than a natural propensity to respect one another's interests. Founding natural law on natural rights undermines the

Aristotelian assumption of natural human sociality and narrows the scope of natural law to mutual noninterference."[20]

For Vitoria, the political community is a natural institution on which human beings fundamentally rely. (As his defense of Amerindian society demonstrates, Vitoria does not rest his justification of political community on any specific historical form it might take, such as the European state.) The resources of the community (moral and not just material) that make up the common good are essential to human flourishing or the achievement of human excellence. Political sociality is rooted in human nature. By contrast, for Grotius and his heirs, the state of nature is an apolitical condition out of which the state emerges through the free agency of self-sufficient, contracting individuals. The relationship between human beings and the political community is more instrumental than constitutive. Such divergent conceptions of human nature and the state are bound to affect any understanding of international relations. In particular, this cleavage in natural law and just war thought has a very considerable impact on the way in which humanitarian intervention is understood.

Though Vitoria accepted the principle of humanitarian intervention (on the grounds of a duty in natural law to protect the innocent), his political conception of human nature and his ethical conception of the state had a restraining effect on its application. This enabled him (along with his fellow Thomists) to resist the paternalist and imperialist tendencies of those, like Sepulveda, who argued the right of a Christian and civilized power such as Spain to subject the barbarian Indian communities of the New World to its rule. By invoking the Thomist principle that "dominion is based on nature and not on grace," Vitoria upheld the pagan Indians' right of dominion. This principle applied even to a society that, from a European perspective, appeared not only un-Christian but also primitive or barbarian. Vitoria shared that perspective. His acceptance of the distinction between a civilized Europe and a barbaric New World testified to his struggle to come to terms with an alien culture, yet he refused to make the distinction an excuse for conquest. Moreover, the barbaric appearance of Indian society was unable to conceal from him its fundamental rationality. "They have some order in their affairs," he observes. "They have properly organized cities, proper marriages, magistrates and overlords, laws, industries and commerce, all of which require the use of reason."[21] Crucially, this recognition of the hidden virtues of Indian society went hand in hand with an acknowledgement of the deficiencies of Christian and European society. Vitoria was no moral relativist, but his natural law conception of a universal moral order found room for the particular, for difference. The realization of that universal order involved its refraction and embodiment, necessarily imperfect and incomplete, in particular moral and political communities, each with its own integrity and legitimacy.

In Grotius's understanding of international relations the role of the political community was much diminished. His concepts of natural law and human nature were rationalist and individualist in comparison with those of Vitoria. He understood natural law itself in abstract rational terms, as the product of individual reasoning rather than the fruit of social and historical experience. Here, the state or political community was without the ethical significance attributed to it by the Thomist tradition. For him, the state was no natural institution (no reservoir of moral and material resources through which social individuals are enabled to realize their humanity) but an artificial construct designed to secure the interests of natural individuals. Political dominion was founded not on nature but on grace or, rather, on grace's secular equivalent, "civilization." Such an understanding had a relaxing and energizing impact on the issue of humanitarian intervention. Whereas the political principle of Thomism dictated a moral presumption against intervention that was surmountable only with difficulty, Grotius's rational individualism inspired the ready acceptance of intervention. Where Vitoria discerned a hidden rationality in alien societies, Grotius saw only barbarity, the recognition of which led to the justification of punitive wars that went far beyond humanitarian intervention.[22]

The divide between Grotius and Vitoria seems fundamental, fundamental enough to be expressed in terms of a rivalry of traditions. That rivalry is of more than historical concern. In the interests of a fuller and more critical understanding of humanitarian intervention, the attempt to recapture the just war thinking needs to take the rivalry in question into account. Any indiscriminate appeal to a traditional or natural law way of thinking that conceals or suppresses this cleavage of thought within the natural law tradition itself diminishes the past and narrows the scope of contemporary debate. In fact, the result of such an indiscriminate appeal has been that the distinctive tradition to which Vitoria and others gave expression has remained largely unrecognized, its absence, or relative silence, contributing to the polarized state of the contemporary ethical debate about humanitarian intervention.

In that debate, typically, *realism* is contrasted with *cosmopolitanism* (moral particularism with moral universalism). Overwhelmingly, humanitarian intervention is seen to be grounded in a cosmopolitan form of universalism. This simple moral schema is sometimes adjusted to take account of that more morally sensitive variant of realism called the *morality of states*.[23] Resisting the moral skepticism of more extreme forms of realism, the latter upholds the ethical determination of international relations. However, because its main object is to safeguard the autonomy of states, it does so in a form that is too limited to accommodate humanitarian intervention. The result is the persistence of the realist-cosmopolitan divide. As John Vincent puts it, "[I]f the central idea of the 'morality of states' is that states should be desensitized to each other's domestic wrongdoings in the interest of order among them, the central idea of cosmopolitanist morality is to heighten the sensitivity of people in one place to wrongs done in another in the interest of the achievement of global justice."[24] This division between *cosmopolitanism*, on the one hand, and the equally statist categories of *realism* and the *morality of states*, on the other, cannot accommodate the more complex—synthetic—tradition to which Vitoria gave expression.

4. POLITICAL AND COSMOPOLITAN UNIVERSALISM

The main reason, perhaps, why humanitarian intervention remains such a contentious moral issue is that there is so little agreement about its normative basis. Realists criticize interventionists for their systematic neglect of particular attachments and for the ease with which they are prepared to set aside such cherished international norms as state sovereignty and nonintervention. In their turn, interventionists bemoan the moral parochialism of realists, the paucity of their moral ambition, their relative indifference to values and concerns that transcend states. In either case, the argument starts, more often than not, from a presumed antithesis of particular and universal. But this antithesis is quite alien to the natural law tradition of thinkers like Aquinas and Vitoria. In that tradition, universalism is always an embedded universalism, that is, a synthesis of particular and universal.[25]

The polarized state of the debate stems from the one-sided concept of universalism employed by advocates and critics of intervention alike. Though moral universalism is the most plausible normative basis of humanitarian intervention, that universalism can take different forms. In particular, a distinction needs to be drawn between the "political" and the "cosmopolitan" forms of universalism that typify the early and the late traditions of natural law respectively. The problem that bedevils the current debate is that the moral universalism underpinning humanitarian intervention has come to be identified with the later, cosmopolitan variant, that is, with a concept of universality that—quite unlike its political counterpart—is inherently unsympathetic toward particular states or political communities.

As the discussion of Grotius suggests, the role of the state in this cosmopolitan tradition is much diminished. Human beings are without the social and political nature, the basic dependency, ascribed to them by the earlier tradition of natural law. Thus, Brian Barry argues that "human beings are . . . only incidentally members of polities."[26] As a result, "membership of a society does not have deep ethical significance."[27] Charles Beitz, another cosmopolitan theorist, agrees that "cosmopolitan liberalism accords no ethical privilege to state-level societies."[28] Peter Singer, too, concurs: "[A] global ethic should not stop at, or give great significance to, national boundaries. National sovereignty has no *intrinsic* moral weight. . . . Instead we should be developing the ethical foundations of the coming era of a single world community."[29] The universal community is monolithic in conception. Where a continuing role for the state is acknowledged, an instrumental view, based on the priority of the rational individual, prevails. The traditional, constitutive and ethical, role of the state is discarded.

One of the fiercest recent criticisms of humanitarian intervention has come from the pen of Danilo Zolo. In *Cosmopolis* (1997) and *Invoking Humanity* (2002), Zolo mounts an attack, in the

name of "realism," on a growing "humanitarian interventionism."
He identifies natural law, together with its corollary just war, as the
philosophical foundation of this "militant humanism." However,
his understanding of both natural law and just war ignores the
cleavage I have identified within the tradition of natural law. The
object of Zolo's criticism is a cosmopolitan version of natural law,
which he sees as rooted in the Enlightenment, that is at odds in
several fundamental respects with the earlier political tradition of
natural law.

Zolo's criticism rests on the judgment that humanitarian intervention is inherently imperialistic. That judgment owes something
to a classical realist view of international relations, according to
which the heightened moral appearance of humanitarian war
serves to conceal the naked realities of power and interest. More
to the point, however, it relies heavily on his interpretation of the
cosmopolitan philosophy that, in his view, underpins the moral
case for intervention. "Can any cosmopolitan project," he asks,
"ever be anything other than an inherently hegemonic and violent undertaking?"[30] According to Zolo, the source of cosmopolitan imperialism lies in its rationalism, its individualism, and its
covert (because unacknowledged) ethnocentrism (three qualities
that are alien to the political tradition of natural law). It is, in
other words, a matter of basic principles and concepts that lead,
logically, to the systematic neglect or conceptual downgrading of
particular states, cultures, and traditions. What lies at the heart of
his criticism is the idea that moral universalism can find little
room for the particular, that it is unable to tolerate difference,
that it must be "cosmopolitan" in this sense. This assumption
explains his conclusion that "the very idea of the moral community of humankind is totalitarian."[31]

Zolo's interpretation of cosmopolitanism, like his reading of
the tradition of natural law as a whole, is misleadingly uniform. In
both cases, the internal variety or plurality of the tradition is overlooked. The contemporary movement of cosmopolitanism is, in
some of its expressions at least, alive to the concerns that lie
behind his criticism—as several contributions to the present volume demonstrate. At the same time, however, the conception of
cosmopolitanism that Zolo singles out for attack is no straw man
and, in respect of this familiar variant, his suspicions are not with-

out foundation. However, the case for humanitarian intervention does not stand or fall with cosmopolitanism. Zolo's criticism of interventionism assumes that intervention is grounded in a cosmopolitan form of universalism, with its natural hostility toward particular cultures, and ignores the claims of an earlier, more political, universalist tradition that has a natural affinity with particular cultures.

Can this older tradition add anything to the ethical debate about humanitarian intervention? I think it can provide a more satisfactory normative basis for intervention, one that by doing justice to both universal *and* particular values overcomes the polarities of cosmopolitanism and realism. Here is a tradition of thought, rooted in natural law, that is unequivocal in its moral universalism, while, at the same time, recognizing the essential role of particular moral and political communities. Its concept of the moral community of humankind not only tolerates but also upholds and affirms difference. That unity is understood as a plural unity in which difference is seen as a strength, not a weakness. The choice is not between "plurality" and "solidarity," as some have suggested,[32] but between a plural and a monolithic concept of unity. Its aim is not the vindication of the universal against the particular, or of the particular against the universal. This political tradition is wholly without that antagonism between particular and universal that is the common currency of much cosmopolitan and realist thought. Its chief merit lies in its ability to hold together those elements that are prised apart in later traditions of thought. As a consequence, many of the normative dilemmas that afflict more one-sided conceptions can be avoided.

The older tradition's political concept of universality avoids the abstractions of cosmopolitanism without surrendering to realist particularism. By conceiving states as parts of a universal moral community, ethical limitations are placed upon them, with the result that state sovereignty does not become here what it becomes in some later (realist) doctrines, namely, the rock on which humanitarian intervention founders. At the same time, by conceiving universality as a plural and concrete unity (grounded in the ethical role of the state and the political nature of human beings), the tradition is able to affirm and do justice to cultural and political differences in a way that is foreign to more abstract (cosmopolitan) versions of universality. This dual aspect has a beneficial impact on the treatment of humanitarian intervention. As a result, the tradition is less eager to endorse intervention in the first place and, when interventions *are* called for, more sensitive to the circumstances and requirements of the communities affected by the intervention. In this way it can help to diminish the prospects of the militant interventionism that realists like Zolo fear.

The form that universalism takes in the earlier, political, tradition means that it is without the expansive tendencies associated with the later, cosmopolitan, tradition. Though unequivocal in proclaiming the moral community of mankind, its principled recognition of particular states or political communities gives it, unlike its cosmopolitan rival, a strong moral presumption *against* intervention. Though cosmopolitans, too, may start from such a presumption, that presumption seems weak without the clear foundation in moral principle that the political tradition so clearly possesses. As Pratap Mehta argues, there is a tendency in cosmopolitan thought to claim the moral high ground and to discount the moral credentials of those seeking to uphold the claims of the particular via state sovereignty and nonintervention.[33] The principled stand is assumed to be cosmopolitan, while the defense of nonintervention is reduced, at best, to a pragmatic or prudential concern with international order rather than justice, and, at worst, to the defense of venal self-interest. The moral basis of *non*intervention is downplayed.

This is not the case with political universalism. In the political tradition, there is a high moral threshold to be surmounted before intervention can be justified. Such inhibition has nothing to do with moral skepticism or moral indifference to the fate of fellow humans, as cosmopolitans are prone to assume. It is a matter of moral principle, not self-interest or political expediency. It betrays no wavering in the defense of moral universalism. On the contrary, its moral presumption against intervention is grounded in an appreciation of the worth of the particular to the cause of universalism. Its defense of the particular is an expression of universalist concerns. The aims of moral universalism are better served by upholding the integrity and plurality of particular communities and cultures than by imposing some monolithic unity based on the temporary hegemony of one particular moral culture or tradition. This is a form of universalism that, unlike cosmopolitanism, privileges states ethically, and it does so without surrendering to state sovereignty, absolutely conceived. It is this political universalism, and not its cosmopolitan rival, that underpins just war theory in its older, classical, conception.

5. Right Intention and the Virtues of Humanitarian Intervention

To determine, more specifically, the potential contribution of the tradition to the debate about intervention, it is necessary to look at its internal principles, as Joseph Boyle does in his contribution to this volume. In this concluding section, I will consider one of those principles, *right intention*. I focus on this principle because it illustrates my general point that, in certain respects, the just war tradition is diminished in its predominant modern form and also because of its strategic importance in the moral limitation of war.

One of the strengths of the older tradition of just war thinking is its attention to the moral psychology of war. Viewed from this perspective, the ethics of war involves more than the rational application of principles. To be effective, it must cultivate the virtues and inhibit the vices of war. The capacity to conduct war justly is not simply assumed (as it tends to be in more rationalist and abstract accounts of moral conduct). Moral agents are in need of moral empowerment, of that "which *inclines* moral agents to attitudes and actions in accordance with the order of right reason."[34] The need is greater in war than it is in any other moral sphere. This is the kernel of truth contained within the moral skepticism of realism. The hostile environment of war is simply not conducive to the moral decision making that some versions of the ethics of war require. The urgency of combat precludes reflective morality. Responses in war must be spontaneous, immediate, certain, the result of acquired habits of behavior, of moral character, and not of the rational application of rules. Because war creates situations that are among "the emergencies of life when time and opportunity for reflection are lacking,"[35] "habitual" morality meets its demands in a way that "reflective" morality never can. It is a matter of a disposition, or predetermination, to act or, per-haps, more important, *not* to act in certain ways.

As Boyle argues, it is Aquinas's emphasis on the virtues (and their correlative vices) that accounts for the economy of principle that, from a modern perspective, is so striking a feature of his discussion of the just war. Aquinas does not mention the *ius in bello* principles of proportionality and discrimination, to which so much importance is now (quite rightly) attached, in that discus-sion. However, those principles are implicit in Aquinas's concep-tion of *ius ad bellum* and, more specifically, in the condition of *right intention*, in the substantive sense in which Aquinas under-stands it. The tendency in contemporary just war theory to inter-pret *right intention* in an exclusively deontological way diminishes its force and undermines its strategic role in the moral restraint of war. What Aquinas (following Augustine) appears to have had in mind is not simply the specific aims or intentions that inform war but the more permanent and preestablished moral dispositions of those who engage in war, dispositions that ultimately determine whether war is fought justly or unjustly, whether principles are upheld or denied.

The greatest moral threat comes not from the defective moral reasoning of individuals in time of war but from the unethical dis-position that belligerents from deformed moral cultures bring with them to war. The moral habits, attitudes, prejudices, and affections of belligerents are the decisive factor in war. Reflecting its Aristotelian roots, the tradition sees the process of moral for-mation (or malformation) taking place in, and largely through, the moral and political communities to which all individuals be-long. The acquisition of the necessary virtues and the avoidance of the particular vices of war are a matter of communal as well as individual agency, of cultural imperatives and influences, not just individual preferences and choices.

In line with this approach, the debate about humanitarian intervention should address not only the principles of interven-tion but also the moral culture of intervention. A moral commu-nity and culture that relies exclusively on the values of realism, or even on the principles of the morality of states, does little to dis-pose its members to accept the need for humanitarian interven-tion on behalf of noncitizens. Habits of moral particularism, or national egoism, inhibit action that is not reducible to promoting the national interest. Humanitarian intervention presupposes widespread acceptance (affective and not only cognitive) of the moral community of humankind. Assumptions of moral universalism, of rights and duties shared beyond borders, must have taken root and found expression in the community in question, if just intervention is to take place. This applies with special force in the case of democratically governed states, in which public opinion plays such a decisive role.

In the absence of a strong universalist disposition among the citizenry, democratic governments may be unable to respond promptly and effectively to cases of humanitarian need. The moral threshold of intervention will appear virtually insurmountable. Even when the protection or rescue of innocent noncitizens is recognized by the electorate as a potential just cause for war, widespread doubts about the proportionality of that cause will persist. The unequal value attached to the lives of citizens and noncitizens in cultures imbued with particularist values ensures that the ordinary reluctance to pay the costs of war increases greatly in wars that are understood to be humanitarian rather than defensive. The readiness for self-sacrifice that war demands is lacking. As a result, the prospects both of just recourse and of just conduct can be much diminished in the case of humanitarian war.

Governments struggle to mobilize public opinion in favor of a war in which vital national interests do not appear to be at stake. In such circumstances, democratic leaders may be tempted to overcome popular inhibitions by means that imperil the just conduct of war. Support for war may be made conditional upon the war's being free of the risks that its just conduct might require belligerents to take. Complying with just war principles can be costly. Fighting war in a way that upholds the immunity of noncombatants, for example, often increases the risks to an attacking force. There is reason to doubt the willingness of democratic governments and publics to accept those risks in the case of humanitarian wars, which often seem acceptable to both only if they are largely risk free.[36] In Kosovo, for example, strategies were adopted that minimized the risks to coalition forces (like the refusal to commit ground troops and the reliance on air power and high-altitude bombing), but doing so increased greatly, and *disproportionately*, the risks to the civilian population. It even seemed to one observer that the Western powers were committed to intervention "only if impunity could be guaranteed."[37]

If a moral deficit—the lack of a strong sense of moral solidarity with noncitizens—is one potential impediment to just intervention, moral zeal or excess is another. "He who would play the angel, plays the beast," wrote Aron (echoing Pascal). The sentiment was shared by Carl Schmitt, who sought to unmask the "bestial" tendency of "humanitarian" war. Like many realists, Schmitt was convinced that there is much more reason to fear a just war than a more prosaic war fought for mundane political objectives. Limited war, he argued, is the natural outcome of the latter, while total war is the inner dynamic of the just war, particularly in its humanitarian form.[38] But the realist's understanding of a just war is deficient. It confuses a mere potentiality with a necessity, ignoring less expansive and more restrained versions of just war thinking. However, the realist's fears are far from groundless. Wars that are conceived as "just" *can* threaten the moral restraint of war. This may apply especially to the case of humanitarian war, in which the moral aim is most pronounced. Paradoxically, the more convinced belligerents are of the justice of their cause, the less concerned they may be about its conduct.

The critical conclusion with which Michael Ignatieff closes his study of the Kosovo War is instructive in this regard. Reflecting on events, he notes how ready the West was to simplify the moral boundaries of the conflict. Moral abstractions like human rights induced an absolutist frame of mind, in which justice was ranged against injustice, civilization against barbarism, good against evil, virtue against vice. Demonization, with all its potential harmful consequences for the moral limitation of war, was the inevitable outcome of deeply ingrained assumptions of moral and cultural superiority. This negative categorization was applied not just to Serbian leaders, like Milosevic, but also to the Serbian people as a whole, ignoring the uncomfortable facts that many Serbians shared the humanitarian values in the name of which armed intervention was carried out and that other ethnic groups were implicated in the perpetration of acts of moral infamy. As a result of such illusions, the prevailing moral image of the war was more "virtual" than real. However comforting it may be, such an image is a shaky basis for making war.[39]

In the light of these concerns, it would be imprudent to interpret *right intention* in a moralistic way by equating it with purity of intention, as some are wont to do. Far from ensuring the justice of war, moral purism seems more likely to undermine it. The idea that, to be just, humanitarian war must be interest free is dangerous as well as false. It ought not to be assumed that the impact of interest on the moral limitation of war is necessarily a damaging one. The concern with interests can help to give humanitarian war the kind of political anchorage that it may require in order to remain limited. As long as the interests in question are neither illegitimate nor preponderant, their presence need not subvert the justice of the war. As Pratap Mehta suggests in his contribution to this volume, to insist on a disinterested war is to fly in the face of the complex moral realities of international politics and war, in which interests are ubiquitous and moral dividing lines always blurred. Such puritanical insistence invites the very self-righteousness that critics of just war fear, the disposition that silences moral doubts and that releases moral inhibitions, to the potential detriment of the just conduct of war.

A just cause, including a humanitarian just cause, should not be understood in absolute or unilateral terms. However just, no war can match the simple moral equation of Good versus Evil. The realm of war and international politics is too complex (too tragic perhaps) to accept any Manichaean definition. Justice is never the monopoly of one side, nor injustice of the other. If war is to remain just, the rights and interests, as well as the failings and injustices, of all belligerents need to be acknowledged. In other words, justice (and injustice) should be understood comparatively, or bilaterally, never unilaterally.[40] This applies with particular force to humanitarian wars. The conflicts that dictate intervention are often of such complexity (Bosnia and Kosovo are cases in point) that even a bilateral concept of justice seems inadequate. If crude moral assumptions are not to distort moral and strategic judgments, a multilateral understanding of justice and injustice may be required.

Political universalism seems better equipped than realism, the morality of states, or an abstract cosmopolitanism to counter the dual threat to just intervention posed by moral deficiency and moral excess. As any form of moral universalism must do, political universalism upholds the primacy of a moral community that transcends states and embraces all humanity. It is this community that generates the rights and the duties that apply across borders and that provide the moral basis of humanitarian intervention. However, the ethical privileging of the state in the Thomist-Aristotelian tradition has a further, naturally restraining effect on intervention. The concrete universalism of the tradition demands a basic respect for other political communities and cultures, and this respect inhibits the sense of moral and cultural superiority that fuels more militant and aggressive forms of intervention.

A moral universalism built on assumptions of moral superiority and inferiority between cultures is an unpromising basis for the conduct of international relations and, in particular, for the practice of humanitarian intervention. Though, in an appropriate form, the idea of moral progress seems indispensable, it should not be assumed that the present always outstrips the past, or that progress is identical with the achievements of a particular moral culture or tradition.[41] The tendency to absolutize a particular culture needs to be resisted, not only on pragmatic grounds but also for the sake of a richer and more authentic moral universalism that recognizes the worth and contribution of other cultures and traditions. As Jean Elshtain argues, the just war thinker's skepticism about "a universal culture of Kantian republics governed by identical normative and legal commitments . . . does not derive from opposition to a robust international regime of human rights or greater international fairness and equity but, rather, comes from a commitment to the intrinsic value of human cultural plurality."[42] The universal moral community that this tradition upholds and fosters is conceived as a plurality. As such, it calls for a dialogue of particular cultures and moral communities, not the monologue that arises when one culture abrogates to itself the title of "civilization." It requires the recognition and affirmation of difference. In this respect, the practice of humanitarian intervention needs "a differential ethics—one that does not so much cancel universality as rather suffuse general discourse with recognition of diverse idioms or voices."[43]

A dialogue of the cultures seems impossible to achieve without rehabilitating the unfashionable and much maligned virtue of humility. Humility stands not (as commonly perceived) for self-abnegation but for the honest assessment of self and others. Through "the ability to recognize and be at ease with one's flaws,"[44] this virtue "opens one's eyes to see and appreciate the gifts of others."[45] In its political and collective form, the virtue involves a process of cultural self-recognition that accepts the weaknesses as well as the strengths of a culture. The unavoidable limits of a particular culture are acknowledged, its (at best) partial, one-sided, imperfect, and incomplete embodiment of moral goodness and human excellence. In particular, it involves, as the case of Vitoria demonstrates, a fundamental skepticism (neither cynical nor relativistic) about the more elevated moral claims made for a home culture. In acknowledging the defects of his own society, Vitoria was able to discern the merits of another. How different his attitude was to that of his compatriots, the conquistadors, whose obsession with the "unnatural vices" of Amerindian society blinded them to their own inhumanity.

In this moral disposition, the key to the recognition of the other lies in self-recognition. Recognition of the other is impossible when the self is understood absolutely (or imperially). However, when the limits of the self are acknowledged, the merits of the other can come into view. Of course, recognition of the other in a collective, or cultural, form presents a challenge that recognition of the other in the individual (culturally sterile) form that more abstract forms of universalism presuppose does not. It calls for the kind of "anthropological" insight that enabled Vitoria to delve beneath the apparent disorder of Indian society to unearth its inner rationality. It presumes a basic openness and receptivity to the moral good that finds embodiment in someone else's culture. In short, what it demands is "humility," which, for that reason, may lay claim to be the preeminent virtue of humanitarian intervention and one that any moral community would do well to cultivate.

6. Conclusion

In deciding whether or not the just war tradition has anything to offer the ethics of humanitarian intervention, it would be a mistake to generalize. The historical tradition of the just war is a divided one that transmits mixed signals. Some just war variants are less promising than others as sources for an ethics of intervention. This applies most evidently to thinking with a statist and particularist orientation, but it also applies to universalist conceptions that are too abstract to give sufficient moral weight to particular states and cultures. In both cases, the problem lies in the one-sidedness of conceptions that uphold the moral claims of particular and universal against one another. I have defended the merits of a Thomist-Aristotelian tradition of just war thinking, based on a political (or concrete) universalism. Its principled affirmation of particular and universal, combined with its emphasis on the moral virtues, establish it as a fruitful source of an ethic of intervention.

NOTES

I am indebted to Terry Nardin for his supportive criticism. I have profited greatly from his many helpful comments and suggestions.

1. Mervyn Frost, "The Ethics of Humanitarian Intervention," in *Ethics and Foreign Policy*, ed. Karen E. Smith and Margot Light (Cambridge: Cambridge University Press, 2001), 52.

2. Michael Walzer, *Just and Unjust Wars: A Moral Argument with Historical Illustrations*, 3rd ed. (New York: Basic Books, 2000).

3. David Rodin, *War and Self-Defense* (Oxford: Oxford University Press, 2002), 195.

4. Ibid., 195 n. 11.

5. Michael Oakeshott, "Introduction to *Leviathan*," in *Hobbes on Civil Association*, ed. Oakeshott (Oxford: Basil Blackwell, 1975), 7.

6. Brian Orend, *War and International Justice* (Waterloo, Ontario: Wilfred Laurier University Press, 2000), 76.

7. Walzer, *Just and Unjust Wars*, xx.

8. J. Bryan Hehir, "Expanding Military Intervention: Promise or Peril?" *Social Research* 62, no. 1 (1995): 43. See also Hehir, "Intervention: From Theories to Cases," *Ethics and International Affairs* 9 (1995): 1–13.

9. C. A. J. Coady, "The Ethics of Armed Humanitarian Intervention," *Peaceworks*, no. 45 (Washington, D.C.: United States Institute of Peace, 2002).

10. Terry Nardin, "The Moral Basis of Humanitarian Intervention," *Ethics and International Affairs* 16, no. 1 (2002): 70.

11. Joseph Boyle, "Traditional Just War Theory and Humanitarian Intervention," this volume, chap. 1, 31.

12. Rodin, *War and Self-Defense*, 194.

13. Janna Thompson, *Justice and World Order* (London: Routledge, 1992), 17.

14. For further illustration, see Robert L. Holmes, *On War and Morality* (Princeton: Princeton University Press, 1989) and Richard Norman, *Ethics, Killing and War* (Cambridge: Cambridge University Press, 1995).

15. Rodin, *War and Self-Defense*, 199.

16. Ibid., 195.

17. James Turner Johnson's pioneering work, for example, stresses "the close relation between the thought of Vitoria and Grotius." It is the continuity of the tradition that is to the fore in Johnson's account, which portrays Vitoria and Grotius as "bridge figures" between the medieval and modern eras, and between religious and secular conceptions of just war. See James Turner Johnson, *Ideology, Reason, and the Limitation of War* (Princeton: Princeton University Press, 1975), 260, 208, 210, 255. Elsewhere Johnson writes that "the line from medieval just war theory to modern international law as described by Grotius and later writers passes importantly through Vitoria." The emphasis throughout is on the continuity of the just war tradition and on the convergence of various lines of development. James Turner Johnson, "Francisco de Vitoria," in *The Blackwell Encyclopedia of Political Thought*, ed. David Miller (Oxford: Basil Blackwell, 1987), 542. See also his entry on "just war," 257–59.

18. Richard Tuck, *The Rights of War and Peace* (Cambridge: Cambridge University Press, 1999), 89.

19. In like manner, Brian Midgely argues that "[Grotius's] individualistic formulations represent a grave emasculation of the traditional doctrine [of natural law]." E. B. Midgely, *The Natural Law Tradition and the Theory of International Relations* (London: Paul Elek, 1975), 159.

20. Terry Nardin, "The Emergence of International Law," in *International Relations in Political Thought: Texts from the Ancient Greeks to the First World War*, ed. Chris Brown, Terry Nardin, and Nicholas Rengger (Cambridge: Cambridge University Press, 2002), 315.

21. Francisco de Vitoria, *Political Writings*, ed. Anthony Pagden and Jeremy Lawrance (Cambridge: Cambridge University Press, 1991), 250.

22. Nardin, "Moral Basis of Humanitarian Intervention," 62.

23. See Charles R. Beitz, *Political Theory and International Relations* (Princeton: Princeton University Press, 1979), vii; R. J. Vincent, *Human Rights and International Relations* (Cambridge: Cambridge University Press, 1986), chap. 7; Joseph S. Nye, *Understanding International Conflicts* (New York: Longman, 1997), 19–24; Nigel Dower, *World Ethics* (Edinburgh:

Edinburgh University Press, 1998), 17–20; and Brian Barry, "Statism and Nationalism: A Cosmopolitan Critique," in *Global Justice*, NOMOS XLI, ed. Ian Shapiro and Lea Brilmayer (New York: New York University Press, 1999).

24. Vincent, *Human Rights and International Relations*, 118.

25. Chris Brown recognizes this when he observes that "medieval thought on the problems of 'international' relations is, for the most part, neither cosmopolitan nor communitarian." Chris Brown, *International Relations Theory* (London: Harvester, 1992), 27.

26. Barry, "Statism and Nationalism," 35.

27. Brian Barry, "International Society from a Cosmopolitan Perspective," in *International Society: Diverse Ethical Perspectives*, ed. David R. Mapel and Terry Nardin (Princeton: Princeton University Press, 1998), 145.

28. Charles Beitz, "Social and Cosmopolitan Liberalism" *International Affairs* 75, no. 3 (1999): 519.

29. Peter Singer, *One World: The Ethics of Globalization*, (New Haven: Yale University Press, 2002), 148 and 198.

30. Danilo Zolo, *Cosmopolis* (Cambridge: Polity Press, 1997), 15. See also Zolo, *Invoking Humanity* (London: New York: Continuum, 2002).

31. The quoted statement was made in response to David Held during the conference Global Democracy held at the University of Reading in January 1997.

32. See Nicholas J. Wheeler, *Saving Strangers: Humanitarian Intervention in International Society* (Oxford: Oxford University Press, 2000).

33. Pratap Mehta, "From State Sovereignty to Human Security (via Institutions?)," this volume, chap. 10.

34. M. M. Keys, "Aquinas and the Challenge of Aristotelian Magnanimity," *History of Political Thought* 16, no. 1 (2003): 53, paraphrasing Aquinas, *S T* II-II 161, 1 ad 3; emphasis added.

35. Michael Oakeshott, "The Tower of Babel," in *Rationalism in Politics and Other Essays*, 2nd ed., ed. Timothy Fuller (Indianapolis: Liberty Fund, 1991), 468.

36. See Michael Ignatieff, *Virtual War* (London: Vintage, 2001), and Christopher Coker, *Humane Warfare* (London: Routledge, 2001).

37. Ignatieff, *Virtual War*, 179.

38. Carl Schmitt, *The Concept of the Political*, trans. George Schwab (Chicago: University of Chicago Press, 1996), 36 and 54. See also Schmitt, "The Legal World Revolution," *Telos* 72 (Summer 1987).

39. Ignatieff, *Virtual War*, 214–15.

40. For further discussion, see A. J. Coates, *The Ethics of War* (Manchester: Manchester University Press, 1997), chap. 6.

41. For example, Beitz writes that "cosmopolitan liberalism [consists

in] the application to the global level of the individualist moral egalitarianism of the Enlightenment" ("Social and Cosmopolitan Liberalism," 516), while Barry argues that "the fundamental human right is to live in a liberal society" ("Statism and Nationalism," 32). Both concepts seem too narrow and particular to do justice to the idea of a universal moral community.

42. Jean Bethke Elshtain, "Just War and Humanitarian Intervention," *Ideas from the National Humanities Center* 8, no. 2 (2001): 5.

43. Fred Dallmayr, "Cosmopolitanism: Moral and Political," *Political Theory* 31, no. 3 (2003): 432.

44. Judith Andre, "Humility," in *Ethics in Practice*, 2nd ed., ed. Hugh LaFollette (Oxford: Blackwell Publishers, 2002), 279.

45. D. A. Horner, "What It Takes to Be Great: Aristotle and Aquinas on Magnanimity," *Faith and Philosophy* 15, no. 4 (1998): 434. Quoted in Keys, "Aquinas," 55.

3

THE DUTY TO PROTECT

KOK-CHOR TAN

1.

Much of the philosophical discussion on humanitarian intervention has been concerned with what we may call the permissibility question, that is, whether and under what conditions intervention is morally permissible. Relatively little attention, however, has been paid to the question whether an intervention, when permissible, can also be morally obligatory.[1] This relative neglect in the literature concerning the obligation to intervene is perhaps understandable given that the just war tradition, within which the debate on intervention is conventionally situated, is concerned with limiting the occasions for war and protecting the sovereignty of states, and so treats intervention as a forceful transgression of state sovereignty that needs to be justified. The burden, in other words, is generally on interveners to prove that their actions fall within the limits defined by the principles of just war.

But in recent years, some of the more urgent criticisms concerning intervention are directed not at unjustified interventions but at the failure to intervene to protect human rights. The case of Rwanda is an obvious example. Here, the main criticism was not the familiar one that an intervention took place when it should not have but that an intervention to stop the genocide did not happen when it ought to have. The tardy and tepid response on the part of Western democracies to the human rights violations in Kosovo and the Balkans more generally, the rapid withdrawal of the intervening force from Somalia when the intervention became no longer risk free, and the indecisiveness in action with respect to the civil war in Liberia are other examples.[2] These cases poignantly suggest that the moral problem of intervention is not restricted to the question of permissibility but further includes the question whether an intervention (when permissible) can also be obligatory. The philosophical debate surrounding intervention must move beyond the permissibility question, which has preoccupied much of the contemporary discussion, and explicitly address the question of obligation. This is not to suggest that the permissibility question is settled and no longer open to debate but only that the question of obligation is a distinct and morally pressing one that deserves more attention in the literature than it currently receives.

One might offer the observation that although the central challenge of intervention during the height of the Cold War was to contain unjustified and violent interference in the affairs of other states, the passing of the Cold War presented the new challenge of getting states to intervene to combat severe human rights abuses. The eagerness of the rival superpowers to intervene in countries for the purpose of extending their spheres of influence during the Cold War has been replaced by a reluctance on the part of the remaining superpower and its allies to commit their military in regions where there are no perceived national security interests, even when human rights violations in these regions acquire genocidal proportions. The new "realities" of the post–Cold War era have made poignant a question that was less urgent when states were eager to intervene.[3] These admittedly conjectural comments aside, it is an indisputable fact that humanitarian intervention in the contemporary world is undertaken selectively by the countries capable of stopping gross human rights violations, and this naturally raises the question of whether it is morally right for a state *not* to intervene when such violations occur.

In this discussion, I want to explore that question, whether there is an obligation to intervene to protect human rights— a duty to protect, for short. Two more specific questions can be identified. First, are the conditions that are *necessary* for making an intervention permissible also *sufficient* in themselves for making that intervention obligatory? That is, is a permissible intervention also straightaway an obligatory intervention? Second, if not, what are the additional conditions that must be met before a permissible intervention becomes an obligatory intervention?

I will address these broad questions in the following, more definite, steps. I begin, in section 2, by examining why one might think that a permissible intervention is also straightaway obligatory. One reason for this is that given the stringency of the conditions that an intervention must meet in order to be permissible, these conditions are also thought to be, by themselves, robust enough to generate a duty to protect. To put it more specifically, it might seem that if human rights violations are severe enough to overrule the principle of nonintervention, they should also be severe enough to overrule the right of third-party states to neutrality. I point out, however, that this argument shows only that there is an *imperfect* obligation on the part of any particular state to intervene, in the sense that the international community as a whole has the duty to protect, but *no specific* agent can be said to have the moral duty to act. It seems, then, that if the duty to protect is to be a perfect duty, there must be the additional condition that an agent capable of performing the duty be identified and assigned the responsibility to act.

I go on (section 3) to consider two situations in which the "agency condition" is arguably met. One is when an agent stands in a special relationship to the people needing protection; the other is when an agent is obviously the most capable among potential actors of successfully providing the protection. But (section 4) even if the agency condition is not satisfied in the above ways, that there is a duty to protect means that all relevantly situated members of the international community are obliged to take the necessary steps to assign and allocate their respective responsibilities to facilitate the discharge of the collective duty. In other words, if there is an imperfect duty to protect, it need not, and ought not, to remain imperfect. Finally (section 5), I try to counter the objection that the duty to protect exceeds the limit of obligation because of the risks of military intervention.

To avoid misunderstanding, it is worth stressing the obvious point that there can be a duty to protect only if it is also permissible to protect. This follows from what I hope is a truism that all obligatory actions must by definition be permissible—one cannot be required to do that which one is required not to do. So my discussion assumes that humanitarian intervention is permissible in at least some cases. My question, to be precise, is whether a *permissible* intervention could also be morally obligatory.[4]

Before beginning, I want quickly to note and leave to one side a possible line of argument in defense of obligatory intervention. One might argue that a state has a duty to intervene when the human rights violations in a foreign country pose a security threat against its own citizens. Given that states have the primary obligation to ensure the security and safety of their own citizens, a state can be said to have a duty to intervene (where the intervention is also permissible) that derives from its primary obligation to its own people. The practical significance of this argument is not to be underestimated. Many commentators have remarked, for example, that the events of 9/11 are stark reminders that human rights violations—and conditions associated with these, such as the phenomenon of failed states, civil war, genocide, and so on—in distant lands can have regional and even global consequences. Failure to take action abroad can have serious security repercussions at home.[5] Still, it is worthwhile asking if there can be a duty to intervene *for the sake* of protecting foreigners. This question clearly raises distinct issues that are of philosophical interest in their own right, for it asks whether there can be moral reasons for going to war that are not tied, directly or indirectly, to national defense. But for this reason, the question also has significant practical implications. Grounding the duty to intervene on the duty to protect national security holds the former hostage to how countries perceive and understand the interdependence between global human rights protection and their national security.

Taking the duty to protect to be derivative of a country's national security commitments allows potential interveners to rationalize their inaction against grave moral atrocities. As suggested above, a primary reason for the failure to respond to the genocide in Rwanda was the *perception*, by those most capable of stopping the atrocity, that Rwanda did not present a compelling national security issue.[6] Indeed, how severe human rights violations elsewhere can affect another country is ultimately speculative, given the complex array of contingencies involved, and so whether any given human rights crisis in a foreign land is thought to pose a threat against a country's national security depends on its own "expert" evaluation of the situation. But if there is a duty to protect that is nonderivative (in the aforementioned sense), it would not be constrained by the difficulties of assessing the national security challenges presented by humanitarian crises abroad, and one can defend such a duty without invoking potentially controversial causal claims about security and human rights. It is, therefore, not just conceptually interesting but of great practical importance that there may be a duty to protect that is independent of national security considerations.

2.

Discussions of humanitarian intervention sometimes assume that a permissible obligation immediately generates a duty to protect. The report of the special International Commission on Intervention and State Sovereignty (ICISS), entitled *The Responsibility to Protect*, illustrates this way of thinking.[7] Its title notwithstanding, the report is narrowly focused on the traditional debate concerning the limits of state sovereignty and the principle of nonintervention. It is mainly concerned with clarifying the conditions under which an offending state's sovereignty may be overridden for the sake of protecting the rights of its own citizens. It does not explain why a permissible intervention also generates "a responsibility" on the international community or some other agent "to protect." Instead, it simply assumes that when the principle of nonintervention is overridden, there is "the international responsibility to protect."[8] The report seems to take it for granted that there is a default responsibility to protect, and the only obstacle to the performance of this responsibility is the principle of nonintervention. So once the nonintervention principle has given way, the default duty can be permissibly carried out.

Establishing the permissibility of intervention is, of course, a necessary first step toward showing its obligatory character, given that an obligatory action must, by definition, be permissible. Because some continue to oppose the permissibility of intervention on the grounds of state sovereignty and the principle of nonintervention, to the extent that the ICISS report persuasively defends the permissibility of intervention by showing the limits of sovereignty and nonintervention, it contributes importantly to advancing this debate. But permissibility alone does not necessarily generate an obligation, and if the ICISS report is, as its title intends, interested in the question of responsibility, the missing premises that are needed to connect the claim about permissibility to the conclusion about responsibility must be fleshed out. It might be the case that intervention presents a special class of action, such that when it is permissible, it is also necessarily obligatory. But this needs to be explicated.

Let us examine, then, whether the conditions for permissible action do in fact sufficiently ground an obligation to act in the special case of humanitarian intervention. Humanitarian intervention involves the use of military force to defend the population of a foreign country against human rights abuses. This use of force is normally directed against the ruling regime of a country. However, in the case of a failed state (e.g., Rwanda or Somalia), the use of force will be directed against insurgents who are attacking the population. What is common to both cases, importantly, is that the territorial integrity and the political sovereignty of an independent state are compromised for humanitarian reasons.

The precise limits of a permissible intervention are, of course, a point of contention in the just war debate.[9] But it is generally agreed that intervention is permissible when the human rights violations in a country are so extreme as "to shock the conscience of mankind," to use the familiar expression. Such violations include mass enslavement, genocide, large-scale massacre (whether genocidal in intent or not), mass expulsion, and so on. Indeed, interventions are termed "humanitarian" (and thus by definition permissible?) when they are motivated by the need to put a stop to grave *human rights* violations.

Of course, other considerations are relevant in determining the permissibility of intervention. As with any defensible military action, the intervention has to meet certain requirements of proportionality (for example, the foreseeable harm to civilians resulting from the intervention cannot be disproportionately greater than the ongoing violation against them that the intervention aims to end). Also, it is normally agreed that the use of force is permitted only after nonmilitary alternatives have been seriously tried, and that the military option (given its inherent high moral costs) has a reasonable chance of success. Moreover, to ensure that the intervention is not an "ideological intervention" (that is, an intervention serving geopolitical ends) under the guise of humanitarianism, there might be the further requirement that a permissible intervention must also be a multilateral one.[10] But serious human rights violation is the crucial and necessary factor that is commonly thought to make a humanitarian intervention permissible. The universality of human rights means that state borders provide no immunity from international moral action when the violations of rights within a country are severe enough.

What the conditions of permissibility overrule is the presumption of state sovereignty and the corollary principle of nonintervention. International relations are premised on the idea that states have sovereign political authority over their territories, and the principle of nonintervention protects this sovereignty. Michael Walzer writes that the principle of sovereignty "derives its moral and political force from the rights of contemporary men and women to live as members of a historic *community* and to express their inherited culture through political forms worked out among themselves."[11] However, Walzer also notes that when human rights abuses in a state are so extreme as to make any talk of community or self-determination "cynical and irrelevant," *that* state forfeits its claim to sovereignty, and military action, under the right conditions, may be taken against it to end the abuses.[12] The idea that states have *absolute* sovereignty and that they may do whatever they want to their own citizens is rapidly becoming an outmoded one.[13]

Taking this relatively widely accepted (and minimalist) account as the paradigmatic case of permissible intervention, it seems that a permissible intervention must also be obligatory. If rights violations are severe enough to override the sovereignty of the offending state, which is a cornerstone *ideal* in international affairs, the severity of the situation should also impose an obligation on other states to end the violation. If the right of the offending state to nonintervention may be overruled in the name of human rights, so too, it seems to me, may the right of other states to stay disengaged.

This seems to me to be uncontroversial. Human rights generate corresponding obligations of different kinds on all parties to conduct themselves in the appropriate ways. Following Henry Shue's well-known typology as one illustration, human rights generate the duty to avoid depriving (a duty that the offending state has failed to live up to); a duty to protect from deprivation (which an indifferent agent fails to live up to); and a duty to assist those who are deprived.[14] The first duty, the duty to avoid depriving, imposes duties on agents not to violate human rights; because the offending state has failed in this regard, it may be acted against, its claim to state sovereignty notwithstanding. The second, the duty to protect, would require that agents take the necessary steps to counter the rights abuses, and this can, it seems to me, include military action under the right conditions. Rights, as Shue argues, entail both positive and negative duties. People whose rights are being violated have a right to protection, and this right will require that others *act* in the appropriate ways to provide the protection.

The force of human rights can, therefore, impose a duty on the part of third parties to intervene to combat rights abuses where necessary; human rights, as James Nickel puts it, "generate corresponding duties," including the duty to protect.[15] Taking rights seriously entails taking seriously the duties generated by these rights. The duty to protect derives from the commitment to human rights, and this commitment can overrule the presumptive right of states to remain neutral.

Now, the right of states to neutrality in war is an aspect of their sovereignty, and it is often accepted as a convention in just war theories that no state may be forced to enter into a war.[16] In examining the issue of obligatory intervention, we are therefore confronting another aspect of the ideal of sovereignty. Although addressing the question of permissible intervention means addressing the sovereignty (and its limits) of the offending or failing state, discussions of obligatory intervention must also address the sovereignty of the neutral state and its presumptive prerogative, as a sovereign state, not to engage in a war for humanitarian ends. In asking whether there is a duty to protect, we are in effect asking whether a state in fact has the sovereign right to remain neutral in the face of a humanitarian crisis, even if military engagement is a necessary means of combating the crisis.

As there is a presumptive right of sovereignty to noninterven-

tion, so too there is a presumptive right of sovereignty to neutrality. But if serious human rights violations can overrule a state's
sovereignty and its right to nonintervention, it can, it seems, also
overrule a state's sovereign right to remain neutral. When human
rights violations are "terrible" enough to constitute sufficient
grounds for overriding the claims of sovereignty in one case, it
should also be sufficient for overriding the claims of sovereignty
in the other. As a matter of consistency, one must conclude that a
permissible intervention also generates a duty (on other states) to
intervene.[17] If the principle of sovereignty yields for one, it should
also yield for the other.

It might be objected here that there is an important moral difference between the offending state and the neutral state such
that the sovereignty of one may be overridden but not that of the
other. The alleged difference is that the offending state has *acted*
in ways that make it *deserving* of the forfeiture its sovereignty,
whereas the neutral state has not.

But this objection mistakes the normative basis that motivates
humanitarian interventions and the overturning of the principle
of sovereignty. It is not the *active violation* per se of human rights
that has overturned the sovereignty of the offending state but the
fact that basic human rights are not being protected. It is a rights-
generated duty to avoid harming that allows for an intervention
against the offending state. Similarly, it is the rights-generated
duty to protect that imposes a duty on a third state to take action
against the offending state. Whether states have positively acted in
ways as to *deserve* the forfeiture of their sovereignty is a morally
irrelevant point in this analysis of intervention.

Intervention, I would argue, is not about punishing an offending state for its human rights failures; it is grounded on the need
to protect the rights of persons. Intervention gains its moral legitimacy not as a claim about punishment but as a claim about protection. It is the need to protect human rights that allows for the
forfeiture of the sovereignty of the offending state. And this need
to defend human rights, I am suggesting, will limit the claim of
neutral states (at least, those in a position to do something about
the rights violation) to stay out of the conflict. So it is not that the
active violation of rights on the part of a state causes it to forfeit
its sovereignty, which in turn renders permissible an intervention

by outsiders. Rather, it is the need to protect human rights, which compels outsiders to intervene, that explains the bypassing of sovereignty when the protection requires it.

Understanding the limits of sovereignty in terms of rights protection rather than in terms of punishment is consistent with the widely held view that a state that is unable to protect its own people against severe violations by substate elements within its borders may also be intervened against (e.g., in Somalia and Rwanda). That is, the territorial integrity and the political sovereignty in the case of a failing or failed state can be legitimately transgressed when the abuses against its population are serious enough, regardless of whether the foundering state regime itself is *actively* doing the violating or is simply *unable* to stop the abuses that are being carried out by substate elements. An account of intervention based on the deserved "forfeiture" of sovereignty does not square with this wide endorsement in international practice of the permissibility to intervene against failing or failed states to protect human rights, where these states cannot be said to have acted in ways as to forfeit their formal right to sovereignty.

To be sure, there is a difference between an offending state and a neutral state. An offending state may be *coercively thwarted* in order to protect the rights of the population it is violating. One need not treat this forceful coercion as a case of punishing the state but as a case of doing what is necessary for protecting the rights of persons. And because intervening in the offending state is necessary to end the rights violation, there is a right to use force within its jurisdiction without obtaining its consent. Still, the important distinction remains that there is no right to coerce a neutral state, as there is to coerce an offending state. But my discussion above respects this morally intuitive distinction. I am not suggesting that the neutral state may be attacked like the offending state just because it can no longer appeal to the principle of sovereignty. I am claiming only that the neutral state cannot appeal to the principle of sovereignty to maintain its neutrality.

Both offending and neutral states lose their appeal to sovereignty in situations of severe rights abuse. For the offending state, this can include losing the right not to be attacked, if attacking it is necessary for ending the violations. For the neutral state, there is no such need to attack it. Losing its claim to sovereignty means only that it loses the right to continue its neutrality, not that it may be attacked—attacking it serves no purpose toward ending the human rights abuse. Now, one may say that when we insist that a country has a moral duty to wage war, we are subjecting its people to force in some sense, for we are demanding that they expose themselves to violence. But this raises the different question of the risks of military engagement and the limits of obligation, a point to which I will turn in section 5.

In short, if human rights are important enough to trump the principle of state sovereignty, they can trump the right of states to neutrality, and so can impose on states the duty to protect. Thus, although ordinarily a permissible act need not be obligatory, humanitarian intervention presents a special case. Given the stringent conditions that are *necessary* for an intervention to be permissible, it follows that these same conditions are *also sufficient* for making that intervention obligatory. One might say that the moral gap between permissibility and obligation is always bridged in the special case of humanitarian intervention. Given the moral seriousness of humanitarian intervention, it can never merely be a prerogative. By default, all permissible interventions generate a duty to protect.[18]

So, as a first formulation, one might say that whenever it is permissible to intervene in a country to stop severe human rights violations, there is an obligation on the part of the international community or some state to intervene. On first glance, then, it might appear that the implication of the ICISS report, that a permissible intervention straightforwardly generates a duty to protect, is not unwarranted, once the underlying premises are spelled out.

The phrase "international community" or "some state," however, underlines a possible shortcoming in the formulation. Since it is not clear which particular state in the international community (only *some* unspecified state) should perform the task of intervening, it appears that there can be no perfect duty on the part of any state to act. As Walzer points out, "The general problem is that intervention, even when it is justified, even when it is necessary to prevent terrible crimes, even when it poses no threat to regional or global stability, is an imperfect duty—a duty that doesn't belong to any particular agent. Someone ought to intervene, but *no specific state* in the society of states is morally bound to do so."[19] The duty to protect, unless some agent is identified as the primary agent of protection, is at best an imperfect one—it is a duty that cannot be morally demanded of any particular state.

What this means is that the duty to protect is not effectively claimable unless it "is actually allocated to specified agents and agencies." Absent such an allocation, any right to protection (such as violated individuals might have) would be what Onora O'Neill, borrowing Joel Feinberg's terminology, calls a "manifesto right."[20] A manifesto right is a right that a claimant has but that nonetheless cannot be effectively enforced because no specific agent has a duty to provide that right. People whose rights are being violated have a right to be protected, as I have argued. Unfortunately, no specific agent bears the duty to provide that protection. What would change the prospects of the claimant is that "specified others" are earmarked as the agents responsible for carrying out the protection.

The distinction between perfect and imperfect duties is central to Kantian ethics. For Kant, a perfect duty "allows no exception in the interest of [an agent's partial] inclinations," whereas an imperfect duty allows an agent discretion and latitude as to when and how, and for whom, the duty is to be discharged.[21] Among Kantian scholars, the basis for this distinction is sometimes said to rest on the distinction between duties that are owed to specifiable persons on the one hand, and duties that are not owed specifically to anyone on the other, rather than on the distinction between duties for which agents are specified and duties for which there are no specific agents. That is, on this view, imperfect duties are imperfect more because of the lack of specificity of *claimants* than the lack of specificity of *agents*. Accordingly, on this interpretation of Kant's distinction, it might not be quite accurate to say that a duty to intervene is an imperfect one, for, in this case, it is clear to whom this duty is owed—it is owed to the people whose basic rights are being seriously violated by their own state. Still, I think that treating a duty as imperfect on the grounds that no agent has been specified, as Walzer and O'Neill do, is not inconsistent with the spirit of the Kantian distinction. If agency is not specified, one can easily see why potential agents can have the discretion of not acting in *all* cases of humanitarian crisis if for each case there are alternative agents who can as well perform the action required by duty. At any rate, what is of significance for my discussion is not whether the duty to intervene is imperfect in the technical Kantian sense but, rather, the substantive moral claim, following Walzer, that in the absence of a clear specification of which country is to intervene, it is not clear if any can be morally bound to do so. For consistency, I will follow Walzer in referring to this as a problem of imperfect obligation.[22]

It seems that for a permissible intervention to generate a perfect duty to protect—that is, a duty that can be demanded of a specific agent and is therefore effectively claimable—a further condition (in addition to the permissibility conditions) must be satisfied. This is the condition that an agent (or class of agents) be *identified* as having the defined duty to carry out the intervention. Call this *the agency condition*. A morally demandable intervention, then, is an intervention that satisfies the permissibility conditions as well as the agency condition. It must be a permissible intervention in which it is also clear who the agent of protection is.

One obvious way the agency condition is satisfied is by some form of institutionalization of responsibilities through which the different requirements of the duty to protect are specified and assigned to specific states or international agencies, and each then can be morally bound (in other words, have a perfect duty) to carry out its assigned tasks. Before discussing the issue of institutionalizing responsibilities, however, I want to consider two situations in which the agency condition might be thought to be met, antecedent to any institutional arrangements. In the first, there is a capable agent who stands in a *special relationship* of some sort to the people needing the protection. In the second, there is an agent who is clearly the *most capable* among potential actors of successfully carrying out the protection duty. The assumption that special relationship and/or special capability can identify an agent of protection is sometimes alluded to in public discussions on intervention. It is therefore worthwhile uncovering and examining the underlying arguments behind this assumption to evaluate its plausibility.

3.

A state (or more precisely the people of a state) can stand in a special relationship to a people needing protecting by virtue of their shared historical ties. The historical relationship between the United States and Liberia is one obvious example. Because of this special tie, the United States is widely seen (by international organizations and by prointervention Liberians themselves) to have the special obligation to intervene to put a stop to the thirteen-year-long civil war ravaging that country. As the British ambassador to the U.N. puts it, the United States is "the nation that everyone would think would be the natural candidate" to intervene given its historical ties with Liberia.[23] Indeed, there is the general sentiment in international practice that as former colonial powers, certain countries have continuing special responsibilities to take action to ensure stability and peace in their former colonies (Britain in Sierra Leone, France in the Ivory Coast, and Portugal in East Timor, for example).

Although this argument is sometimes presented as an argument for reparations—that is, the special responsibility to intervene is thought to derive from an obligation to make amends for the past injustices of colonialism—it need not take this form.[24] Indeed, it is not immediately obvious how a duty of reparation can generate a duty to intervene to protect human rights, especially where the injustices are historic ones. It is controversial whether there can even be any general duty of reparation for historic injustices (such as colonialism or slavery), let alone a duty of reparation that can take specific forms, such as military action. In fact, in the case of Liberia, the emphasis in the popular debate has been on the historical ties between Americans and Liberians —ties based on cultural affinity and a shared past—rather than on colonial exploitation. I am not saying that an argument for intervention based on the duty of reparation for colonial exploitation can never be made. I want only to note that the argument from special relationship need not limit itself to the problem of past injustice and be understood exclusively as an argument for reparation but that it can also be an argument that appeals to a shared culture, a common history, and other common ties that are unrelated to past injustices.

The sentiment behind this claim is not that the United States *alone* has the duty to protect because of its special ties; the duty to protect in this case is generally recognized as a duty that falls on the international community as a whole. Rather, its historical ties with the people needing protection presumably *identify* the United States as the country that has the special responsibility to carry out the protection. This argument has some plausibility. A special relationship can rightly identify an agent who can be said to have the perfect duty to act.

As an analogy, consider Joel Feinberg's well-known example of a swimmer drowning off a beach that has no lifeguard. For Feinberg, every bystander keen to the situation has the duty to cooperate and coordinate his or her efforts to rescue the drowning swimmer. I will return to the details of Feinberg's example later. For now, imagine that among the bystanders is the swimmer's spouse, and that the bystanders know this. Assume also that none of them is especially capable of rescuing swimmers in distress but that they are equally capable. It would not be unreasonable to say, and for members of the group to expect, that the spouse of the swimmer is the primary agent of rescue in this case, absent any arrangement or coordination to the contrary. There is no problem of agency because there is an identifiable agent who has the perfect obligation to rescue, given the agent's special (in this case, spousal) relationship with the drowning swimmer.

The special relationship does not mean that no other bystander has an obligation to assist; indeed others are obliged to do what they can to assist the agent's rescue effort. It only means that an agent "morally stands out" from the crowd as having the special responsibility to act. The rest of the bystanders (should they know that the spouse of the swimmer is among them) can have the *reasonable expectation* that the spouse will carry out the rescue. To be sure, if the expected agent does not act, then others must accept the duty to act, and some allocation of responsibilities would be necessary to specify each person's responsibility. I will return to this issue in section 4.

The point here is only that there is an identifiable agent who can be reasonably expected to act on the group's behalf (or to discharge the duty that the group as a whole has), given the agent's special ties with the claimant. "Everyone would think" that the spouse would be the "natural candidate" for carrying out the rescue, and, indeed, everyone would be entitled to think that the spouse acted poorly and oddly if he did not assume a primary role in the rescue effort, if he did not show and express through his actions more concern for the drowning victim than did strangers, and so on.

The agency problem is that because the duty to protect falls on some unspecified agent, *no one* can be said to have the perfect duty to protect even though the collectivity (the international community in the case of humanitarian intervention) has a duty to act. But if some members of the international community stand out because they have a special relationship with the people whose rights are being abused, the agency question is, it seems, overcome. The special relationship can generate the expectation, among the victims and in the potential actor, that a particular agent actually carries out the duty. The exact content of the special relationship need not be an issue. The historical relationship could be one based on past ties or even on past injustices. What is sufficient is that the relevant parties perceive the relationship as one in which those related treat each other in a particular way. The existence of these ties generates a reasonable expectation among all in a situation that from a group of agents who are morally obliged to assist, the agent related to the person in need of assistance will be the one to act. It is the reasonable expectation that a particular agent will act that identifies the agent as the primary actor.

This is not to say that the special relationship *alone* generates the duty to protect—that is a different claim, and different arguments would be needed to support it. The claim can be read, more modestly, as saying only that the special relationship *identifies* the specific agent of protection in the context where it is already acknowledged that *someone must act.* The fact of a special relationship is invoked here to solve the agency problem, that is, to determine who is to act, and not to generate the obligation itself. The moral need to protect human rights generates the duty to intervene, but this duty is only imperfect. This is the problem that appealing to the existence of a special relationship between victim and agent is meant to resolve.

The other common way of attempting to solve the agency problem is to appeal not to the relationship between the protector and the victim but to the capability of the protector. A particular state might be said to have the special responsibility to act because it is the best candidate, compared to others, for doing the protecting. This might be because of its military capacity or its geographical location, for example. Thus, one might say that the neighbors of Rwanda or Liberia or Kosovo are the natural agents of protection, given their geographical proximity, which could give them a deployment advantage over more distant countries. Or that the United States, because of its military strength, is the obvious agent to be asked to use force to counter human rights violations when there are no obvious equally capable agents. Of course, spatial proximity need not single out an agent if that proximate agent is clearly unable to perform the protective task; similarly, the most capable agent may be ruled out as a "qualified" agent if that agent's past record makes it an unsuitable protector. But the point here is that independent of institutionalizing responsibilities, a state's special capability can cause it to meet the agency condition under the appropriate conditions.

In short, special capabilities, like special relationships, can distinguish one potential agent from others as the proper agent to perform the duty. To illustrate, let me return to the drowning example. This time, assume that no particular bystander has a special relationship with the drowning swimmer. However, imagine that it is known that there is a qualified but off-duty lifeguard among the bystanders. It seems to me that the agency problem is here solved. There is a collective duty of rescue that is not assigned to any particular agent. But even though no one from the collectivity has been previously designated as the actual rescuer, it is reasonably clear that the off-duty lifeguard should be given this assignment because she is the person best qualified to get the job done. Furthermore, the other bystanders can reasonably expect that this member of the group will initiate the rescue. Or, suppose that near the swimmer is a person in a boat who is aware of the emergency, and that the crowd on the beach knows that the boater is alert to the situation. Here, it is not unreasonable for the bystanders to expect the boater to attempt the rescue of the swimmer in the absence of any explicit coordination of efforts. In short, an agent's ability, proximity, and other such relevant factors can generate a reasonable expectation among potential agents as to *who* should act in a given situation.[25] Again, there is no implication here that others besides the most capable agent need do nothing at all. The rest are required to do their best to assist the capable agent who is undertaking the rescue operation.

The presence of a reasonable expectation, on the part of those on the scene, that the agent with the special capacity should be the first to act can be explained in this way. All parties in the group, including the most capable agent, if they take their collective duty seriously, would want the rescue effort to be successful. The rescue effort is more likely to succeed if the most qualified agent carries out the rescue. Therefore, absent any arrangement to the contrary, the agent best positioned to ensure the successful discharge of the group's duty is the natural candidate for carrying out the duty, given the objective of the group. In other words, on the assumption that a group has a duty to protect, and given the importance of how effectively the duty is carried out and the degree to which proximity or ability increases the chance of success, members of the group can reasonably expect that the most proximate or capable agent will be the one to act. This expectation naturally arises, even in the absence of any explicit assignment of the duty, given the shared desire of the group that the rescue effort should succeed.

As above, the claim here is not that special capability (due to expertise or proximity or some other relevant fact about the agent) generates the duty to protect. Rather, the claim is if a duty to protect is acknowledged, having a special capability identifies who could be expected and called on to perform the actual protection. Put weakly in this way, as an identifying feature rather than an obligation-creating one, special capability can point out the agent on whom others can reasonably expect to act on the group's behalf.

As I noted, these claims about special relationship and special capacity are often invoked in public discourse, and I have tried to identify some possible moral arguments (sometimes already implicit in these claims) that might be given to support them. While these arguments are plausible, as I contend they are, it is important to acknowledge their limitations. Claims of special relationship are sometimes tenuous (how far back can these historical ties go?) and vague (what are the criteria of such ties?). Moreover, there may be more than one potential agent with historical ties to those in need of protection, in which case the agency problem reappears. The problem reappears because it is now unclear *who* is to act, given that there is more than one equally suitable candidate. As for the second case, the appeal to special capacity might appear to impose unreasonably heavy burdens on a country just because it is capable of acting. The U.S. government often explains its inaction by declaring that its foreign military commitments are already overextended and that it "can do only so much." Whether or not the claim is reasonable, the general principle behind it is not unattractive. It tracks our moral intuition that an agent should not be given a significantly larger share of the collective moral burden just because it happens to be the most capable agent (while others are also capable even if not equally so).

4.

A surer way of solving the agency problem is by institutionalizing the duty to protect. That is, there can be an explicit assignment of roles and responsibilities specifying who should act and what they should do. This means that a duty to protect need not remain imperfect just because a protecting agent has not (yet) been designated. What is important is that the agency problem is not a conceptual one; that is, it does not deny that there is a duty and that someone ought to act. It is a strategic problem: there is no identifiable agent who can be called upon to act. Resolution of the problem requires that some agent be identified and assigned the task of protecting. As Onora O'Neill puts it, that some duties are imperfect means that they should be institutionalized to make their assignment and content clear. The crucial question, then, is whether there is an obligation to assign and allocate the duty to protect, and who has this obligation.

Let us return again to Feinberg's example, this time referring also to his analysis of the problem. When a group of bystanders sees a person drowning (and no one stands out from the crowd in the either of the ways described above), then, according to Feinberg, "everyone should use his eyes and his common sense and cooperate as best as he can. If no one makes any motion at all, it follows that no one has done his best within the limits imposed by the situation, and *all* are subject at least to blame."[26] In other words, *all* persons present at the scene have a moral obligation to act; they may be held morally culpable if, because of their collective inaction, the swimmer drowns. This, of course, does not mean that everyone ought to rush into the ocean to attempt the rescue; indeed, a nonswimmer certainly does not have the obligation to attempt the actual rescue. What it does mean, though, is that all parties are to contribute to the rescue in ways commensurate with their ability and the needs of the rescue operation. They may have to coordinate their efforts, appoint a primary rescuer from among their ranks if necessary, and provide support to the primary agent and the victim in the different ways that a rescue effort of this sort would need. That is, the duty to rescue, though initially an imperfect one because it is not clear which person(s) from among the crowd is to act, need not remain imperfect (that is, unallocated); all bystanders are duty bound to ensure that the duty is made perfect (in other words, that someone is assigned to carry out the rescue).

What Feinberg's analysis suggests is this: that a duty is imperfect does not mean that no one has an obligation to do anything, or that everyone may act as he or she wishes or not act at all. On the contrary, the fact that there is a duty, even though imperfect, would mean that relevant parties have an obligation to take the necessary steps to make sure that the imperfect duty can be properly discharged. This usually implies that the parties would have the immediate duty of cooperation and coordination, that is, to assign and allocate the duty in order to facilitate its performance.

So the fact that it might not be obvious, when the international community is confronted by a given abuse of human rights, which state has the duty to act does not mean that no state is obliged to act. All states in a position to do something are to coordinate their efforts so as to effectively discharge the protection duty. This will require identifying who is actually to perform the intervention. And in an era in which organizations, such as the U.N., can provide a ready-made forum for internationally coordinated responses to human rights crises, the failure of their member states to do anything can hardly be excused. If no state does its "*best* within the limits imposed by the situation" then all are subject to moral blame.[27] To acknowledge that a duty is imperfect is not to deny the force of that duty but simply to recognize that some intermediate steps must be taken before the obligation can be effectively discharged. There is, in short, a duty to make what starts as a "manifesto" right into a right that is enforceable and claimable. That a duty is imperfect need not be seen as limiting that duty, as some commentators suggest. On the contrary, to describe a duty as imperfect is to announce the commitment to take the intermediate steps necessary to allocate and specify it.[28] Some duties are just too important to be left imperfect, to paraphrase O'Neill.

There is, therefore, an obligation on the part of the international community to institutionalize the duty to protect (if we accept that there is such a duty) so that it may become a morally claimable one. And this obligation to institutionalize the protection duty is one that falls on all relevantly situated members of the international community. Each is to coordinate its efforts so as to facilitate the performance of the duty to protect. Just as everyone in the crowd in Feinberg's example is morally obliged to do what is necessary to advance the rescue of the drowning swimmer, so all members of the international community are to do what is necessary to ensure that the abused are protected. We can say that members of the international community have the obligation to *make perfect*, through cooperation and coordination, what might be otherwise an *imperfect* duty to protect.

Whether the duty to institutionalize an imperfect duty to make it perfect is itself, strictly speaking, a perfect duty or imperfect duty will depend on our precise definition of the terms "perfect" and "imperfect." But, fortunately, this quibble over definition need not distract from the substance of my point: that the duty to institutionalize the duty to protect is one that falls on *all members* of the international community (or, at least those able to cooperate with one another, as all members of organizations such as the U.N. are), and that all members are obliged to *do what is necessary* to establish and support the cooperative arrangement required to carry out the duty to protect. Unlike a duty to protect that is imperfect in this very definite sense—no one has been assigned the duty, and it is not specified what anyone is to do (which presents a practical problem about the claimability of the right to protection)—the duty to create whatever arrangements are needed for enforcing the duty to protect does not raise this problem of agency and responsibility, and so is not imperfect in this way.

In Feinberg's example, the coordination of efforts is ad hoc, that is to say, undertaken as and when an emergency presents itself. Those on the beach must act together only when the need arises. What is required is that something be done, some duty assignment be made, when a situation calls for it. No institutionalization of responsibilities is actually required. But if it can be reasonably predicted, based on experience, that many such emergencies will arise, and that a prior assignment of role and responsibilities is needed if the response is to be successful, there arises an obligation to *institutionalize* the duty of rescue so as to have, on a standing basis, a prior assignment of roles and responsibilities.

The recurrence of humanitarian crises suggests the need to institutionalize the protection duty before a crisis occurs. If experience has shown that the international community cannot respond effectively to a crisis when it arises (because influential countries are indifferent, troops cannot be quickly mobilized, or for any other reason), the community has a duty to clarify, in advance of any crisis, how the collective duty to respond is to be performed. This will require putting in place institutional arrangements to allocate and distribute responsibilities to ensure that the duty to protect is effectively performed when the situation demands it.

This might mean establishing a permanent international humanitarian defense force whose role is to protect human rights where the need arises. If, without such a force, human rights cannot be effectively protected, the creation of this force is morally obligatory. Failure to establish the necessary arrangements beforehand, when it is reasonably foreseeable that such arrangements are necessary for the proper discharge of an imperfect duty, is to fail to treat the imperfect duty as a *duty*. The duty to protect, in spite (or, rather, because) of its being imperfect, can generate the duty to create a global humanitarian defense force if the creation of this force is required to ensure that the response to humanitarian emergencies is acceptably efficient.[29]

It is generally accepted that (most) states require a standing army and cannot afford to wait until they are under attack before assembling a military force. Military preparedness for national self-defense requires carefully planned and coordinated allocations of responsibilities and a permanent readiness to act if necessary. Military preparedness to defend human rights should be no different.

Interestingly, then, the claim that the duty to protect is imperfect can be turned to the advantage of defenders of humanitarian protection. They should press the point that an imperfect duty is still a duty, and the fact that it is a duty means that necessary steps must be taken to facilitate its performance. Failing to do so might imply the adoption of a principle not to comply with the duty. And if these necessary steps include the creation of a humanitarian defense force, there is an obligation to establish such a force. Any outright opposition to the creation of such a force, when it is known that absent this force human rights protection in extreme cases cannot be offered, is morally culpable.[30]

5.

Because it involves the use of military force, humanitarian intervention is clearly a high-risk activity. This might be taken to imply that there can be no obligation to intervene, on the ground that one cannot have a duty to rescue others at great risk to oneself. Or, at the very least, interveners have the prerogative to minimize the risks to themselves, as they see fit, allowing this consideration to determine their intervention strategy, if they intervene at all. This objection follows from ordinary morality. We ordinarily accept that individuals do not have an obligation to seriously risk their own lives to protect the lives of others. Such sacrifices are supererogatory, not morally obligatory.[31]

But the individual-state analogy suggested by the objection does not quite work. Although no natural person can be expected to risk his or her life to save others (other things being equal), it is not clear what the equivalent of such a risk might be for a collective entity like the state. Perhaps we can assume that a state ceases to exist if it loses its identity—as it might, if it were to be annexed by another state or broken up into different states. Still, a state need not risk its identity in this way by intervening in most historical cases.

There are, to be sure, some cases where the risks of getting involved are significant—Norway's refusal to enter into a war against Nazi Germany is one example. But humanitarian crises often involve failed states, and intervening in these situations scarcely endangers the independent statehood of those countries that are most capable of dealing with the crisis. Indeed, given that a permissible intervention is likely to enjoy broad international support, it seems that the worry that the offending state may *fatally* retaliate against the intervening state is quite unfounded. The intervening party has the international community on its side, whereas the offending state is often on its own. In any case, a proper allocation of the duty will ensure that the duty actually falls onto a state that is capable of intervening without risking a serious retaliation from the targeted state that it cannot defend itself against. Of course, if the cost of intervention is high not only for the intervener but also for international peace and stability, there can be no duty to intervene, but only because it cannot be *permissible* to intervene in such cases. An intervention that has met the strict permissibility criteria—for example, it is intended to thwart a looming genocide—is likely to be one whose costs are within acceptable limits, given the importance and limited character of its end.

If intervention does not necessarily present a meaningful risk to the intervening *state*, however, it might be argued that it does risk the lives of the *individuals* who are called upon to perform the intervention. On this interpretation of the objection, what can place an intervention beyond the call of duty is not so much the risks a state as a corporate entity faces by intervening, but the risks its soldiers face when it commits them to an intervention. By intervening, the state "condemns an indefinite number of its citizens to certain death," as Walzer puts it.[32] The real concern of the objection, then, is with the physical risk of intervention that falls directly on the soldiers doing the intervening. So, the objection may be redescribed as saying that it is beyond the call of duty for a soldier to risk his or her life to protect the lives of foreigners.

To be sure, soldiers are expected to risk their lives; this is part of what it means to be a soldier. When a country's vital interests are at stake, soldiers must assume certain risks to protect these interests. This is, in fact, the raison d'être of the soldier's office. But it is different, the objection argues, in wars defending the human rights of foreigners. It follows that soldiers cannot be called upon to risk their lives for humanitarian ends. It is not part of their "role obligation." For this reason, Samuel Huntington writes, "[I]t is morally unjustifiable and politically indefensible that members of the [U.S.] armed forces should be killed to prevent Somalis from killing one another."[33]

But the objection rests on an unduly and arbitrarily narrow view of the soldier's professional duty, a view that, I think, is rapidly changing (assuming that it was ever the norm, historically speaking, that a soldier's duty is limited to national defense).[34] This is evidenced by the number of countries that have routinely committed their troops for peacekeeping operations in recent years. Indeed, for a country like Canada, peacekeeping missions seem now to be the primary function of its military. United Nations peacekeeping operations constitute a major aspect of the U.N.'s global role. Since 1956, more than 750,000 troops from different countries have participated in as many as forty-two U.N. peacekeeping operations.[35] Given this precedent, soldiers in many democratic countries today cannot in good faith claim that their job does not include humanitarian protection.

Moreover, even if it were true that a soldier's present role obligation does not include protecting human rights, this does not entail that the soldier's job description cannot be revised and expanded to include this role. Nothing about humanitarian protection is conceptually at odds with the definition of soldiering, and the risks that humanitarianism would impose are not different from those already imposed on soldiers as a (professional) class. As Walzer puts it curtly, soldiers, unlike ordinary citizens, "are destined for dangerous places, and they should know that (if they don't they should be told)."[36]

Indeed, were the limited view of the soldier's duty to be accepted, it would follow that there can be no permissible intervention. For, if we grant that a state cannot have a duty to intervene *because* this would offend against the rights of its soldiers not to be risked for humanitarian ends, this reason would also block the state's prerogative to intervene. That is, the state would act impermissibly when intervening because it has violated the limits of its soldiers' duty. So, the objection, if sound, actually proves too much.[37]

It might be argued that leaders of a democratic state are specially obligated to their own citizens not to commit their country to a war solely to protect strangers. Although soldiers in a democracy may be told that it is part of their job to go to "dangerous places" to protect their country's interests, they should not be told that it is also part of their job to go to dangerous places to protect foreigners. The definition of the soldier's duty should not be expanded to include human rights protection, lest democratic ideals are violated. This argument is not concerned, to be exact, with the risks that are imposed on soldiers in sending them to war but with the alleged breach of democratic trust between leaders and the people that have elected them to represent and protect their interests. There are limits to what state leaders of democracies can expect their own citizens, whose interests they are democratically elected to represent, to do for foreigners. As Jack Goldsmith and Stephen Krasner write in defense of realism, "[E]lectorates in advanced industrialized democracies have been reluctant to expend blood and treasure to deal with humanitarian catastrophes that do not affect their material interests."[38] Thus "political leaders cannot engage in acts of altruism abroad much beyond what constituents and/or interest groups will support."[39] A purely humanitarian intervention (that is, an intervention that is not also motivated by national security considerations) would be in violation of the democratic ideal, according to this argument.

Again, as it should be clear, this objection against obligatory intervention, if correct, tells against the permissibility of intervention as well. So the objection, if successful, proves more than its proponents might like. But the argument, at any rate, is refutable. Its premise, that democratic citizens are reluctant "to expend blood and treasure," is an inaccurate description of actual democratic citizens. Moreover, it does not follow that democratic ideals, properly understood, can allow a citizenry to stand idly by while serious atrocities are going on elsewhere. I will explain these two points in turn.

The democratic citizen is not narrowly self-interested in the way the objection describes. Indeed, democratic citizens have historically been critical of overzealous interventions on the part of their countries, but they have also been critical when their leaders do not act to protect human rights. The motivations and moral interests of democratic citizens are more complex and varied than the objection implies. It is not true that electorates in democracies have a narrow view of their interests such that these interests must exclude human rights concern. Some do hold this narrow view of their interests; others do not. The relatively broad public support for the NATO intervention in Kosovo among North Americans, which many commentators describe as a rare example of a purely altruistic intervention, shows that electorates in democracies have a broader view of their moral commitments and their militaries' role in fighting for these commitments than the argument suggests. The interests of Americans, as members of a democracy, can include the commitment to global justice and human rights. Historically, democratic citizens have renounced their own country's unjust interventions (e.g., the opposition to the war in Vietnam) and criticized their country's failure to intervene in other cases (e.g., criticism of the indifference with regard to Rwanda).[40]

But even if actual citizens in a democracy do in fact oppose their country's involvement in the protection of human rights, as of course some would, or even if they would consent to an intervention only if the risks to their own troops were strategically kept to a minimum (as in the case of the aerial intervention in Kosovo), it does not follow that leaders who commit their troops to combat in spite of this lack of popular support are violating democratic norms. The democratic citizen, ideally conceived, is one who is able to take the global point of view and able to appreciate that the scope of his or her moral concern extends beyond the borders of her state. One of the central virtues of democratic citizenship is the commitment to justice and to further its cause around the world.[41] There is nothing at odds with democratic responsibility when a leader of a democracy commits troops to protect human lives elsewhere. The objection that intervening to protect the rights of foreigners violates democratic trust is ultimately premised on an impoverished account of democracy. So, even if it is true that actual democratic citizens never support humanitarian intervention, the normative conclusion, that leaders of democracies should not commit troops to protect human rights, does not follow.

"[I]t is the task of the [ideal] statesman," John Rawls writes, "to struggle against the potential lack of affinity among different peoples. . . . Since the affinity among peoples is naturally weaker (as a matter of human psychology) as society-wide institutions [cover] a larger area and cultural distances increase, the statesman must continually combat these shortsighted tendencies."[42] Rawls is not speaking about intervention here, but the point of his remarks is that when democratic citizens endorse a form of patriotism that always puts the interests of compatriots before the needs of strangers, this is not an aspect of the democratic ideal. On the contrary, the task of democratic leaders is to overcome this form of moral favoritism and to avoid letting it determine their foreign policy decisions. The underlying principles and commitments of democratic citizenship—equal respect, mutual trust, and a shared commitment to justice—defy the parochial reading of democratic citizenship suggested by this objection.

I have argued that given the stringency of the conditions for permissible intervention, these conditions are also sufficient for making intervention obligatory. If it is permissible to override the ideal of sovereignty to put an end to a serious violation of human rights, it is also permissible to override the right of neutral states to keep out of the fighting. Although this duty is generally imperfect, the fact that it is imperfect means that the international community has an obligation to assign responsibilities so that this duty will be discharged. That the duty to protect is imperfect in the absence of institutionalized procedures for intervention should not be seen as a limitation against arguments for obligatory humanitarian intervention but as a case for greater international cooperation to protect human rights, including, if necessary, the creation of a permanent humanitarian defense force. That a duty is imperfect points only to the need for coordinating efforts and the need to cooperate. It does not mean that the duty need not be taken seriously by anyone.

NOTES

A version of this essay was presented at the symposium on Global Politics at the 2003 meeting of the American Philosophical Association, Central Division, in Cleveland. I thank my fellow panelists and members of the audience for their helpful comments. I am also grateful to participants at the Montreal Political Theory Workshop (McGill University, 2003) and the Legal Studies Seminar (The Wharton School, February 2004) for their helpful questions and suggestions. Although I did not write this essay for the ASPLP Humanitarian Intervention sessions held in conjunction with the American Political Science Association Meeting (Boston, 2002), I benefited from those sessions and am grateful to Terry Nardin and Melissa Williams for inviting me to participate in them. Thanks to Ryoa Chung, Michael Green, Marilyn Friedman, Bill Laufer, Catherine Lu, Alan Patten, and Scott Weinstein for helpful discussions; to David Reidy for his written comments on an early draft; and to Rosemary Nagy for her suggestions on the penultimate draft. Most especially, I thank Terry Nardin, whose insightful, detailed, and thorough comments on both the content and style of various drafts have vastly improved the paper. I am very grateful for his generous editorial and intellectual guidance throughout the different stages of writing this paper.

1. I will be using the terms "duty" and "obligation" interchangeably, for stylistic reasons. As will be clear, I am ultimately interested in whether there can be a moral duty to protect, independent of whether this duty is voluntary assumed, legislated, and so on. The standard distinction between duty as nonvoluntary and obligation as voluntary does not affect the discussion.

2. See Samantha Power, *A Problem from Hell: America and the Age of Genocide* (New York: Basic Books, 2003).

3. Generalizing and adapting loosely from Kant, one might say that there is no urgent need to talk about an "ought," a duty, when the agent is already disposed to act as the duty would command. See Kant, *Groundwork of the Metaphysics of Morals* (1785), trans. H. J. Paton (New York: Harper and Row, 1964), chap. II, 413–14.

4. Thus, if one believes that "Operation Iraqi Freedom" is an unjust intervention, nothing I say here about the obligation to intervene will apply to this intervention. Arguing that an intervention can be a duty does not prove that every intervention is permissible; rather, it assumes only that some are permissible. The question is whether such interventions are also morally obligatory.

5. For one discussion on this point, see Michael Ignatieff, "State Fail-

ure and Nation-Building," in *Humanitarian Intervention: Ethical, Legal, and Political Dilemmas*, ed. J. L. Holzgrefe and Robert O. Keohane (Cambridge: Cambridge University Press, 2003).

6. Regarding Rwanda, see Power, *A Problem from Hell,* chap. 10. Senator Robert Dole op-posed the U.S. participation in the United Nations–sanctioned operation to restore democracy in Haiti, saying that "risking American lives to restore Aristide to power is not in America's interest." See "Administration Determined to Send U.S. Forces to Haiti," *Washington Post*, September 2, 1994, 2.

7. See the ICISS report, *The Responsibility to Protect* (December 2001), available at www.dfait-maeci.gc.ca/iciss-ciise/report2-en.asp.

8. For example, the report says, "Where a population is suffering serious harm, as a result of internal war, insurgency, repression or state failure, and the state in question is unwilling or unable to halt or avert it, the principle of nonintervention yields to the international responsibility to protect" (1B). That there is a gap in this reasoning is clear. The "yielding" of the principle of nonintervention means only that intervention in the offending state is permissible; the responsibility to intervene does not necessarily follow. The responsibility to protect is simply assumed here.

9. See Joseph Boyle, "Traditional Just War Theory and Humanitarian Intervention," this volume, chap. 1.

10. On this point, see Pratap Mehta, "From State Sovereignty to Human Security (via Institutions?)," this volume, chap. 10. But, contra Mehta, I think one should not take multilateralism to be more than a means of ensuring that an intervention meets certain moral requirements. To make it a necessary condition of a permissible intervention that it is not unilateral seems to confuse means for ends. For more discussion on this, see Terry Nardin, "The Moral Basis of Humanitarian Intervention," *Ethics and International Affairs* 16, no. 1 (2002): 57–71. See also Joseph Boyle, "Traditional Just War Theory and Humanitarian Intervention," this volume, chap. 1; Thomas Franck, "Legality and Legitimacy in Humanitarian Intervention," this volume, chap. 5; and my commentary on Mehta, this volume, chap. 11.

11. Michael Walzer, "The Moral Standing of States," *Philosophy and Public Affairs* 9 (1980): 211.

12. Michael Walzer, *Just and Unjust Wars: A Moral Argument with Historical Illustrations*, 3rd ed. (New York: Basic Books, 2000), 90.

13. See, e.g., John Rawls, *The Law of Peoples* (Cambridge: Harvard University Press, 1998), 25–27. The ICISS report also stresses this point.

14. Henry Shue, *Basic Rights* (Princeton: Princeton University Press 1980).

15. James Nickel, "How Human Rights Generate Duties to Protect and Provide," *Human Rights Quarterly* 15, no. 1 (1993): 83–84.

16. Walzer, *Just and Unjust Wars*, 233; also chap. 15.

17. Thus, although Walzer defends the right of neutrality, he wonders about the limits of this right in the case of intervention: "But can a state claim neutrality when one nation or people is massacring another?" *Just and Unjust Wars*, xv.

18. This conclusion, that permissible interventions are also obligatory, is also defended by Darrel Moellendorf, *Cosmopolitan Justice* (Boulder: Westview Press, 2002), 122–23. See also John W. Lango, "Is Armed Humanitarian Intervention to Stop Mass Killing Morally Obligatory?" *Public Affairs Quarterly* 15, no. 3 (2001): 173–92.

19. Walzer, *Just and Unjust Wars*, xiii.

20. I rely here on this passage by Onora O'Neill: "[U]nless the obligation to provide food to each claimant is actually allocated to specified agents and agencies, this 'right' will provide meagre pickings. The hungry *know* that they have a problem. What would change their prospects would be to know that it was others' problem too, and that specified others have an obligation to provide them with food. Unless obligations to feed the hungry are a matter of allocated justice rather than indeterminate beneficence, a so-called 'right to food', and the other 'rights' of the poor, will only be 'manifesto' rights." O'Neill, *Faces of Hunger* (London: Allen and Unwin, 1986), 101.

21. Kant, *Groundwork*, 421.

22. I thank Alan Patten for helpful discussion on this point. See also Kok-Chor Tan, "Kantian Ethics and Global Justice," *Social Theory and Practice* 23, no. 1 (1997): 53–73.

23. See Kathryn Westcott, "Liberia's Historical U.S. Ties," *BBC News Online*, June 26, 2003, available at http://news.bbc.co.uk/1/hi/world/africa/3022740.stm. President George W. Bush himself concedes that the United States' "unique history with Liberia" has "created a certain sense of expectations" that the United States should be more actively involved in stopping the massacres in that country. He quickly noted, however, countervailing factors and conditions to rationalize U.S. limited involvement. "Bush Insists Liberian President Go before Troops Come," *New York Times*, July 4, 2003, A3.

24. For one discussion on responsibility for injustices and intervention, see Erin Kelly, "The Burdens of Collective Liability" in *Ethics and Foreign Intervention*, ed. Deen K. Chatterjee and Don E. Scheid (Cambridge: Cambridge University Press, 2003), 121. Although Kelly is primarily concerned with the responsibility of members of the rights-violating state to

accept the costs of being intervened against, she also suggests in passing that "a state has an obligation to intervene on behalf of a group whose unjust suffering it has helped to cause."

25. See Larry May, *Sharing Responsibility* (Chicago: University of Chicago Press, 1992), 114–15.

26. Joel Feinberg, *Doing and Deserving* (Princeton: Princeton University Press, 1970), 244.

27. Ibid.

28. This is the point behind O'Neill's discussion of imperfect duties. The importance of institutions in mediating duties is discussed in Henry Shue, "Mediating Duties," 88 *Ethics* (1998): 687–704.

29. The still nascent Multinational Stand-by High Readiness Brigade for U.N. Operations (SHIRBRIG) launched in 1994 (in part as a reaction to the inaction regarding Rwanda) can provide the institutional motivation and framework toward a global humanitarian defense force. For some background on SHIRBRIG, see United Nations, "Multinational Stand-by High Readiness Brigade for United Nations Operation" (Norway: Presidency, SHIRBRIG Steering Committee, MOD Norway, n.d.), available at http://odin.dep.no/archive/fdvedlegg/01/01/Shirb044.pdf. I thank Katherine Cinq-Mars and Nicholas Ward for helpful discussion and the reference.

30. Kant, *Metaphysics of Morals*, 390, writes of imperfect duties that "failure to fulfill them is not itself culpability . . . unless the subject should make it his principle not to comply with such duties." That is, while an imperfect duty allows a certain discretion on the part of the agent (as to when, how, and for whom) the duty is to be performed, there is a moral violation, a culpability, if the agent makes it a point of hers not to carry out the duty. If it is known that failing to create an international humanitarian defense force means, in consequence, that there can be no effective performance of humanitarian protection duty, this would sufficiently suggest, it seems to me, that parties opposing the creation of such a force have made it their "principle not to comply with" this duty, and thus are morally culpable.

31. See James Fishkin, *The Limits of Obligation* (New Haven: Yale University Press 1982); J. O. Urmson, "Saints and Heroes," in *Moral Concepts*, ed. Joel Feinberg (Oxford: Oxford University Press, 1969).

32. Walzer, *Just and Unjust Wars*, 236.

33. Huntington, "New Contingencies, Old Roles," *Joint Forces Quarterly* 2 (1993): 42. Quoted in Michael J. Smith, "Humanitarian Intervention: An Overview of the Ethical Issues," *Ethics and International Affairs* 12 (1998): 63. In his article, Huntington goes on to say that "[t]he military

should only be given military missions which involve possible combat . . . when they advance national security interests and are directed against a foreign enemy of the United States."

34. Historically, soldiers, conscripted or professional, have fought for causes (such as the Crusades), rightly or wrongly, and not just for the protection, narrowly conceived, of their homeland. Some just war traditions explicitly note the responsibility of soldiers to protect victims of religious persecutions even if these victims are not fellow citizens or subjects of the same political authority.

35. See UNA-Canada, "The U.N. and Peacekeeping," available at http://www.unac.org/en/link_learn/fact_sheets/peacekeeping.asp.

36. Michael Walzer, "The Politics of Rescue," *Dissent* 42, no. 1 (1995): 38.

37. See also Moellendorf, *Cosmopolitan Justice*, 124.

38. Jack Goldsmith and Stephen Krasner, "The Limits of Idealism," *Daedalus* 132, no. 1 (2003): 58.

39. Ibid., 59.

40. Consider also the relatively wide public support for the U.N. intervention in Haiti in 1994. The recent war against Iraq is justified to the American public and its military not only as a war against terrorism but also as a war of liberation (for the Iraqi people). My point is not that this justification is beyond scrutiny but only that it is not true that citizens of democracies are in practice unwilling to expend blood and resources to protect the human rights of strangers.

41. See, e.g., Amy Gutmann, "Democratic Citizenship," in *For Love of Country*, ed. J. Cohen (Boston: Beacon Press, 1996).

42. Rawls, *The Law of Peoples*, 112. And if a leader risks making an unpopular decision in committing her country to a purely altruistic intervention, this is not to be seen as a political risk that is beyond the call of the statesman's duty: "[T]he politician looks to the next election; the statesman looks to the next generation" (ibid., 97). The leader does not shy away from her moral duty, even if doing her duty means she will lose her job at the next election.

4

HUMANITARIAN INTERVENTION AS A PERFECT DUTY: A KANTIAN ARGUMENT

CARLA BAGNOLI

1. Introduction

Humanitarian intervention is generally treated as an exception to the nonintervention principle, which requires us to respect the integrity of a foreign country and not to interfere in matters of domestic jurisdiction.[1] The appeal of this principle is apparent, but the reasons for treating it as exceptionless do not seem equally compelling. Indeed, when a foreign government commits unspeakable atrocities against its own citizens, the burden of justifying nonintervention may seem as weighty as the burden of justifying intervention.

It is tempting to cast these cases as moral dilemmas. On the one hand, we should respect the integrity of another country out of respect for the principle of national self-determination and in order to sustain a stable international order. On the other hand, we should defend the rights of the oppressed, regardless of their nationality. According to this approach, humanitarian intervention represents a situation in which the principle of state integrity conflicts with the requirements of universal morality. Attempts to overcome the dilemma are ultimately efforts to show that the requirements of universal morality are overriding, and therefore to provide a moral grounding for an exception to the principle of

117

noninterference where noninterference implies a violation of the *requirements* of universal morality. Grievous violations of human rights, including ethnic cleansing, massacre, and other acts that "shock the moral conscience of mankind," are just too serious to be regarded merely as a matter of domestic jurisdiction.[2]

Current debates on the normative status of humanitarian intervention have been significantly influenced by the language and arguments of traditional just war theory. When assessing whether armed intervention is justified, we ask whether there is a *casus belli*, who has the proper authority, and whether the intervention is motivated by the right intention. Just war theory assumes that the political leader is entrusted with the good of the community and acts with that good in mind. Humanitarian intervention is morally legitimate when it is shown to be for "the common good." The scope of armed humanitarian intervention is limited to cases where the fundamental human rights of noncitizens are seriously violated or jeopardized by the action of their government. Even the more recent (and rare) Kantian philosophers who argue for humanitarian intervention borrow the vocabulary and conceptual framework of just war theory. Partly, this is because traditional just war theory supports humanitarian intervention, not merely as an exception to a general principle of noninterference but in its own right.

Arguments justifying humanitarian intervention usually aim to establish the grounds on which warfare is a *permissible* response. It is only recently that anyone has raised the issue of whether intervention can be morally *required*. However, even when people argue that serious violations of fundamental human rights provide the moral grounds for a duty to intervene, they cast such a duty as a duty of charity. On this view, there is a duty to protect or to assist the victims, and this duty of beneficence is meritorious or broad —a matter of mercy rather than justice. This implies that states have the right to remain neutral in the face of human rights violations in other countries and that their neutrality is not morally objectionable.

In what follows, I argue that there is a strict moral duty to intervene when fundamental human rights are violated. I analyze this duty as comprising two complementary duties, to protect the vic-

tims and to coerce the wrongdoer, and defend it by appealing to Kant's conception of respect for humanity. My argument is
that both duties follow from respect for humanity and hence are a
matter of justice, not of mercy. Failing to fulfill them calls for moral
blame; hence neutrality is morally culpable and blameworthy.

There are two important qualifications to add. First, a moral
case for the duty of armed intervention to protect fundamental
human rights should not be confused with a legal case. To claim
that there is a moral requirement to intervene is not to claim that
there is a legal (and legally sanctioned) requirement to do so.[3]
Second, neither argument yet establishes who has the proper
authority to intervene. The duty applies to the universal moral
community as such and therefore is everybody's responsibility.
Because this duty concerns the international community as a
whole, it should be discharged by that community by institutionalizing its responsibility.

2. MORAL REASONS TO PROTECT THE VICTIMS

The claim that the threshold between lawful and outlaw states is
set by human rights does not yet warrant a duty to intervene; at
best it justifies a permission to do so. In this section, I argue that
there are moral reasons to protect the victims of serious violations
of human rights. In the next sections, I will show that these moral
reasons warrant a perfect duty to protect and a complementary
perfect duty to coerce the wrongdoer. My argument is that human
rights are ways to express our humanity and that the duty to intervene proceeds from respect for humanity.

What is humanity, then? According to Kant, humanity is what
characterizes us as persons; it consists in the capacity to decide
what is valuable and what is not. This decision is not a mere whim
but the very capacity for rationally setting ends of one's own.[4] A
person is a special *locus* of value in that it is also the origin of
value. Kant calls "dignity" the peculiar kind of value that persons
embody insofar as they are themselves sources of value. Originat-
ing value is a lawlike activity: it requires that we be capable of setting ends by conceiving maxims that can be willed as universal
laws. This also requires that we be capable of self-legislation and

therefore of prescribing obligations for ourselves. This activity of self-legislation is tantamount to the autonomous exercise of rationality. Hence, humanity is tantamount to autonomous rationality, and it is this feature that makes persons inviolable.[5] We cannot view persons as indistinguishable units of value insofar as persons embody a peculiar kind of value, dignity. The recognition that somebody is a person makes a claim on us: it demands that we respect such a person as an autonomous source of value.

Armed intervention is "humanitarian" when it is undertaken for the sake of protecting the dignity of persons, that is, the value of their humanity. Human rights are necessary to express and exercise our humanity; they are fundamental to being a person. When we appeal to the idea of human dignity, we make a *moral* case for intervention, that is, one that applies universally and unconditionally.

Framing a moral universalist argument for intervention has important consequences whose significance is greater than the intervention debates suggest. First, to claim that respect for humanity grounds a moral basis for humanitarian intervention is to say that intervention is morally justified *whenever* human rights are seriously violated. If intervention to protect human rights is defended on moral grounds, any reference to whether the state against which we act is dangerous or aggressive is irrelevant.[6] Its threat can be considered a secondary supporting reason for undertaking war, but it is neither a primary nor a moral reason. In some cases, the violation of human rights might occur exactly because such a state failed as a state, that is, it failed to guarantee law and order, and it is in such a state of dissolution that it does not represent a threat to anyone. By paying attention to the threat that such a state may pose to other countries, when considering the moral status of intervention, we make a prudential case for intervention. Prudential and moral reasons may pull in the same direction, but I am urging that in discussing the wrongdoing that justifies armed intervention, we should keep these two kinds of reasons separate. My claim is that a moral argument applies universally and unconditionally, that is, independently of (although not necessarily incompatibly with) prudential considerations.

Second, to ground the duty to intervene on the principle of respect for humanity makes any consideration of special relationships or other contingencies irrelevant. There is a duty to intervene independently of considerations of proximity, friendship, capability, expertise, or effectiveness.

Third, to appeal to humanity importantly affects both the normative status of armed intervention and the question of proper authority anticipated in section 1. I will address these issues in turn.

3. HUMANITARIAN INTERVENTION AS A PERFECT DUTY

Most of the debates surrounding humanitarian intervention concern the permissibility of intervening for humanitarian reasons. When we recognize that there is a reason to protect human rights grounded on respect of humanity, however, it is inappropriate to say that such a moral argument warrants merely a permission. It is like saying that we are permitted to respect others as well as ourselves. Morality does not simply "allow" us to respect people: it demands, it requires, it commands that we do so. The very nature of the argument based on the protection of fundamental human rights qualifies the normative status of humanitarian intervention as a requirement of morality, a duty. To say that protecting human rights is a moral matter is to say that human rights are universally binding, and therefore they are enforceable even in those polities that do not recognize them. They have a normative force even when they are not supported locally.

Those in favor of treating humanitarian intervention as a duty are nonetheless inclined to treat it as an imperfect duty of charity or beneficence.[7] This is to say that it is not a strict duty, whose violation is a prohibition, but a meritorious duty, one we can be praised for performing but cannot be forced to perform. Characterizing humanitarian intervention as an imperfect duty brings with it several unwelcome consequences, but I would like to start by noticing what it *does not* imply.

First, some assume that a duty is imperfect by virtue of being unassignable to any specific agent, of not identifying the agent who should discharge it. So to speak, there is a duty but because nobody is specifically called to fulfill it, nobody is specifically obligated by it. This interpretation of imperfect duty is sometimes invoked as an argument that if there is anything like a duty to intervene, it must be an imperfect duty, given that it is not obvious who has an obligation to discharge it. Notably, Michael Walzer refers to this qualification as a problem for humanitarian intervention: "[T]he general problem is that intervention, even when it is justified, even when it is necessary to prevent terrible crimes, even when it poses no threat to regional or global stability, is an imperfect duty—a duty that doesn't belong to any particular agent. Someone ought to intervene, but *no specific state* in the society of states is morally bound to do so."[8]

Now, this seems to raise several worries. It seems to imply that the duty to protect cannot be effectively claimable because it cannot be actually allocated to specified agents and agencies. It then becomes a mere "manifesto right," which cannot be effectively enforced because, although the claimant is justified in asserting it, there is no definite addressee for the claim.[9] Conversely, treating humanitarian intervention as an imperfect duty risks the implication that polities can intervene at their own discretion. This leaves the door open to polities' opportunistic use of humanitarian arguments to justify interventions that are motivated by other interests. A further consequence—and in this context the most important one—seems to be that neutrality is morally admissible, not blameworthy or culpable.

Yet if we look closely at Kant's distinction between perfect and imperfect duties, these worries vanish. Kant's distinction relies uniquely on the relationship between the performance of a duty and the motive from which this performance derives.[10] For both perfect and imperfect duties, the moral worth of an action depends on its having been performed from the right motive, that is, for the sake of duty alone. In the case of perfect (or what Kant calls "juridical") duties, the content of the duty is independent of the motive for performing it. It is not a logical contradiction to fulfill a perfect duty from the wrong motive. Put differently, the performance of the duty is externally obliging, in the sense that one must perform it whether or not one is motivated by a sense of duty. One acts rightly even if one is motivated by fear of coercion, for example.[11] In the case of imperfect (or "ethical") duties, however, the rightness or wrongness of an action consists wholly in the quality of the will from which it is performed. Ethical duties are not duties to perform a particular act but to endorse a specific kind of end; they are therefore inseparable from a specific motivation. In contrast, one is required to perform juridical duties whatever the motive. There is a difference between performing a juridical duty out of fear of coercion or for the sake of duty, but such a difference concerns only the moral worth of the action. The person who performs the juridical duty out of fear acts rightly, but his action does not have moral worth.

The defining feature of juridical duties—that the duty to perform them exists whether or not one has the right motive in doing so—has important implications. First, it means that perfect duties are externally enforceable (to the extent that they are independent of internal motives). Second, it implies that membership in a civil society regulated by this notion of right requires no specifically moral motivation.[12] Conformity to the law is a perfect duty; making it our motive is a requirement of virtue alone. This difference will bear important consequences in the argument that follows. While perfect (or "juridical") duties are externally enforceable, imperfect (or "ethical" duties) are not. Although we can be compelled or coerced to perform perfect duties, we cannot be likewise compelled to perform imperfect duties. Failure to perform an imperfect duty is a moral failure, a lack of virtue (*defectus moralis*), but it is not an offense (*demeritum*) and it does not constitute a vice (*vitium*).[13] Although lack of virtue is a moral defect, we cannot speak straightforwardly of "culpability" for this kind of failure unless there is lack of intention to comply; but this is only because of the peculiar manner of imperfect duties' internal legislation, which makes obscure when we can attribute culpability.[14] Failure to perform an imperfect duty is a transgression (*peccatum*). When such a violation is deliberate, it becomes a vice as much as failure to perform a perfect duty is a vice.[15]

So, to call X an imperfect duty does not imply that those who fail to fulfill it are not guilty of doing wrong. Kant emphasizes that "by an imperfect duty is not understood a permission to make exceptions to the maxim of the actions, but only the permission to limit one maxim of duty by another."[16] Imperfect duties, that is, what Kant calls "ethical duties" or "duties of virtue," command only maxims of action and not actions themselves.[17] This might seem to imply that imperfect duties are more indeterminate than perfect duties are because they do not command specific actions.

Consider, however, that both right and ethics command laws. Right prescribes laws for actions; ethics prescribes maxims of ends that can be expressed in various kind of actions.[18] In both cases, that is, the law prescribes types of action (which is supposed to be incorporated into the agent's maxim of action). In neither case is an act-token prescribed. The difference is that right prescribes types of actions; ethics prescribes types of ends expressed in a maxim of action. In this latter case, then, it is up to the agent how to specifically frame her end, that is, how to conceive of her particular acts. But consider exactly what this indeterminacy amounts to. Imperfect (ethical) duties leave some latitude to the agent as to how to interpret and carry out the maxim. However, such latitude concerns exclusively the fact that an imperfect duty "cannot definitely assign *in what way and to what extent* something should be brought about by an action directed toward an end which is also a duty."[19] To admit of some latitude as to *how* to perform a duty is not to admit any latitude as to whether we are bound by it. It does not imply that such a duty is either discretionary or that its agency is unspecified. To call a duty "discretionary" is in fact a contradiction in terms: a duty for Kant is a practical necessity. To suggest that it leaves agency unspecified is also a contradiction in terms: whether perfect or imperfect, a duty is binding for all rational beings. Therefore, there is no question of allocation.

In the case of humanitarian intervention, the issue of identifying the appropriate agency certainly arises. But this is a political issue that concerns *proper authority*. Whether perfect or imperfect, a duty applies to all rational agents. Specifically, then, in the case of a serious violation of human rights, everybody, that is, the entire international community, is bound by the obligation to protect the victims of human rights abuse. How should we collectively handle this moral responsibility? This is not a question of allocation deriving from the broadness of the duty to protect. Rather, this is a political problem of how to institutionalize a response that should be voiced by the international community as a whole.

I agree with Kok-Chor Tan's argument in this volume that if the duty to protect is imperfect in the absence of collective institutions, the proper conclusion is that states must cooperate to improve those institutions, not that they are free individually to ignore the duty.[20] There clearly is a problem as to how to institutionalize the moral responsibility to intervene, but it is not exactly a problem of allocation: the problem is a political one and concerns how to institutionalize the responsibility. Furthermore, this political problem does not depend on the fact that humanitarian intervention is at best an imperfect duty. In fact, the problem remains even when we take the duty to intervene as a perfect duty generated by respect for humanity.

Although treating humanitarian intervention as an imperfect duty does not have the consequences I have just discussed, it is nonetheless a mistake. The underlying claim is that the duty to intervene is imperfect, insofar as it is a duty of charity or beneficence, because we cannot be compelled to act on motives of charity. Charity is a duty of virtue that cannot be coerced. This argument seems to me mistaken. Beneficence is the moral ground for assisting societies burdened by unfavorable political or economical conditions. It is related to the principle of respect because the duty of beneficence includes promoting the conditions for respecting human rights and for self-respect.[21] But resisting the violation of basic human rights is not simply a duty of charity, or something that one may or may not choose to perform. It is a perfect duty whose performance is morally obligatory. It is a duty that proceeds from respect for humanity. Human rights, such as right to life, liberty, personal safety, social security, and membership or recognition[22] are necessary for expressing who we are and exercising our rational agency.

It is worthwhile to consider what the recognition of humanity involves in order to appreciate the stringency of the duty to protect. Humanity is the criterion for membership in the moral community, for moral personality.[23] It is what gives us dignity, that is, what make us sources of value or "self-originating sources of valid claims," as Rawls puts it.[24] Dignity (*dignitas interna*) is a category of value that is specific to persons, makes persons inviolable, puts them "above all price," and entitles its bearers to equal standing in a community of equals.[25] Such a community is regulated by moral norms to which all members, as free and rational agents, are accountable. These moral norms express and give substance to the equal dignity of persons, and dictate how they must address and treat one another, what they may properly exact from one another, and what they owe to one another.

Since these moral norms are constitutive of the moral community, complying with such norms cannot be merely a matter of virtue or good character. We are bound by such norms insofar as we are members of the moral community. Respect for those norms is tantamount to respect for our humanity and is therefore something that not only may but must be demanded by all our equals and is owed to all.[26] It is the condition on which the possibility of appropriate relationships and interactions is grounded. We owe one another respect not because we stand in a special position toward one another (as neighbors, friends, or traders) but because we are persons, that is, self-originating sources of claims.[27]

Duties of respect are therefore a particularly important category of duties we have toward others and are distinct from duties of beneficence. Duties of beneficence such as charity put others under some corresponding obligation (to express gratitude, for example), but duties of respect do not generate any reciprocal obligation. They are simply owed to others and can be legitimately demanded by them: "Every human being has a legitimate claim to respect from his fellow beings and is in turn bound to respect every other."[28]

Defending human rights is a duty of respect because human rights are claims persons have *as persons*. Human rights are, in this reading, principles that warrant that we are able to represent ourselves as self-originating sources of claims and to act upon the conception of ourselves that we have formed. But it should be noted that *promoting* human rights and *defending* basic human rights are different activities and fall under distinct categories of duty. This difference also affects the nature of the means for pursuing them. To assist a country in promoting the social and political conditions for the fulfillment of human rights cannot be successfully carried out by warfare: it is a much more complex endeavor that requires many different activities and structures. Instead, stopping a particular violation of basic human rights can sometimes be achieved only by inflicting sanctions, specifically, by military action.[29]

4. THE PERFECT DUTY TO COERCE THE WRONGDOER

According to a long-standing tradition, war is a just response only in the presence of wrongdoing and has a distinctive punitive meaning. The right to punish is understood as legal retribution, not as an expression of hatred or revenge. In the context of humanitarian intervention, it seems extraordinarily problematic to justify the right of the officials of one polity to punish another polity or its subjects.[30] The more recent doctrine embraced by the Second Vatican Council (*Gaudium et Spes*) does not invoke military intervention as a punitive action but only as a defensive resort. In this way, the focus shifts from the wrongdoer to the victim.

In the previous section I argued that there are moral reasons for armed humanitarian intervention and that these reasons ground a perfect duty. My aim in this section is to show that those same moral reasons ground a perfect duty to coerce states that fail to protect the fundamental human rights of their citizens. By appealing to Kant's conception of right, I argue that the duty to coerce the wrongdoer and the duty to protect the victims are complementary aspects of the moral requirement to respect humanity. Recognizing humanity in others amounts to respecting their freedom *and* obstructing any action meant to curb that freedom.

In the *Rechtslehre*, Kant states that the juridical condition (*Recht*) is "the whole of the conditions under which the choice of one can coexist with the choice of the other according to a universal law."[31] By the notion of "right," Kant aims at providing a complete set of conditions for moral cooperation, that is, the constraints that make cooperation possible. It should be apparent that the notion of right does not refer to a body of rules, but it is a set of conditions for the cooperation of persons, that is, beings who are capable of choice. Being capable of choice amounts to being autonomous, that is, capable of acting upon our own representation of the action and for the sake of ends that we have set for ourselves. This is a distinctive property of persons. Since persons can make choices, they can also obstruct one another's choices. Furthermore, they can choose to obligate themselves and others. Obligation and obstruction are both constraints that pertain

to actions undertaken by beings endowed with the capacity to
choose. A lawful state is one in which this conception of right is
instantiated through appropriate institutions, and informs personal relations. A lawful state, then, is one in which external freedom is secure insofar as its citizens coexist under an effective legal
order that protects mutually secure domains of external freedom.
In one of its most famous formulations, the fundamental principle of right is "So act externally that a way that the free use of
your choice can coexist with the freedom of everyone according
to a universal law."[32] This formulation resembles a variant of the
categorical imperative, but it is worth noticing that the emphasis
here is not on what I can do as an agent but on what others can
do to me, if I fail to respect others' freedom, that is, if I act in a
way that is not consistent with the external freedom of others.[33]
The principle in fact states the bounds of my external freedom,
which (exactly like my freedom of choice) proceeds from reason:
"Reason says only that my freedom is in its idea restricted to those
conditions and also *may forcefully be restricted by others*."[34]

Both the source of external freedom and its bounds come from
reason. To recognize that the bounds of external freedom are set
by reason is to say that we are free only when we act in a manner
that respects the dignity of others. When we fail to respect that
dignity, we also fail to be internally free. When I fail to recognize
the dignity of others, I also fail to exercise my own dignity, that is,
the capacity to rationally set my ends. Rationality does not simply
require that we choose the appropriate means to some given
ends, that is, instrumental rationality. Rationality also and most
importantly prescribes which ends are appropriate and that some
ends are also duties. This latter domain of practical rationality,
which is noninstrumental, is specifically linked to moral personality. Animals are capable of instrumental rationality insofar as they
are capable of selecting means to satisfy their ends (set by instinct
or habituation), but they are not capable of setting ends of their
own. For Kant, what makes us human is the capacity to rationally choose our ends, which is equivalent to being autonomous
agents. Recognizing a person amounts to recognizing that she is
an autonomous agent, an independent and inviolable source of
value. This recognition is both a moral and a rational achievement, insofar as we understand what makes it a source of value.

Rationality therefore determines the limits of how we may treat one another.

In violating another person's dignity, I fail as a moral as well as a rational being in that I fail to act upon a maxim that can be conceived and willed as a universal law.[35] Others are then permitted and required to coerce me, if coercion is needed to obstruct my wrongdoing. Although the underlying reasoning is clearly moral, Kant defends the permission to coerce as a *juridical permission*, according to which one person may force another to act rightly; that is, we may obstruct wrong actions.[36] This conception of coercion is based on the idea that the wrongdoer and the victim are both members of a moral community of mutually accountable equals. The moral norms that regulate the moral community are merely the standards of respect for the equal dignity of all members. All members of the community have equal standing to demand compliance. When those standards are violated, the victims have a claim on the wrongdoer, and they have grounds for complaint if he does not comply.

Membership in a community of mutual respect and accountability helps us to see that human rights are claims to which we are entitled *as persons*. As Joel Feinberg points out,

> having rights makes claiming possible; but it is claiming that gives rights their special moral significance. This feature of rights is connected in a way with the customary rhetoric about what it is to be a human being. Having rights enables us . . . to look others in the eye, and to feel in some fundamental way the equal to anyone.[37]

This conception is backed by a long-standing tradition; my aim here is simply to ground it on a Kantian conception of respect for humanity. Membership in humanity is tantamount to membership in a community of equals, "persons" who have equal standing and are mutually accountable. Morality, according to this Kantian view, is mutual accountability based on mutual recognition, not on special moral customs and conventions or common sense.[38] By linking morality to mutual accountability, we can argue not only that the failure to protect human rights is a failure to acknowledge and defend the claims to which persons are entitled as members of the moral community but also that a failure to hold someone accountable for wrongdoing is tantamount to a failure to respect his dignity as a rational being.[39] That is, the right to coerce springs from the recognition of the wrongdoer as an equal, as having equal standing in the moral community, and therefore as somebody to be addressed as a wrongdoer, rather than obstructed as a moral incompetent. On this view, then, coercion of the wrongdoer is a form of moral address, a relation that presupposes the recognition of mutual accountability.

What is legally right according to the existing laws may not correspond to what is categorically right. This is the case where the actual laws do not meet the complete conditions for mutual external freedom. In other words, it can be that we live under unjust institutions, governed by laws that do not adequately express or protect our humanity. *Recht* is a regulative ideal. Therefore, when we ask ourselves how to act, we should ask not only what is required by the existing law but also, more importantly, whether our maxim can be willed as a universal law. When the conception of right is instantiated, instead, there is no further test for our maxims because what is legal according to the existing law is also consistent with the external freedom of others.

This argument makes further sense of the claim that a state that does not grant fundamental human rights to its citizen is a state that fails its most important task; it fails *as* a state. In Kantian terms, it is a state that does not warrant mutually secure domains of external freedom. Hence, not only is there no obligation to respect the integrity of a state that fails as a state, there is also a legal permission (that is, an obligation) to use coercion against it. To argue that there is a moral obligation to obstruct the obstruction of freedom is already an argument for humanitarian intervention. It follows from it that neutrality is morally inadmissible, that the decision not to intervene calls for blame and other moral sanctions. The perfect duty to coerce the offender is complementary to the perfect duty to protect the victim.[40]

5. The Question of Proper Authority

Reluctance to treat humanitarian intervention as a perfect duty has its rationale. To consider humanitarian intervention as a strict duty seems to imply that political leaders have a standing duty to interfere with other states to enforce morality. If we treat intervention as permission or as a meritorious duty, instead, we justify it as morally nonobjectionable without burdening states with the onus of guaranteeing moral order outside their domestic jurisdiction. In this way, we also prevent leaders of sovereign states from abusing their power and acting outside their capacity, hence themselves committing a criminal aggression in the name of assisting the oppressed. As I am about to explain, however, the claim that the protection of human rights makes intervention a strict moral duty does not decide anything about proper authority: it does not determine whether our political leaders should or could be invested with the role of global enforcers of morality.

To treat humanitarian intervention as an imperfect duty is to make respect for basic human rights a minimal criterion for declaring a state minimally just. This implies that if a state violates basic human rights it has no right not to be interfered with because it does not meet the criteria of domestic legitimacy. It also implies that intervention by other states to protect human rights is a moral duty. This duty is sanctioned by moral blame. Blame is not the only cost that the proper authorities incur when they violate the duty to protect human rights. Another cost is international stability, which I qualified as a practical aim.

However, these considerations do not (and are not meant to) settle the issue of proper authority. The claim that humanitarian intervention is a perfect duty imposes no burdensome responsibility on any particular state, nor does it excuse a bellicose policy. The appeal to fundamental human rights only determines that intervention is a strict moral duty. Who should perform the duty is a separate question, one that must be decided by reconsidering the grounds for proper authority.

Although the violation of human rights calls for action, it is not obvious that any particular state has the authority to respond, especially in cases where the state in which the violation occurs is not aggressive and does not pose any immediate threat. If the outlaw state manifests an expansionist policy, the threatened neighbors have the right to act in self-defense.[41] But in responding to an immediate threat, the intervening state is invoking self-defense as a ground for action, not the defense of noncitizens' basic human rights. When the outlaw state is not aggressive, however, it is not obvious that any particular state should take on the burden of enforcing morality. This is not because political leaders will not always heed the call of duty or because the duty of humanitarian intervention is episodic and extraordinary. Of course, armed intervention should never be precipitous; it should be chosen only after diplomatic alternatives have been seriously explored and proven unsuccessful.[42] But this does not ground a normative qualification of the duty of humanitarian intervention, and it does not affect its status: there is a perfect duty of humanitarian intervention. However, this discussion suggests further considerations about proper authority.

First, it suggests that we rethink the basis of proper authority, in cases of humanitarian intervention, outside the framework of traditional just war theory. Traditional just war theory views the justification of war from the standpoint of a national sovereign who is entrusted with the common good of a local community. Alternatively, we might conceive authority more broadly. We might, that is, make room for the idea that only international authorities can authorize states to use force to obstruct human rights violations outside their territories.

One might argue that governments never act for purely beneficent purposes where such action compromises national interests. One might even claim that, because it is entrusted with the good of the community it governs, it would not be appropriate for a government to act only for such purposes. A government that acts to assist noncitizens fails its own citizens; and because those citizens have entrusted it with their good, they are entitled to expect something in return. After all, it is putting their lives at stake, depleting their resources, and relying on their trust. To allay these concerns, one may argue that those citizens profit from restoring law, order, and eventually peace in the troubled country they assisted. But to enjoy this benefit, the state need not participate in the war *as a state*, for example, by acting unilaterally. Correspondingly, to grant that human rights are respected, and that law, order, and peace are restored, it is not necessary that any state act unilaterally. In fact, one might argue that to act unilaterally to protect human rights in other countries is not a practical aim that a state should have.

This introduces a second important point. To argue that individual states do not have the moral capacity and the legal authority to intervene to protect human rights does not impugn the status of humanitarian intervention as a perfect duty. As I argue in the previous sections, the duty to intervene is perfect insofar as it is grounded on respect of humanity. We bear this duty as individuals bound by rationality and morality to regard others with respect. However, not all individual duties are to be discharged individually. This is true in a number of trivial cases. The duty to repay one's debt is something that we all bear as rational and moral beings, but it may be fulfilled as a collective duty and, most importantly, through communal practices and institutions. *How* we fulfill our duty to repay our debts depends on the actual institutions and practices that are in place. Notice, once again, that this issue is independent of the normative status of the duty to repay one's debt. Delegation to the appropriate institution (for example, the institution of debt collectors) can be the only appropriate way to satisfy some individual duties. In other words, some duties we bear as individuals may and sometimes ought to be discharged collectively. This conclusion is particularly relevant in the case of humanitarian intervention. My argument for the justification of humanitarian intervention does not pretend to answer the legal issue of proper authority. Rather, it aims at showing that although there is a compelling moral argument that we all are under the perfect duty to protect human rights, how to fulfill such a duty is a separate issue.

When we ask who is under the call of duty in a case of humanitarian intervention, we ask both a moral and legal question. From a moral perspective, we all, as rational and moral beings, are under the call of duty. From a legal perspective, however, the duty is to be discharged as a collective through an appropriately designed institution, invested with the proper legal authority. In the case of humanitarian intervention, it seems to me that the proper authority should be supranational. We should respond to the violation of human rights not as Italians or Americans, as subjects of a certain state, but as moral agents who delegate to an agency. My rationale for this suggestion is both prudential and moral. From a prudential perspective, it seems to me that an international agency might be less prone to be thwarted by the interests of any particular state. From a moral perspective, I argued that because the perfect duty falls on the moral community as such, and not on specific states, an international agency would best represent such community; it would be rather arrogant if a particular state pretended to have the exclusive prerogative to voice and protect the moral concerns of the whole community of rational beings. Only an international agency can make such a claim.

This leaves open the question of how to institutionalize this requirement and the corresponding action. I hope that distinguishing institutional issues from those of moral principle makes clear why the fact that there is no international agency to discharge the duty to intervene is no argument that such a duty is imperfect. That there is no international institution with the proper authority to intervene means that we *ought* to design such an institution so that the perfect duty could be appropriately fulfilled. This bears, once again, on the conditions of justice. There might be cases where we cannot perform our perfect duties because the actual legal institutions are defective or, in Kantian terms, do not meet the conditions of justice. The modest contribution of a moral philosopher is to point out the discrepancy between what we ought to do and what we can do, given the limitations of legal institutions, and to indicate why a reform is needed.

Let me add a final remark. This discussion makes it apparent that if we are to justify enforcing morality against an outlaw state that is not aggressive and does not immediately threaten any other country, further normative criteria are needed. One plausible additional criterion would be whether the rescuers have been freely invited to do so by the oppressed people of the outlaw state.[43] This criterion, advocated by Kantian internationalists, has the merit of preventing paternalistic interference, although it is not sufficient to determine the motive of the intervening state. That state might be responding to the call for help not from beneficent motives but for economic or political advantage. For this criterion to be successfully applied, moreover, it is necessary that the oppressed people of the outlaw state have the opportunity to organize and call for help and the political and diplomatic resources to do so. But where the violation of basic human rights is extreme and intervention most needed, the oppressed people may lack the resources to organize and ask for help. I have in mind situations in which, for example, ethnic or religious hatred has divided families, villages, and communities, destroying the most natural *loci* of resistance. In this case, oppression works by dissolving social ties, breaking natural bonds, and corroding the fabric of society; this impedes any form of organized resistance. I also have in mind situations where oppression works by imposing an ideology the oppressed themselves embrace: in this case, the oppressed would not feel entitled to any treatment other than the one they are subjected to; they feel unworthy rather than oppressed, and see no cause for rescue. This latter case is, I believe, particularly delicate because intervention to defend basic human rights where people do not recognize them for themselves can seem paternalistic and illegitimate. Still, these seem to me two situations in which there is a grievous violation of basic human rights and in which refraining from action is morally objectionable.

Political leaders must be constrained from abusing their power and violating, under the color of humanitarian intervention, the territorial integrity of other countries with the aim of ruling, exploiting, and profiting. We cannot formulate this constraint as a clause concerning the intentions of political leaders entrusted with the good of a community, as it is the case in traditional just war theory. Rather, the issue must be addressed by constituting an international institution whose constitutive and sole aim is to protect fundamental human rights. We can keep that institution from abusing its power by framing its constitutive rules intelligently.

6. Conclusion

I have attempted to show that in constructing a moral case for humanitarian intervention based on the defense of human rights, we are bound to recognize it as a duty rather than permission, and as a perfect duty rather than an imperfect one—a duty that proceeds from respect for humanity rather than from charity. This qualification implies that the gross violation of human rights calls for intervention and that a state that grossly violates the human rights of its citizens is outlaw and has no right not to be interfered with. To qualify humanitarian intervention as a strict duty does not settle the issue of proper authority, but it encourages us to rethink the ground of proper authority and the institutionalization of moral responsibility. My conviction is that when human rights are at stake, the whole international community must respond, and only an international organization can have the proper authority to do that. How exactly to design such an international institution is something that falls well beyond the scope of competence of a moral philosopher; so I should leave the matter at this point.

NOTES

I would like to thank Joseph Boyle, Luca Ferrero, Julius Sensat, Richard Wilcox, Melissa Williams, and most of all Terry Nardin for their comments on previous versions of this essay.

1. See Nicholas J. Wheeler, *Saving Strangers: Humanitarian Intervention in International Society* (Oxford: Oxford University Press, 2000); Brian D. Lepard, *Rethinking Humanitarian Intervention: A Fresh Legal Approach Based on Fundamental Ethical Principles in International Law and World Religions* (University Park: Pennsylvania State University Press, 2002); Pierre Laberge, "Humanitarian Intervention: Three Ethical Positions," *Ethics and International Affairs*, 9 (1995): 15–35.

2. This view finds a variety of supporters: see, for example, Elizabeth Anscombe, "War and Massacre," in *War and Morality*, ed. Richard A. Wasserstrom, 41–53 (Belmont, Calif.: Wadsworth Publishing Company, 1970); Michael Walzer, *Just and Unjust Wars: A Moral Argument with Historical Illustrations* (New York: Basic Books, 1977), 106–8; John Rawls, *The Law of Peoples* (Cambridge: Harvard University Press, 1999), 80–81; and Terry Nardin, "The Moral Basis of Humanitarian Intervention," *Ethics and International Affairs*, 16, no. 1 (2002): 57–71.

3. See Terry Nardin, "Introduction," this volume.

4. I take "humanity" as also including "personality."

5. Kant writes that "rational nature exists as an end in itself. We necessarily think of our own existence in this way; thus far it is a subjective principle of human actions." Kant, *Groundwork of the Metaphysics of Morals*, trans. Mary Gregor, ed. Christine Korsgaard (Cambridge: Cambridge University Press, 1998 [1785]), 4:429.

6. The issue is addressed by Rawls, *Law of Peoples*, 80ff.

7. See Nardin, "Introduction"; Joseph Boyle, "Traditional Just War Theory and Humanitarian Intervention," this volume, chap. 1. Kok-Chor Tan, in "The Duty to Protect," this volume, chap. 3, 111, writes, "I have argued that given the stringency of the conditions for permissible intervention, these conditions are also sufficient for making intervention

obligatory. If it is permissible to override the ideal of sovereignty to put an end to a serious violation of human rights, it is also permissible to override the right of neutral states to keep out of the fighting. Although this duty is generally imperfect, the fact that it is imperfect means that the international community has an obligation to assign responsibilities so that this duty will be discharged."

8. Walzer, *Just and Unjust Wars*, xiii.

9. Tan takes this problem very seriously. He takes it to be a problem in the formulation of the principle of humanitarian intervention: "The phrase 'international community' or 'some state,' however, underlines a possible shortcoming in the formulation. Since it is not clear which particular state in the international community (only *some* unspecified state) should perform the task of intervening, it appears that there can be no perfect duty on the part of any state to act." Tan, "The Duty to Protect," this volume, 94.

10. Kant, *Metaphysical Principles of Virtue*, in *Immanuel Kant's Practical Philosophy*, trans. and ed. J. Ellington (Indianapolis: Hackett Publishing Company, 1983 [1797]), 6:220.

11. Kant, *Metaphysical Principles of Virtue*, 6:218–19.

12. See Allen Wood, "The Final Form of Kant's Practical Philosophy," *Southern Journal of Philosophy* 36 (1997): 7–9; Thomas Hill Jr. "Punishment, Conscience, and Moral Worth," *Southern Journal of Philosophy* 36 (1997): 51–71.

13. Kant, *Metaphysical Principles of Virtue*, 6:390.

14. Tan also denies that we cannot talk of culpability in case of failure to perform an imperfect duty, but his argument differs from the one I am advancing here.

15. Kant, *Metaphysical Principles of Virtue*, 6:390.

16. Ibid.

17. Ibid., 6:388.

18. For an illuminating investigation of this kind of indeterminacy, see Onora O'Neill, "Instituting Principles: Between Duty and Action," *Southern Journal of Philosophy* 36 (1997): 79–96.

19. Kant, *Metaphysical Principles of Virtue*, 6:390. Emphasis added.

20. Tan writes "[t]hat the duty to protect is imperfect in the absence of institutionalized procedures for intervention should not be seen as a limitation against arguments for obligatory humanitarian intervention but as a case for greater international cooperation to protect human rights, including, if necessary, the creation of a permanent humanitarian defense force. That a duty is imperfect points only to the need for coordinating efforts and the need to cooperate. It does not mean that the duty need not be taken seriously by anyone." Tan, "The Duty to Protect," this volume, 111.

21. Wheeler, *Saving Strangers*, 34ff., defines humanitarian intervention as aiming at the promotion of a positive humanitarian outcome. I think it is important to distinguish between "promoting" and "correcting": they differ not only in nature but also in the means they require.

22. Rawls, *Law of Peoples*, 80. Universal Declaration of Human Rights, Articles 3–18.

23. In later works, Kant distinguishes between humanity and moral personality. See Kant, *Religion within the Limits of Reason Alone*, trans. Theodor Green and Hoyt Hudson, ed. John Silber (New York: Harper Torchbooks, 1960 [1793]), n. 26. Cf. Allen Wood, *Kant's Ethical Thought* (Cambridge: Cambridge University Press, 1999), 364–66. For the sake of simplicity, I take humanity as to include personality, as Kant does in the *Groundwork of the Metaphysics of Morals*.

24. Rawls, "Kantian Constructivism in Moral Theory," *Journal of Philosophy* 77 (1980): 546. "Humanity insofar as it is capable of morality is that which alone has dignity." Kant, *Groundwork of the Metaphysics of Morals*, 4:434–35.

25. Kant, *Metaphysical Principles of Virtue*, 6:436.

26. As Kant writes: "A human being regarded as a person, that is, as a subject of a morally practical reason . . . possesses dignity . . . by which he exacts respect for himself from all other rational beings in the world." Ibid., 6:434–35, 557.

27. Darwall labeled this kind of respect "recognition respect" as opposed to "appraisal respect." Stephen Darwall, "Two Kinds of Respect," *Ethics* 88 (1977): 36–49. "Recognition respect" does not involve any consideration of appraisal of excellence, status, special relation, position or merit: it is owed to others insofar as they are recognized as persons. I am not suggesting that respect is the only way to value others but that it is the way we value others insofar as they are persons; for a comparative analysis of respect and other evaluative attitudes directed toward persons, see Bagnoli, "Respect and Loving Attention," *Canadian Journal of Philosophy* 33 (2003): 483–516.

28. Kant, *Metaphysical Principles of Virtue*, 6:462.

29. I am thinking of scenarios where diplomacy, threats, and sanctions proved unsuccessful and there is no hope of restoring a meaningful communication. As for inflicting economic sanctions rather than attacking, several authors have pointed out that the imposition of systematic economic sanctions violates the principle of discrimination of *jus in bello* since it applies to all indiscriminately and most affects the poor and vulnerable. See, for example, Walzer, *Just and Unjust Wars*, xxv–xxxii.

30. See Boyle, "Traditional Just War Theory and Humanitarian Intervention," this volume. Boyle argues that in its defensive interpretation,

the argument for humanitarian intervention does not require this much, and is therefore more restrictive and more likely to find a plausible foundation.

31. Kant, *Metaphysical Principles of Virtue*, 6:230:24–26

32. Ibid., 6:231:10–12

33. See Thomas Pogge, "Is Kant's *Rechtslehre* Comprehensive?" *Southern Journal of Philosophy* 36 (1997): 167–72.

34. Kant, *Metaphysical Principles of Virtue*, 6:231:13–17. Italics mine; see also ibid., 6:231:3–9.

35. "Maxim" is a technical term that refers to the formulation of an intention to act. In contrast to animals' acting on instinct without the mediation of the will, human beings act on the basis of conceptions of their own. Maxims state these conceptions. Perhaps they are best rendered in their teleological formulation, that is, as specifying an end; for example, "I will talk to him in order to help him out." Maxims are not yet motives or decisive reasons for action. They become decisive and motivating through deliberation, by an act of will.

36. I am indebted to Thomas Pogge on this point. Pogge, "Is Kant's *Rechtslehre* Comprehensive?" 168–69.

37. Joel Feinberg, "The Nature and Value of Rights," in *Rights, Justice, and the Bounds of Liberty* (Princeton: Princeton University Press), 1980.

38. On the relation between respect and mutual recognition, see Bagnoli, "Respect and Loving Attention." For an extended argument about morality and the practices of mutual accountability, see Thomas Scanlon, *What We Owe to Each Other* (Cambridge: Harvard University Press, 1999).

39. This is Hegel's insight. See George Frederick Hegel, *Elements of the Philosophy of Right*, ed. A. Wood, trans. H. B. Nisbet (Cambridge: Cambridge University Press, 1991), 126–27. I take his conception of punishment to be one that can be grounded on a Kantian argument. See Thomas Hill, "Punishment, Conscience, and Moral Worth," and also Nelson Potter, "Comment on Hill: Punishment, Conscience, and Moral Worth," *Southern Journal of Philosophy* 36 (1997): 51–72 and 73–78, respectively.

40. In this respect, my argument differs from Boyle's, Tan's, and Nardin's. Boyle offers only a defensive argument, Tan does not see the duty to protect as a strict duty that is complementary to the duty to coerce, and Nardin focuses on the duty to punish the wrongdoer.

41. Notice that this is not to imply that the criteria for justifying armed humanitarian intervention are more stringent in nonaggressive countries than in aggressive countries. Rather, this is to say that when we deal with aggressive outlaw states, the grounding for undertaking war is self-defense rather than the defense of human rights. There is a

difference in how we should respond to aggressive outlaw states and non-aggressive outlaw states, but the difference concerns how we should respond to aggression, not how we should respond to their violation of basic human rights. This seems to me an important qualification concerning the status of armed humanitarian intervention that gets lost in many accounts. See, e.g., Brian Orend, *War and International Justice: A Kantian Perspective* (Waterloo, Ontario: Wilfried Laurier University Press, 2000), 187.

42. This claim does not amount to saying that war should be the last resort. As Walzer noted, there is no such thing as the last resort since, in principle, one can always try something else. See Walzer, *Just and Unjust Wars*, xiv.

43. See Orend, *War and International Justice*, 187. Orend mentions another criterion: that the intervening state must commit itself to meaningful participation in the reconstruction of the outlaw state, after war. I do not see why this commitment should be considered a criterion for justifying any particular intervention; it seems to me to pertain to *jus post bellum*, rather than to *jus ad bellum*. Under the rubric of *jus post bellum*, I think it is important that the intervening state takes the responsibility of committing itself to share the cost of reconstruction. If one treats this as a criterion for selecting the interveners, however, one basically suggests that only states powerful enough to bear the economic costs of intervention and reconstruction can legitimately undertake war.

PART II
INSTITUTIONS

5

LEGALITY AND LEGITIMACY IN HUMANITARIAN INTERVENTION

THOMAS FRANCK

Saint Paul tells us that "the letter killeth but the spirit giveth life."[1] The U.N. Charter, now nearly sixty years old, cannot rationally be applied in strictly literal fashion, as if its drafters could have foreseen such supervening events as the development of the hydrogen bomb, the end of colonialism and communism, and the emergence of terrorism as weapon of choice for the disempowered. They could not have anticipated the consequences of responsible regionalism in Europe, Africa, and the Americas, nor the proliferation of states from fewer than sixty to almost two hundred. Given the immensity of changes in the state system's configuration, together with the intractability of the Charter to change through formal amendment, it is not surprising that there arise conflicts in practice between what is prescribed by the text and good sense.

The U.N. Secretary-General has recently addressed this tension between what needs to be done and the normative constraints on doing it. In the aftermath of the genocide perpetrated against 800,000 persons in Rwanda, he has asked: what if there had been a coalition of the willing able to act preemptively, but consent had been blocked by the opposition of one permanent member of the Security Council? Had there been a choice, would it have been better to sacrifice the Charter's rule prohibiting intervention and thereby save a multitude? Or would it have been better to sacrifice those lives in order to uphold the letter of a law widely deemed, at least in general principle, to be essential to the preservation of the international security system? What are the costs to the system of allowing the rules to be bent to allow unauthorized use of force by states in a situation of exceptional humanitarian necessity or, on the other hand, in Annan's words, of "setting dangerous precedents for future interventions without a clear criterion to decide who might invoke those precedents and in what circumstances"?[2] What, in other words, would have been the cost to the credibility of the normative system were strict adherence to the law to have been the proximate cause of a mass slaughter of innocents?

Some lawyers seek to escape this conundrum by insisting on a strict separation of law from good sense, a factor that might also be rendered as "morality." They argue that it is not the role of law to ensure moral outcomes to every crisis but, rather, to protect the integrity of law itself, which is undermined when it is not enforced and thereby is diminished in its primary role as the guardian of good order. In this vein it can even be argued that the highest form of good sense and morality *is* good order.

To this, Britain's eminent international lawyer Professor J. M. Brierly, writing in the middle of the past century, responded— swimming rather against the then-prevalent positivistic tide—that law

> is not a meaningless set of arbitrary principles to be mechanically applied . . . but . . . exists for certain ends, though those ends may have to be differently formulated in different times and places. . . . This is so because the life with which any system of law has to deal is too complicated, and human foresight too limited, for law to be completely formulated in a set of rules, so that situations perpetually arise which fall outside all rules already formulated. Law cannot and does not refuse to solve a problem because it is new and un-provided for; it meets such situations by resorting to a principle, outside formulated law . . . appealing to reason as the justification for its decision.[3]

In other words, any straining to save law's determinacy by applying it strictly, even when to do so leads to absurd or horrific consequences, is futile and of no benefit either to the law or morality.

This requires some further emphasis. Those who insist on enforcing "the letter of the law" do it no favor as an institution of social control. Nowadays, when law's obsession with positivism has crested as part of the general reassessment of the monopoly of the state in norm creation and norm implementation, it has been widely accepted both by rulers and the ruled that the power of law to secure compliance is undermined if the gap between it and the prevalent sense of justice, morality, and common sense is allowed to become too wide. The capacity of the law to pull toward compliance those to whom it is addressed is diminished whenever it is seen no longer to comport with shared notions of what is right. The law's self-interest, therefore, demands that a way be found to bridge any gap between its own institutional commitment to the consistent application of formal rules and the public sense that order should not be achieved at too high a cost to widely shared moral values.

If law permits—or even *requires*—behavior that is widely believed to be unfair, unjust, or immoral, it is not only persons but also the law that suffers. So, too, if law *prohibits* that which is widely believed to be just and moral. It is apparent, therefore, that law has a strong interest in narrowing the gap between its strictures and the common sense of what is right in a specific situation.

This is not a requisite apparent only to international lawyers but is well understood also by those versed in the domestic law of states. Courts in many countries have had to deal with a broad array of cases in which "the letter killeth but the spirit giveth life." An instance, unusual but surprisingly found in many legal systems, is that of persons who commit murders in order to save lives. A British case involved passengers, adrift and starving in a lifeboat, cannibalizing one of their number in order to save the rest;[4] an American case turned on the act of passengers in an overloaded lifeboat jettisoning persons to prevent all being lost through capsizing.[5] Both kinds of killings, however excusable and morally defensible in the circumstances, can be categorized in law as murder. In both instances, however, the trials resulted in extremely lenient penalties of six months, or time already served.[6] The law was interpreted to accommodate the public sense of right and wrong. It was construed in such a way that the case would not tear a large hole in the fabric of the prohibition, while yet accommodating what was seen as a highly exceptional circumstance of a kind not within the contemplation of society in fashioning the legal prohibition on killing. This can be seen as analogous to the U.N. Security Council's reaction to the Israelis' postwar kidnapping of the Nazi mass murderer Adolf Eichmann from his sanctuary in Argentina, a response by the interstatal community that amounted to no more than an admonition and reaffirmation of the law's general prohibition on that sort of conduct.

In virtually every legal system, there is some way a prohibition can be transformed by extreme necessity into something more akin to a rebuttable presumption. Thus, the law prohibiting the killing of a person is, in effect, a presumption rebuttable by a convincing demonstration of circumstances of extreme necessity. As Professor H. L. A. Hart has pointed out, "[I]n the criminal law of every modern state responsibility for serious crimes is excluded or 'diminished' by some 'excusing conditions.'"[7] An example is section 3.02 of the U.S. Model Penal Code, which provides: "Conduct that the actor believes to be necessary to himself or another is justifiable, provided that . . . the harm or evil sought to be avoided by such conduct is greater than that sought to be prevented by the law defining the offense charged." The International Court of Justice, too, has concluded that an illegal act by a state may be excusable if it was performed in circumstances where its nonperformance could reasonably have been expected to result in the occurrence of some greater wrong.[8] More recently, the report of the Independent International Commission on Kosovo (the "Goldstone" Commission) concluded that NATO's action in using force against Yugoslavia, although not strictly legal, was "legitimate." It called for the applicable law to become more congruent with "an international moral consensus."[9]

Legal theory, whether directed at national or international law, need not be impervious to moral considerations that arise as a result of law's inherent didacticism. Laws, of necessity, are usually drawn in bold brushstrokes, but they can and should be applied flexibly and in keeping with common sensibility, especially to circumstances of extreme necessity. To the extent that this sort of flexible response has been opposed by China and many Third World states in the U.N. context, it is not because they favor rigidity *per se* but because they fear the skewed manner in which flexibility is likely to be implemented in practice. The problem is not simply that there is a "slippery slope." All normativity entails an excursion onto the slippery slope of language, simply because it is inherent in all verbal formulation that it can be read in more than one way. Rather, especially in application of the norms of international law, the problem is with the "jury" that makes the definitive decision as to how the law—or the exception—is to be applied in specific instances. Indeed, the problem is not with what a jury does but with how it is constituted. This problem is made more acute by the fact that, in the arena of international normativity, the jury is a fiction introduced without literal application.

In those domestic legal systems that use the jury, it is the jury that filters the strict letter of the law through a sensibility informed by common sense and a certain innate human receptivity to moral considerations. Since this is bound to involve applied art rather than science, it is extremely important—as every trial lawyer well knows—to inquire *who* these jurors are: those to whom is to be entrusted the crucial work of finding the facts, applying the law to them situationally, and, in doing so, narrowing, when necessary, the gaps between law's legality and legitimacy: between society's normative and ethical constraints.

It is this synthesis of law and moral reason that lawyers call "fairness." The willingness of a society (whether of persons or of states) to agree to be governed by a law depends not only on the content of that law but also on the credibility of the process by which the law is to be applied. Those to whom a law is to be applied must be convinced not only that the general principle implemented in the form of a law is fair and reasonable but also that the law will be applied fairly in all potential instances of its being tested.

In other words, agreement on a general principle (the law) depends not only on its content (the text) but also on the modalities of its application to specific circumstances (the cases). In an earlier era, at least in Western Europe, popes and kings were the supreme judges, and they were thought to act under divine guidance, thereby making the problem of case-by-case application of the rules more manageable. Their fairness was guaranteed by Heaven. Today, those beliefs are largely obsolete and the human process, by which laws are applied, although still seen to be central, now stands exposed as fallible. Like the process by which rules are written, the process by which they are applied is nowadays the cockpit of negotiations among mere mortals.

Neither text nor modalities, however, can be negotiated in isolation. Although the two negotiations are inherently separate, they are also intrinsically interdependent. The rules to which members of a community will agree—rules by which they voluntarily limit their freedom of action through legal constraints—are in large part dependent on, and responsive to, agreement on a fair and credible process by which such constraints will be applied. In domestic law, the jury, as the relevant institution, has a strong constituency among the public and, in particular, among the trial lawyers who represent litigants. In the global system of norms, all that we have been able to invent, so far, is a sort of "jury of peers": sovereign states constituting a Security Council or a General Assembly, hearing evidence of facts, special pleadings pertaining to the way the norms should be applied, and then voting to convict or acquit a state accused of counternormative conduct. The international legal system thus lacks the bedrock intuitive support the law enjoys in more developed legal systems, not because it lacks laws but because it lacks an instantaneously recognizable system for applying the norms fairly.

This problem is rendered more acute by the highly politicized nature of the subjects to which international law addresses itself. Humanitarian intervention is but one example of this. It would be difficult to imagine a law more potentially fraught with tough calls and hard choices than one pertaining to the right of states to use force in situations of extreme necessity. But the difficulty lies less in the formulation of applicable norms than in their application to an infinite variety of potential situations where the rule might be invoked. We might all agree to a rule that permits willing states to send an expedition to save large numbers of innocent lives. But who decides whether a situation has risen to the level of such a crisis? Who defines whether the crisis is truly one of extreme necessity? Who decides whether the force deployed is appropriate and commensurate with the necessity? Who decides whether the motive of the intervener is humanitarian, as distinct from self-aggrandizing? Who, in other words, will be doing the "jurying"? Until that issue has been resolved, the community of states is unlikely to agree to even the most textually reasonable law permitting recourse to force by states except—very narrowly—in self-defense against an armed attack or in response to a Security Council authorization.

This problem of finding a credible process for applying rules is especially acute when the rule to which agreement is sought does not self-evidently apply itself: this is what, elsewhere, I have called a "sophist" rule in contrast with an "idiot" rule.[10] Traffic lights exemplify the idiot rule. So, essentially, does article 2(4) of the U.N. Charter. Humanitarian intervention, on the other hand, if it were to be legally validated, would require a "sophist rule." These are very hard to negotiate in the absence of a divine king or infallible pope to act as the rule's referee.

The reasons for the foregoing statement are evident.

Very few states are in a position to engage in unilateral acts of humanitarian intervention. Only a small number even belong to regional organizations or mutual defense groupings that might engage in collective interventions. Yet, most states can imagine a hypothetical situation in which another, more powerful, state might seek to take advantage of the weaker state's domestic crisis —minor, or imagined—to settle an old score or pursue a long-standing objective. It cannot be astonishing that these states would look askance at even the most textually reasonable proposed rule permitting an armed attack by any nation against another for any reason. Their concern cannot be alleviated solely by refining the normative text to allow some carefully specified interventions but only by also, simultaneously, addressing the "jurying" process by which the international system proposes to implement any new rule. They know too well that, in the absence of such an agreed, credible process, the rule, however expressed, would become a license for the strong to teach manners to the weak. Although this may be true, there is as yet nothing in the system that is the formal surrogate for kings, popes, or juries.

In his address to the Millennium Assembly of the United Nations, Secretary-General Kofi Annan pointed out: "Few would disagree that both the defense of humanity and the defense of sovereignty are principles that must be supported. Alas that does not tell us which principle should prevail when they are in conflict."[11] In this and several other pronouncements, Annan has called for a clarification of the circumstances in which sovereignty should yield in the face of extreme necessity;[12] but even if such a summons is prescient, it does not sufficiently make an effort to address the absence of a credible institutional mechanism for implementing—that is, "jurying"—even the most universally endorsed criteria for distinguishing between real and bogus pleas of moral necessity. Yet that is the essential prerequisite for any rule that seeks to implement a formula for balancing the cherished factor of sovereignty with the humanitarian impulse.

This aspect of the problem needs to be brought to the fore. But its intractability should not discourage us from searching for answers. Dame Rosalyn Higgins, judge at the International Court of Justice and prominent academic scholar of international law, has written that while the problem has not been resolved at the formal institutional level, it might resolve itself in a more pragmatic fashion through the improving practice of existing, mostly political, transnational institutions. There are, she says, "a variety of important decision-makers, other than courts, who can pronounce on the validity of claims advanced; and claims which may in very restricted exceptional circumstances be regarded as lawful should not *a priori* be disallowed because on occasion they may be unjustly invoked."[13] She points out that "there have been countless abusive claims of the right of self-defense. That does not lead us to say that there should be no right of self-defense today. . . . We delude ourselves if we think that the role of norms is to remove the possibility of abusive claims ever being made."[14]

How credibly have these political institutions been in performing this "jurying" function? It is evident that, in the debates of the Security Council and the General Assembly both preceding and following a recourse to force by a state or group of states, there occurs a form of "jurying." In situations of armed intervention, representatives argue the validity of facts alleged by those initiating recourse to force, assess the proportionality of the action taken in relation to the evidence of extreme necessity, and debate the motives of the parties to the dispute. Eventually, they decide. Sometimes—more like a grand jury—they decide not to take any action. Does the record of this process demonstrate a credible assay at institutional "jurying" sufficient to justify the codification of exceptions to article 2(4) of the Charter? Probably not. On the other hand, the process, as it has developed in the practice of the Security Council, may embody elements of another jurying function: applying the law—or selectively *not* applying it—in such a way as to narrow the gap between the strictures of strict legality and the importunings of popular moral intuition.

The practice of the Council demonstrates its ability to respond rather like a jury to instances of the unauthorized use of force in response to what are alleged to be circumstances of extreme necessity. One example is the Security Council's willingness to give retroactive *post hoc* approval to the use of force by the West African community (ECOMOG/ECOWAS) in the extreme circumstances of the Liberian and Sierra Leonean civil wars. Although this humanitarian intervention was not preapproved by the Council, as required by the letter of the law, it was adjudged to be in keeping with the spirit of the Charter. Another example is the Security Council's decisive defeat of Russia's and China's effort to admonish NATO's action in Kosovo. Instead, the Council ratified that action by entering into a partnership with NATO in rehabilitating that territory. Still other examples are the Council's silent acquiescence in some unauthorized uses of force by France against Emperor Bokassa in the Central African Empire and by Tanzania against Field Marshal Idi Amin in Uganda, and the mildness of its disapprobation of India's intervention in the civil war leading to the creation of Bangladesh, of Vietnam's invasion of Khmer Rouge Cambodia, and of Israel's incursions into Uganda to rescue the Entebbe hostages and into Argentina to bring to justice the arch–war criminal Adolf Eichmann.

The verdict, in these latter instances, appears to have been that the use of force produced a salutary result but set a potentially dangerous precedent that could best be contained by tempered admonitions. But, in contrast, the Council is also able to condemn forthrightly the flagrant violations for which no excuses availed, such as North Korea's invasion of the South, Iraq's invasion of Kuwait, Al Qaeda's attack on the United States, and the Afghan Taliban's harboring of Al Qaeda. It is impossible, in the light of these events, to conclude that the Security Council is incapable of discharging the "jurying" function in a credible fashion. It has demonstrated a certain, admittedly fallible, ability and readiness, when faced with states' unauthorized recourse to force, to calibrate the verdict by making quite sophisticated judgments that take into account the full panoply of specific circumstances in each case.

That the Council has chosen in one way or another to approve or to excuse some recourse to force in situations of extreme necessity can be construed either in terms of exculpation or of mitigation. If the former, the practice of the Council may be said to have created, in practice, a reading of Charter article 2(4) that grafts onto it certain contextual exceptions. If the latter, the Council may be said to have continued to protect the coherence of the absolute prohibition of article 2(4) but also to have fashioned a practice that treats violations differently depending on such factors as whether alternative remedies had been exhausted and whether the consequences that were likely to have ensued had the violation not occurred would have exceeded in gravity the consequences of the violation. The differences in national law between exculpation and mitigation may be considerable; however, in international law, the differences are almost imperceptible.

The outcome of this process may not always accord with everyone's sense of justice and morality. But it can reasonably be asserted that there are now in place at least the rudiments of a process by which to weigh considerations of strict legality against the common sense of moral imperatives. It is also a process capable of separating facts from self-serving avowals. The political organs, aided by augmented Secretariat capability, have demonstrated an increasingly credible capacity for fact-finding. This does not entirely abate but puts in perspective the objection that the Council, an intensely political body in which are represented the unvarnished self-interests of states, cannot be seen as a disinterested appraiser of facts or of the public interest.

Can a representative political body be a credible "jury"? Perhaps so. In practice, most of the conflicts pertaining to the use of force that do—or could—come before the Council do not directly engage the national interest of any but a very few states. The judgment of the others is thus largely unencumbered. The response to crises in Bosnia, Sierra Leone, and the fight against terrorism are recent instances of many members acting more as responsible "jurors" than committed partisans. Also increasingly evident is a tendency of states to want to be seen as good institutional citizens and desire to be held in the high regard of their peers.

Beyond that, one's answer is likely also to depend on whether one's model of a jury is that of *impartial* or *cross-sectional* assessors or a balance between these prototypes. In all likelihood, the international standard for credible jurying, like the usual standard applied in domestic legal systems, will mix a degree of disinterestedness with a degree of cross-sectional representativity. In both international and domestic jurying, this is bound to be "a matter of degree." In my opinion, the effectiveness of a jury in persuading persons or states to live by laws is dependent less on whether they share a common moral judgment than on whether they perceive themselves to share a sense of social cohesion (i.e., that they have a greater stake in peaceful, orderly governance than in their unlimited autonomy) *and* whether the jury that will apply the laws will be constituted by those who have no (or only a weak) commitment to preordained outcomes and who are not disproportionately representative of any eco-socio-political part of the community. These two tests are relatively construed, in probabilistic calculus, when decisions are made by autonomous actors to submit or not to rule by law. My point is that this calculus will take into account not only the content of the norms but also the way the jury will be constituted.[15]

"Jurying," however defined, admittedly remains at best a rudimentary process in the emerging global system. As long as this is so, the process for legitimating (or not) a recourse to force remains a fragmented function. The U.N. Security Council is not the only site at which a form of "jurying" may be said to occur. Although Charter Article 53 specifically prohibits regional organizations from resorting to force without the prior approval of the Security Council, in practice they have acquired considerable credibility as "juries" when it comes to determining whether a situation of *bona fide* extreme necessity has arisen in their vicinity that requires an extraordinary recourse to force. When the U.N. manifestly fails to respond to a situation widely perceived to constitute a humanitarian crisis, and its failure is due only to the arbitrary resistance of one or two permanent members of the Council, other institutions may fill the void, legitimating a remedy not foreseen by a Charter that did not envisage that kind of crisis nor the failure of its institutions to respond to it.

The Economic Community of West African States (ECOWAS) was accorded such credibility when it used force during the regional civil wars of the 1990s, and it was to NATO that the United States chose to demonstrate its evidence of Taliban complicity in the aggressive actions of Al Qaeda in order to justify its military measures in Afghanistan. The underlying rationale appears to be that there is credibility in numbers: that if a plea of extreme necessity is accepted by a multiplicity of governments, it is more likely to be believed than when asserted unilaterally by the government directly at interest. This, too, is recognition by the United States and others of the need to submit to a "jury of peers."

That there is growing recognition of this is evident from the new (2002) Constitutive Act of the African Union, which replaces the Charter of the old Organization of African Unity. Whereas the latter had firm commitments to the overriding importance of the principle of nonintervention, the new organization has adopted the "right of the Union to intervene in a Member State pursuant to a decision of the Assembly in respect of grave circumstances, namely war crimes, genocide and crimes against humanity" and provides that such decisions shall be taken "by consensus or, failing which, by a two-thirds majority of the Member States of the Union."[16]

That an argument can nowadays be made for the evolution of a (dispersed) international "jury" reinvigorates the case for attempting to negotiate new criteria for exceptional cases warranting recourse to force even in the absence of a direct, transnational armed attack or a specific authorization by the Security Council. In hearings before the Foreign Affairs Committee of the British House of Commons, Oxford Professor Vaughn Lowe has proposed a specific list of criteria for legitimating humanitarian interventions.[17] These would require, as a minimum,

- prior determination by the Security Council of a grave crisis threatening international peace and security;
- articulation by the Security Council of specific policies for the resolution of the crisis, which policies have not been

implemented but which can demonstrably be achieved by timely armed intervention;

- credible presentation of evidence that this objective can be achieved at a cost much lower than the human cost of nonintervention and attendant imminent catastrophe;
- an incapacity by the Security Council to act forcefully due to the use of the veto;
- intervention by a bona fide *multinational* force, as opposed to a unilateral action by a single state.

Any proposal to engage in the negotiation of such criteria would be more likely to strike a responsive chord, however, only if it were linked to specific commitment to employ force upon having convinced an appropriate, credible "jury" that the criteria have been met in any particular instance.

The onus, however, is always on the proposers of new criteria by which to justify exceptions to the Charter's fundamental and still essentially valid norms; it is up to them to demonstrate how exceptions would be applied by a credible "jurying" process. This involves more than just identifying the appropriate institution. It involves as well a commitment not to circumvent it unilaterally.

In summary: the strict letter of the Charter prohibits humanitarian intervention. In the practice of individual states, regional and mutual-defense organizations, and the U.N. organs, a pattern of exceptions is emerging that conduces to the making of case-by-case judgments in which necessity and common sense have a role in tempering the law, in narrowing the gap between legality and legitimacy, between the letter of the law and its spirit, between normativity and morality.

At the heart of this is the notion that it is excusable to violate the strict letter of the law if, in doing so, less harm results than would have occurred had there been inflexible adherence to its strictures. The Security Council, in its case-by-case consideration of uses of force not in compliance with the strict letter of the Charter, has shown considerable acumen in interpreting the law so as to narrow the gap between its injunctions and the admonitions of ethical intuition.

States, however, are unlikely formally to acknowledge, let alone adumbrate, the right to use force for humanitarian intervention unless they can be assured of the legitimacy of the process by which such a right is to be applied. It would thus seem to be strategic for those who favor closing the gap between legality and legitimacy to focus not only on the rules by which common sense and morality temper law's strictures but also on the process by which the rules are applied or "juried" in practice. The rudiments of such a process exist, but it can be perfected only if states agree to use it, and abide by it, even, or especially, when they have the means to do otherwise.

NOTES

These issues also were addressed in Thomas M. Franck, "Interpretation and Change in the Law of Humanitarian Intervention," in *Humanitarian Intervention: Ethical, Legal and Political Dilemmas*, ed. J. L. Holzgrefe and Robert O. Keohane, 204–31 (Cambridge: Cambridge University Press, 2003).

1. St. Paul's Epistle, 2 Cor. 3:6.

2. Kofi Annan, *We the Peoples: The Role of the United Nations in the Twenty-First Century*, Report of the Secretary-General (New York: United Nations, 2000), 2.

3. J. L. Brierly, *The Law of Nations*, 3rd ed. (Oxford: Clarendon Press, 1949), 24.

4. *Regina v. Dudley and Stephens*, 14 Q.B.D. 273 (1884).

5. *U.S. v. Holmes*, 26 Fed. Cas. 360 (1842).

6. See A. W. Brian Simpson, *Cannibalism and the Common Law* (Chicago: University of Chicago Press, 1984), 225–70.

7. H. L. A. Hart, "Legal Responsibility and Excuses," in *Justification and Excuse in Criminal Law*, ed. M. L. Corrado (New York: Garland, 1994), 31.

8. *Corfu Channel Case*, Judgment of April 9th, 1949, ICJ Reports, 1949, 4 at 35.

9. Independent International Commission on Kosovo (the "Goldstone" Commission), *Kosovo Report: Conflict, International Response, Lessons Learned* (Oxford: Oxford University Press, 2000), 4; 163–98.

10. Thomas M. Franck, *The Power of Legitimacy among Nations* (New York: Oxford University Press, 1990), 67–83.

11. Annan, *We the Peoples*, 35, para. 218.

12. See, for example, Annan's 1999 report to the Assembly: 54 G.A.O.R., 4th Plen. Mtg., 20 September 1999, A/54/PV.4, at 2.

13. Rosalyn Higgins, *International Law and the Avoidance, Containment and Resolution of Disputes,* General Course on Public International Law, Recueil des cours, 230 (1991-V).

14. Ibid.

15. An excellent exploration of this subject is being undertaken by Professor Melissa S. Williams for a project entitled Reconstructing Impartiality. See Melissa S. Williams, "Towards a Deliberative Understanding of Justice toward Groups: Five Models of Jury Impartiality" (unpub. MS).

16. Constitutive Act of the African Union, art. 4 and art. 7, available at http://www.au2002.gov.za/docs/key_oau/au_act.htm.

17. United Kingdom, House of Commons, Foreign Affairs Committee, *Kosovo,* 4th Report, vol. 1 (23 May 2000), available at www.publications .parliament.uk/pa/cm199900/cmselect/cmfaff/28/0020805.htm.

6

MORALIZING HUMANITARIAN INTERVENTION: WHY JURYING FAILS AND HOW LAW CAN WORK

THOMAS POGGE

Thomas Franck believes that the strict constraints imposed by the U.N. Charter on military intervention have become too constraining and that, so long as the Charter remains unrevised, we should condone violations of these rules as legitimated by a jurying process. The relevant U.N. Charter constraints he seeks to subvert are two. First, the Charter directs that "[a]ll Members shall refrain in their international relations from the threat or use of force against the territorial integrity or political independence of any state, or in any other manner inconsistent with the Purposes of the United Nations" (Article 2(4)). Without specific authorization by the Security Council, states may use military force across national borders only in "individual or collective self-defense if an armed attack occurs against a Member of the United Nations, until the Security Council has taken measures necessary to maintain international peace and security" (Article 51). Second, regarding the use of force by the U.N. itself, the Charter proclaims that "[n]othing contained in the present Charter shall authorize the United Nations to intervene in matters which are essentially within the domestic jurisdiction of any state or shall require the Members to submit such matters to settlement under the present Charter; but this principle shall not prejudice the application of enforcement measures under Chapter VII" (Article 2(7)).[1]

Why does Franck want to see these constraints undermined through selective noncompliance? One reason he gives is "the immensity of changes in the state system's configuration, together with the intractability of the Charter to change through formal amendment."[2] The changes he lists are "the development of the hydrogen bomb, the end of colonialism and communism, and the emergence of terrorism as weapon of choice for the disempowered[,] . . . the consequences of responsible regionalism in Europe, Africa, and the Americas, [and] the proliferation of states from fewer than sixty to almost two hundred."[3] Franck does not explain how these changes make strict adherence to the U.N. Charter constraints implausible, but in some cases it is not difficult to guess what he has in mind: to protect ourselves from terrorist attacks, we should be allowed to intervene militarily in other states that seem either unwilling or unable to root out on their soil terrorist organizations capable of attacking our citizens. And, with modern weapons of mass destruction, such as hydrogen bombs delivered by intercontinental ballistic missiles, we should not be required to wait until an armed attack on us or our allies is actually in progress but may instead, under appropriate circumstances, take preemptive action by striking first, as the United States now takes itself to be entitled to do.[4]

But rather than producing arguments that appeal in this way to our security interests, Franck invokes a quite different line of thought, one that appeals not to our entitlements but to our moral duties and has nothing to do with how the world has changed over the past sixty years. He invokes the Rwandan genocide—or rather, he draws on how U.N. Secretary-General Kofi Annan has invoked this case. Here is what Annan wrote:

> To those for whom the greatest threat to the future of international order is the use of force in the absence of a Security Council mandate, one might say: leave Kosovo aside for a moment, and think about Rwanda. Imagine for one moment that, in those dark days and hours leading up to the genocide, there had been a coalition of states ready and willing to act in defense of the Tutsi population, but the council had refused or delayed giving the green light. Should such a coalition then have stood idly by while the horror unfolded?[5]

With Annan, Franck concludes from this case that there is a genuine predicament here, giving rise to serious conflict between the letter of international law, on the one hand, and "good sense and morality,"[6] on the other. Going beyond Annan, Franck stresses that committing or condoning violations of the law can be justified in such cases by reference to the rule of law itself:

> [T]he power of law to secure compliance is undermined if the gap between it and the prevalent sense of justice, morality, and common sense is allowed to become too wide. The capacity of the law to pull toward compliance those to whom it is addressed is diminished whenever it is seen no longer to comport with shared notions of what is right. The law's self-interest, therefore, demands that a way be found to bridge any gap between its own institutional commitment to the consistent application of formal rules and the public sense that order should not be achieved at too high a cost to widely shared moral values.
>
> If law permits—or even *requires*—behavior that is widely believed to be unfair, unjust, or immoral, it is not only persons but also the law that suffers. So, too, if law *prohibits* that which is widely believed to be just and moral.[7]

It is curious that the Rwandan genocide should be invoked in illustration of these points. It is curious, first, because this case is quite disconnected from the changes in the state system that Franck supposes to have been immense and unforeseeable by the drafters of the U.N. Charter. Indeed, the founding of the U.N. was in good part motivated by the German Holocaust of the same decade, so the possibility of another genocide was certainly not inconceivable to the drafters.

Appeal to this case is curious, second, because, as described by Annan, it is purely hypothetical. Perhaps it is good that, high up in remote ivory towers, there should be philosophers searching for moral guidelines for all possible agents in all possible worlds. But, surely, the U.N. Charter should answer to a narrower ambition: it should be formulated to work as well as possible in this actual world of human (and often inhuman) politicians. In order to judge whether certain articles of the Charter should be revised or subverted, we should then examine realistic cases in which strict application of international law actually did or actually would lead to morally intolerable results.

To be sure, the genocide in Rwanda was real enough, and it was certainly morally intolerable. What is entirely fantastic about Kofi Annan's case is his reference to states willing and able to stop the slaughter but held back by an unreasonable vote or veto in the U.N. Security Council. In the real world, there was only the coalition of the *un*willing: of those who did all they could *not* to get involved in Rwanda while suppressing any use of the word "genocide" (in favor of "chaos" and "civil war" and finally "acts of genocide") as long as possible. There were no saviors, willing and able, held back merely by the Charter text.

The choice of Annan's hypothetical example is curious for yet a third reason: Its author, Kofi Annan, played an absolutely essential role—with President Clinton, Clinton's U.N. ambassador Madeleine Albright, and Secretary of State Warren Christopher—in the grand coalition of the unwilling that enabled the genocide. His contributions as head of the U.N. Department of Peacekeeping Operations are well known from many sources, including the official reports by the U.N. itself and by the Organization of African Unity (OAU, since renamed African Union).[8]

On January 11, 1994, General Roméo Dallaire, commander of UNAMIR (United Nations Peacekeeping Mission for Rwanda, already legally stationed in the country), had sent his so-called Genocide Fax to U.N. headquarters. The fax recounts how Dallaire was put in contact with a high-level informant who told him of plans to distribute weapons to Hutu militias (Interahamwe, cooperating closely with the Rwandan army), to kill Belgian members of UNAMIR in order to "guarantee Belgian withdrawal from Rwanda," and then to kill large numbers of moderate Hutus and Tutsis. ("[The informant] has been ordered to register all Tutsis in Kigali. He suspects it is for their extermination. Example he gave was that in 20 minutes his personnel could kill up to 1000 Tutsis.")[9] In the fax, Dallaire indicates that he trusts the informant and is planning to take action, within thirty-six hours, to seize a major weapons cache whose location the informant is prepared to divulge. Dallaire requested authorization to grant the informant, his wife, and their four children U.N. protection and safe exit from Rwanda in return for his information. Dallaire did not ask for authorization to seize the weapons cache, an action he apparently viewed as falling squarely within his mandate "to contribute to the security of the city of Kigali inter alia within a weapons-secure area established by the parties in and around the city."[10]

Without informing the then Secretary-General Boutros Boutros-Ghali of this fax, Kofi Annan, in a sequence of messages (January 10–13, 1994), repeatedly and categorically forbade the operation: "No reconnaissance or other action, including response to request for protection, should be taken by UNAMIR until clear guidance is received from headquarters." "The overriding consideration is the need to avoid entering into a course of action that might lead to the use of force and unanticipated repercussions."[11] Annan similarly refused various subsequent proposals and reinforcement requests sent to U.N. headquarters by Dallaire on January 22, February 3, February 15, February 27, March 13, mid-March, and March 26.[12] Even on April 9, with the massacres in full swing, Annan still instructed Dallaire to

> cooperate with both the French and Belgian commanders to facilitate the evacuation of their nationals, and other foreign nationals requesting evacuation. You may exchange liaison officers for this purpose. You should make every effort not to compromise your impartiality or to act beyond your mandate but may exercise your discretion to do [so] should this be essential for the evacuation of foreign nationals. This should not, repeat not, extend to participating in possible combat, except in self-defense.[13]

We can safely infer from the historical evidence[14] that Dallaire with his 2,500 troops could have done a great deal more toward preventing, and later toward reducing, the slaughter had he not been continuously obstructed by Annan—and that Annan would never have become U.N. Secretary-General, and thus would not have won the Nobel Peace Prize, had he not acted in accordance with U.S. wishes.[15] In light of these facts about what actually happened, Annan's hypothetical is truly astounding.

Annan's words and deeds diverged unfavorably from the less-than-admirable conduct of his boss. On April 20, Boutros-Ghali at last sought "immediate and massive reinforcement of UNAMIR to stop the fighting and the massacres, requiring several thousand additional troops and enforcement powers under Chapter VII"[16] —in vain, as the Security Council voted unanimously the next day to *reduce* UNAMIR from 2,539 soldiers to 270.[17] Boutros-Ghali was also among the first key officials to use the word "genocide,"[18] a word the Clinton administration strictly forbade its staffers to use.[19] He thereby embarrassed Clinton, who, just the day before, had signed Presidential Decision Directive 25, imposing strict conditions on U.S. support for any future U.N. peacekeeping operations.[20]

Now one may be tempted to think that—although there were no states willing and able to stop the genocide—Kofi Annan's hypothetical is realistic at least in this regard: the actions General Dallaire was proposing to take would have violated the U.N. Charter. As head of the U.N. Department of Peacekeeping Operations in 1994, Annan thus found himself in a serious *actual* conflict that illustrates the point he and Franck want to make about the need to condone violations. Perhaps Annan made the wrong decisions, but he did what the U.N. Charter required him to do.

However, this view is also mistaken. The actions Dallaire urgently wanted UNAMIR to undertake clearly would not have violated Article 2(4) of the Charter because they would have constituted an intervention by the U.N. itself, not by a member state.

Would Dallaire's proposed actions—confiscating arms and protecting the informant in January, protecting endangered Rwandan civilians in April—have violated Article 2(7) of the U.N. Charter, which forbids the U.N. to intervene in matters essentially within the domestic jurisdiction of any state? The UNAMIR force was established on the recommendation of the U.N. Secretary General by Security Council Resolution 872 on October 5, 1993, with the consent of both parties to the civil war: the government of Rwanda (headed by President Habyarimana) and the Rwandese Patriotic Front (RPF). UNAMIR's mission was to help implement the Arusha peace agreement concluded on August 4, 1993. Among UNAMIR's official tasks was "to contribute to the security of the city of Kigali inter alia within a weapons-secure area established by the parties in and around the city."[21] The confiscation of weapons about to be distributed to a Hutu militia in Kigali falls squarely within this mission parameter. UNAMIR could not have been charged with intervening in essentially domestic matters for carrying out a mission that was specifically consented to, indeed requested, by both parties to the former civil war and authorized by the U.N. Security Council.

To be sure, any U.N. force monitoring the implementation of a cease-fire will sometimes do things that are unwelcome to one side or the other. But both sides understood and agreed to this when requesting the mission. I conclude that the U.N. had no legal reason to stop the actions Dallaire had proposed to take in January (and later). These actions were blocked not by a strict reading of the U.N. Charter, nor by a veto in the Security Council, but solely at Kofi Annan's discretion.

By the time the last crucial exchange of cables took place (April 9, 1994), the situation in Rwanda had deteriorated dramatically. On April 6, a plane carrying Rwanda's President Habyarimana and Burundi's President Ntaryamira was shot down on its approach into Kigali airport, killing all on board. Mass killings of Tutsis and moderate Hutus started immediately after the crash, producing a *daily* death toll of about 10,000 and resulting in the murder of more than 10 percent of Rwanda's population within three months. Quite apart from Rwanda's prior consent to the UNAMIR mission, such mass killings are not matters essentially within its domestic jurisdiction. By acceding, on April 16, 1975, to the 1948 Convention on the Prevention and Punishment of the Crime of Genocide, Rwanda had itself affirmed that genocide "is a crime under international law."

Article 1 of the convention states: "The Contracting Parties confirm that genocide, whether committed in time of peace or in time of war, is a crime under international law which they undertake to prevent and to punish." It is arguable, then, that the U.N., and the members of its Security Council in particular, had a legal and moral *duty* to stop the genocide, which they could have done quite easily.[22] This, at least, is the plain meaning of the text, as any ordinary person would understand it—whatever governments and their diplomats and international lawyers may tell us to the contrary after the fact. A good case can be made, then, that the situation in April 1994 was the very contrary of what Kofi Annan and Thomas Franck suggest. International law did not merely permit a U.N. use of force to stop the genocide; it actually *required* all parties to the Genocide Convention to work toward and to give material support to such U.N. action.

Only this plain reading of international law as *requiring* intervention can explain why the lawyers of the U.S. State Department were worried and why the Clinton administration went to such extraordinary lengths to suppress any use of the word "genocide."[23] And this plain reading also explains why the United States, the United Kingdom, France, and U.N. officials were so reticent about sharing their information about the situation with other U.N. Security Council members. When they finally understood, late in April, what was happening in Rwanda, some of the nonpermanent members (Argentina, Czech Republic, New Zealand, and Spain) pushed hard for reexpanding UNAMIR peacekeeping operations, which on April 21 had been reduced to 270 soldiers by unanimous Security Council resolution 912. Madeleine Albright considerably delayed this reexpansion of UNAMIR,[24] but resolution 918, authorizing a new force strength of 5,500, was finally adopted unanimously on May 17—too late materially to affect the situation in Rwanda, where the battlefield victories of the RPF were slowly bringing the genocide to a halt.

My reason for reviewing the Rwandan genocide is in part, of course, to do my little bit—against the far more visible efforts by Annan, Clinton, and Albright[25]—to preserve awareness of how these 800,000 horrible deaths were facilitated. If conscientious citizens do not learn from this case, there is little hope that genocides will be effectively prevented or stopped in the future.

A review of the Rwanda genocide may seem tangential to Franck's paper. How important is it to show that one of his examples is ill chosen because of the great distance between what really happened and Annan's offensive hypothetical? Let me explain why I think it is important.

There are, as I have stated, two quite distinct kinds of reasons the United States and its allies might have for not wanting to take international law too literally. Reasons of the first kind, call them humanitarian, derive from their moral commitments: the rules of international law constrain how they may aid and protect foreigners in mortal danger. Reasons of the second kind, call them self-interested, derive from what is euphemistically called their national interest: the rules of international law often constrain these governments in their pursuit of their security and foreign-policy objectives. Selective subversion of the rules—especially those constraining the use of military force—would benefit them by reducing these constraints. To be sure, such subversion might also encourage other states to use military force more freely. But the United States–led alliance has now managed to increase its military and economic dominance so much that a subversion of the constraints on the conduct of states is bound to benefit the United States on balance. It has far more to gain from its own freer use of military force worldwide than it has to lose from a freer use of military force by other, regional powers (China, Russia, India, Indonesia, and so on) in their own areas. In most cases, in fact, it can effectively deter or contain any unwelcome freer use of force by others.

It can hardly be surprising that those who favor subverting the legal rules against the use of force—or the replacement of the existing "idiot rules" by "sophist rules"[26]—emphasize humanitarian over self-interested reasons. And in a world full of humanitarian disasters, these reasons do indeed deserve careful attention. However, these reasons must be judged by the correct criterion. The question is not: What additional human suffering the United States and its allies *could* avert if international law gave them a freer hand to use military force abroad? Rather, the correct question is: What additional human suffering *would* the United States and other states avert *and produce* if international law gave them a freer hand to use military force abroad? Annan's hypothetical bears on the first, irrelevant question. The actual story of the Rwandan genocide bears on the second, highly relevant question.

Annan and Franck make the plea that we should not be too attached to legal niceties when there are humanitarian heroes out there, statesmen willing and able to mobilize their peoples to sacrifice blood and treasure to free others from mortal danger. I agree wholeheartedly. And yet, this conditional injunction is quite irrelevant so long as its antecedent is false. There are no such humanitarian heroes out there. Minor exceptions aside, the people who govern us and determine our foreign policy and the people they appoint to run the U.N. show monstrous indifference to mortal dangers encountered by those who are not citizens of our countries. The Rwanda episode shows this: the French made clandestine deliveries of heavy weapons (some of which were confiscated by UNAMIR) and provided military training to the Rwandan army in early 1994.[27] In June and July of 1994, the French conducted the military "Operation Turquoise," which rescued the genocidal Rwandan government from total military defeat at the hands of the RPF by establishing a safe area, in which the slaughter of Tutsis continued for a time, and by evacuating various leading figures of the genocide to the Democratic Republic of Congo.[28] The Belgians recalled their UNAMIR contingent as the genocide began, abandoning two thousand people to certain slaughter.[29] The United States tried hard to suppress the word "genocide" and to reduce UNAMIR's cost and troop strength. Kofi Annan shackled UNAMIR in accordance with U.S. preferences, instructing it to protect only "foreign nationals." And our governments still hold Rwanda responsible for servicing Western loans that enabled the murderous Habyarimana regime to arm and organize its supporters for genocide.[30]

Now, one may well think that the genocide in Rwanda posed an unusually difficult challenge, as the political costs of involvement were not clearly foreseeable and potentially considerable (as illustrated by the botched U.S. operation in Somalia the year before). Since I cannot here present a large number of other cases illustrating Western complicity in and indifference to humanitarian crises, let me speak briefly to the greatest crisis of all, the problem of world poverty.[31] According to the U.S. government, "Worldwide 34,000 children under age five die daily from hunger and preventable diseases."[32] The total number of deaths from poverty-related causes is approximately 18 million annually, roughly one-third of all human deaths, adding up to 270 million deaths since the end of the Cold War. No less than the 800,000 people butchered in Rwanda, these 270 million painful deaths from starvation, diarrhea, pneumonia, tuberculosis, malaria, measles, perinatal conditions, and other avoidable causes are a well-known humanitarian catastrophe. However, to alleviate this catastrophe, no soldiers would have had to be sent to kill or be killed. Most of those living in life-threatening poverty could easily be protected through the funding of locally providable vaccination programs, basic schooling, school lunches, safe water and sewage systems, housing, power plants and networks, banks and micro lending programs, and road, rail, and other communication links. For example, the World Health Organization (WHO) Commission on Macroeconomics and Health (chaired by Jeffrey Sachs) has outlined how deaths from poverty-related causes could be reduced by 8 million annually at a cost of $62 billion per year.[33] This amount is less that one-quarter of 1 percent of the combined gross national incomes of the high-income countries.[34]

Yet in the face of this catastrophe, the affluent countries have steadily *reduced* their official development assistance (ODA) throughout the prosperous 1990s from 0.33 percent of their combined GNPs in 1990 to 0.22 percent in 2001.[35] Most ODA is allocated for political effect.[36] Only 23 percent goes to the least developed countries.[37] And only $4.31 billion annually is spent on basic social services—basic education, basic health, population programs, water supply, and sanitation—by all affluent countries combined.[38] This is 7.4 percent of all ODA—much less than the 20 percent agreed to at the 1995 World Summit for Social Development.[39] It is one-sixtieth of 1 percent of the rich countries' aggregate GDPs, less than 1 percent of their "peace dividend,"[40] and less than $5 per year from each of their citizens on average.[41]

As could be shown at much greater length, governments and their foreign ministers, diplomats, and negotiators are clearly *not* significantly motivated by humanitarian concerns that international law as it stands obliges them to suppress. And I hope that Thomas Franck and other international lawyers of great reputation and unquestionable integrity will do more to distance themselves from this notion or else to defend it if they can.

There are no humanitarian heroes among those who exercise power in our names. This is why we are treated to a purely *hypothetical* example. This hypothetical appeals irresistibly to the good sense and morality of any person whose humanity has not been thoroughly corrupted. Yes of course, we exclaim, the law (and much else) may and *must* be set aside to save 800,000 people from being hacked to death merely because they are Tutsis or want to live in peace with them. But when the lesson is accepted and the plain meaning of the Charter set aside as unworthy of defense, it is not the good sense of Thomas Franck and us citizens that will fill the vacuum. Rather, outcomes will then be determined by the "good sense" of those whose humanity *has been* corrupted through their ascent to national office, through their power, and through the adversarial character of their role: by the good sense of people like Clinton, Albright, and Annan, who enabled the genocide in Rwanda; by the good sense of people like George W. Bush, Dick Cheney, and Donald Rumsfeld, who use the language of human rights and liberation to justify interventions aimed at enhancing U.S. control of the world's oil reserves.[42]

A study of the overt and covert violence such politicians have employed—and regularly rationalized as humanitarian—in the period since World War II, say, cannot sustain the belief that their forceful interventions do more good than harm.

And there is a further important reason against giving them a freer hand. As smaller states feel increasingly threatened, they will redouble their efforts to protect themselves through the possession of nuclear arms and comparable weapons of mass destruction. (The world has paid a high price for the U.S. "victories" in Afghanistan and Iraq, for these involved accepting Pakistan and India as nuclear powers.) There is decisive moral reason, then, to oppose the suggestions by Annan and Franck in favor of supporting respect for the plain meaning of the U.N. Charter.

Franck, by contrast, approves and encourages an increasingly significant role of the U.N. Security Council in determining whether particular violations of international law matter and, if so, how much:

> In situations of armed intervention, representatives argue the validity of facts alleged by those initiating recourse to force, assess the proportionality of the action taken in relation to the evidence of extreme necessity, and debate the motives of the parties to the dispute. Eventually, they decide. Sometimes—more like a grand jury —they decide not to take any action. Does the record of this process demonstrate a credible assay at institutional "jurying" sufficient to justify the codification of exceptions to article 2(4) of the Charter? Probably not. On the other hand, the process, as it has developed in the practice of the Security Council, may embody elements of another jurying function: applying the law—or selectively *not* applying it—in such a way as to narrow the gap between the

strictures of strict legality and the importunings of popular moral intuition.[43]

Is such "jurying" by governments, as exemplified in the U.N. Security Council, a promising model for how to reconcile the law with "widely shared moral values"?[44]

Franck is right to stress that it is very important that states should have the assurance that claims they make by appeal to international law will be fairly adjudicated. But I am far more skeptical than he is about "jurying" by governments. The basic dilemma I see is this. Fairness centrally requires an adjudication process that is unaffected by power differentials among the disputants.[45] Domestic juries come close to this ideal; jurors have no outside relationship with the parties appearing before them prior to or after their verdict, and their deliberations are not affected by power differentials among themselves.[46] A jury of states lacks all of these features and is highly susceptible to undue influence by the strong.

To be sure, there can be credible jurying—resulting in a morally plausible assessment of a rule violation—within the Security Council and the General Assembly when nothing much is at stake for the great powers. The removals of Idi Amin and Emperor Bokassa are examples of this. But as great-power stakes rise, so do the discrepancies between the jury's reaction on the one hand and facts and morality on the other. For a full decade after Pol Pot's genocidal regime had been overthrown by Vietnamese forces, his Khmer Rouge, still active and posing a threat within Cambodia, retained this country's seat at the U.N. This was achieved by intense lobbying by the Reagan and Thatcher governments, which also got Cambodia barred from all international trade and communications agreements and cut off from all development aid through the U.N. and its agencies (such as the WHO), even while Pol Pot's forces received U.N. World Food Program aid (as well as considerable financial support from the United States).[47]

Or consider Franck's report that "[b]enign silence greeted America's air strike against the Sudan [on August 20, 1998] after the destruction of U.S. embassies in Dar-es-Salaam and Nairobi [on August 7, 1998] by the forces of Osama bin-Laden."[48] Perhaps there was indeed such silence in the deliberative forums of the U.N. At least the United States easily managed to block a U.N. investigation of the destroyed Al-Shifa pharmaceutical plant in Khartoum, which it claimed was producing nerve gas and other chemical or biological weapons.[49] But was benign silence justified? The evidence to date overwhelmingly suggests that the Al-Shifa pharmaceutical plant—not to speak of the nearby sugar and candy factory that was also hit and destroyed—produced no weapons of any sort and also had no ties to Al Qaeda or any other terrorist organization. Sued by Al-Shifa's owner, Saleh Idris, for return of $24 million of his money frozen by the U.S. Treasury Department, the United States had every opportunity to make its case in court.[50] Instead, the United States authorized the full and unconditional release of Idris's assets (May 3, 1999) just before the deadline set by the court. The United States has made no effort to make good for the destruction of the factory or for the severe shortages this destruction has caused. (The Al-Shifa plant covered most of the pharmaceutical needs of the Sudanese people and their livestock.) The case does not reveal, then, an "increasingly credible capacity for fact-finding"[51] or an "innate human receptivity to moral considerations"[52] in the U.N. organs or in their participants.

Let me give one last example of jurying under pressure, with something at stake for a great power. When Yemen voted, in 1990, against U.N. Security Council resolution 678 authorizing the attack on Iraq, a senior American diplomat, caught on an open microphone, told the Yemeni ambassador: "That was the most expensive 'no' vote you ever cast." The United States stopped $70 million in aid to Yemen; other Western countries, the IMF, and World Bank followed suit. Saudi Arabia expelled some 800,000 Yemeni workers, many of whom had lived there for years and were sending urgently needed money to their families.[53] Similar pressure was later brought to bear on Ecuador and Zimbabwe as they joined the Security Council at the beginning of 1991. And similar pressure was brought to bear on Security Council members in the winter of 2002–03, when the United States was once again seeking support for resolutions on Iraq.[54] When much is at stake for a great power, then weaker states are anything but "largely unencumbered."[55] Rather, they are subject to extremely heavy pressures and inducements from stronger states to vote "the right way."

So long as states are self-interested and very unequal in power, the outcomes of any realistically conceivable jurying process will reflect the existing power imbalance. Any such process will be unfair, though it may also of course involve a heavy dose of fairness rhetoric. In the present era, this unfairness benefits especially the United States, which, through arm-twisting of and side payments to jury members as well as through the threat of marginalizing the jury by noncompliance, can generally get the verdicts it wants.

To be sure, the United States and Britain failed to win Security Council authorization for their 2003 invasion of Iraq. This may be adduced to show that jurying can work. In Franck's words,

> [T]he Security Council, however obsolete its composition, does work. When only 4 of its 15 members were willing to approve our invasion of Iraq, the Council was working exactly as intended. It sent us a clear message that, if there were indeed weapons of mass destruction in Iraq, they could be found and dismantled by the most intrusive system of international inspections ever devised. Nothing found by the invading forces in Iraq has proven this wrong. The system also cautioned us that the world could not tolerate one powerful nation unilaterally determining when to occupy another nation and reorganize its society. It warned that thousands, perhaps hundreds of thousands, of innocents might be sacrificed at the altar of such unipolar ambitions. And it expressed skepticism at the unilateralists' claim that America could succeed in imposing its democracy on the Shiites and Sunnis of the Middle East as it had once done in Shinto Japan.[56]

Yes, the Security Council acted well in refusing to authorize this invasion by its most powerful member. And yet, it quickly fell into line, cooperating with the invader, giving moral support and recognition to the new Iraqi authorities installed by the United States, condemning any resistance to the occupation, and urging everyone to help clean up the mess.[57] Appealing to Franck's view that "the mildness of its disapprobation of India's [unauthorized and illegal] intervention in the civil war leading to the creation of Bangladesh" reflected the Security Council's appreciation of the

moral legitimacy of India's 1973 intervention, the Bush administration can thus argue that the mildness (or rather *absence*) of
Security Council disapprobation of the unauthorized and illegal
2002 invasion of Iraq reflects its appreciation of the (even
greater) moral legitimacy of this invasion. Yet it is rather obvious
that the lack of disapprobation of the recent invasion of Iraq has
little to do with its moral legitimacy, and much with the need to
maintain good relations with the world's overwhelmingly dominant military and economic superpower (not to speak of the veto
powers wielded by the United States and United Kingdom).

The kind of jurying Franck approves and encourages is not,
then, of much help for bridging the gap between law and widely
shared moral values. The reason is that the interests and conduct
of the strongest members of the jury diverge far more from widely
shared moral values than the text of the U.N. Charter. Preserving
Cambodia's seat at the U.N. for the genocidal Khmer Rouge was
not required by morality or by the U.N. Charter but by the interests of the U.S. and U.K. governments. Ever expanding settle-
ments in the territories occupied by Israel violate international
law and widely shared moral values, yet are nonetheless condoned
by the U.N. Security Council, its earlier resolutions (242 and 338)
notwithstanding. The destruction of the Al-Shifa plant violated
international law, and widely shared moral values demand that
U.S. claims about its being a chemical weapons factory should be
investigated; but at the U.N. such an investigation was rejected
and the episode passed over in "benign silence."

My judgment is not that in U.N. Security Council jurying, when
the stakes are high, the moral values of a few strong states prevail
over the moral values of the rest. The moral values of the developed West also militate against seating the Khmer Rouge, against
Israel's settlement policy, and against the refusal to investigate the
Khartoum bombing. What prevails in such cases is the proclaimed
national interest of the strongest states as defined by their political and business elites.

Let me close with a general, more philosophical thought.
Normative discussions of humanitarian intervention often suffer
from a lack of clarity concerning what exactly is being discussed.
This happens, because the questions posed—such as "Under
what conditions is humanitarian intervention legitimate?"—look

deceptively simple and yet can be interpreted in many different ways. The various questions produced by these interpretations do not merely have different answers. They may raise quite different normative and empirical issues and may therefore require diverse investigations and reflections.

Let me here focus just on the most important ambiguity. It concerns the status of the criterion for judging whether any humanitarian intervention is justified. In thinking about moral justification, we might look for the *ideal criterion* that (as it were) God should use in assessing military interventions. Here God is conceived as a distant observer who, at the end of history perhaps, judges all that happens but whose judgments are unknown and inconsequential and thus have no effect on the course of history. Alternatively, we might be thinking about the criterion we would want to be in public use: enshrined in international law; appealed to by states, by the U.N. Security Council, and by other international agencies; and prevalent in world public opinion. Such a *public* criterion may well have a strong feedback effect on the course of history by influencing what military interventions are undertaken and how they are justified and conducted. And it makes sense, therefore, that certain exceptions that we think God would recognize should nonetheless be kept out of this public criterion when including them would, through false appeals, do much more harm than good.[58]

Against this background, my response to Franck is this: a literal reading of the U.N. Charter is indeed a poor criterion for God to use as the basis for judging, at the end of time, the conduct of politicians. But the rules of the Charter were never meant for this role. They were meant to be plausible rules by which fallible and corrupt politicians would be called to account by their foreign peers as well as by their compatriots and the media. If we take this to be their purpose, then the analogue to section 3.02 of the U.S. Model Penal Code, which Franck cites for emulation—"Conduct that the actor believes to be necessary to himself or another is justifiable, provided that . . . the harm or evil sought to be avoided by such conduct is greater than that sought to be prevented by the law defining the offense charged"[59]—is a recipe for disaster. In the international arena, even as Franck envisions it, there is no effective court in which a state would have to show that it sincerely and reasonably believed that its conduct would avoid more harm than it produced. With such a rule, then, the say-so of the strong prevails. This is good for the United States, and for Russia and China perhaps. But it adds insult to injury for the weak by covering with a veneer of legal legitimacy the military interventions and threats thereof they so often suffer.

International relations are characterized by great inequalities of power, great moral corruption of those in power (in the poor countries no less than in the rich), high stakes, and the absence of effective mechanisms of binding adjudication. In such a context especially, the optimal public rules are not ones that instruct agents to do what they believe is optimal or ones under which a military operation becomes legitimate merely because it is approved by some group of governments.

I conclude that marginalizing international law in favor of Security Council jurying is a terrible idea and a terrible reality— considerably worse, in the world as it is, than maintaining respect for the plain meaning of the U.N. Charter.

Still, even strict adherence to the Charter is hardly ideal, and so we should ask whether there is a *superior* alternative that is both feasible and reachable from where we are.

Progress requires reform on two fronts. Most important, we need on the international level an effective judicial organ for the authoritative interpretation and adjudication of international law —in real time if needed. Only judges who have tenure and a secure commitment to international law and to the U.N., and who must explain and justify their decisions in writing, can possibly render verdicts that are largely unencumbered by the distribution of power. And even this is doubtful in situations where they have reason to believe that a great power will, in response to an unwelcome verdict, simply withdraw from international legal adjudication altogether.[60] In such a situation, judges may feel that the law is best served by bending it in favor of the powerful in order to keep them on board.

If the authoritative interpretation and adjudication of international law were in the hands of an effective and reliable judicial organ capable of quick decisions, then it would make sense to contemplate revisions of the U.N. Charter that, in particular, broaden the conditions under which military interventions are permitted. Appropriately revised rules might envision that states may conduct a military intervention against a country so long as two conditions are both satisfied:

1. This court has found that genocide or other crimes against humanity are being perpetrated in the country or that this country poses a serious security risk to others or fails to comply with its obligations under the Treaty on the Non-Proliferation of Nuclear Weapons or similar constraints governing weapons of mass destruction.
2. The military intervention has not been forbidden either by the U.N. Security Council or by a supermajority of the U.N. General Assembly.

This proposal has some chance of solving the problems Franck finds in the strict application of the present U.N. Charter text: it enables states to respond forcefully to grave crimes and dangers abroad. And it does not subject such a response to a veto by any one permanent member of the U.N. Security Council. Although it relaxes the constraints on the use of military force in this way, the proposal also provides three powerful safeguards against abuse: the decision about whether a *casus belli* exists is made by a judicial body on the basis of a nonpolitical evidence assessment that must be justified in writing. The authority to make war pursuant to such a court decision can be rescinded by either the Security Council or by a supermajority of the General Assembly—also on political grounds, because they prefer the intervention to be undertaken under U.N. auspices, for example, or because they believe an intervention to be counterproductive or excessively dangerous.

This proposal, too, faces serious problems. Its practicability requires that great powers do not withdraw from or violate the rules or threaten to do so in order to bend the judges to their will. This in turn requires that their own populations develop a serious commitment to international law, so that a government that quits or violates the regime would incur a substantial loss in domestic legitimacy. This goal seems far off.[61]

Difficult also is the task of reaching detailed agreement on such a revision of the U.N. Charter. The fundamental dilemma is that, to be fair, rules and their adjudication must treat disputants evenhandedly, without fear or favor induced by power differentials among them. But stronger parties have prudential incentives to hold out for rules and adjudication procedures that favor themselves over weaker parties. This in turn gives the weaker parties incentives to accede to such an unfair regime because they have far more to lose than the strongest do from the absence or erosion of rules and of authoritative adjudication.

In a world of enormous inequalities in power, there exist, then, strong prudential pressures against the creation of fair rules and adjudication procedures—pressures toward a regime that is officially rigged in favor of the more powerful states (by giving them veto powers, as in the U.N. Security Council, or extra votes, as in the World Bank and IMF) and that, even insofar as it is facially neutral, is tilted toward the strong in its application. (Security Council jurying as endorsed by Franck displays both these features as exemplified by great-power vetoes, on the one hand, and by arm-twisting and side payments, on the other.)

It seems unlikely that these pressures can be overcome in the near future, which will be dominated by the United States as sole superpower. There may be a better chance by midcentury, when China will be a substantial counterweight to the United States and may give the United States more of a prudential reason to allow a genuine rule of law to emerge on the international level. At least until then, the humanitarian concerns Franck so eloquently invokes are unlikely to have much influence on state conduct unless there is a substantial moralization of the citizenries of the developed countries.

NOTES

Many thanks for very helpful criticisms and suggestions are due to the members of the Oxford Jurisprudence Discussion Group, especially Dweight Newman and John Tasioulas; to the members of the Murphy Institute at Tulane University, especially Jerry Gaus and Leif Wenar; to my colleagues at the Centre for Applied Philosophy and Public Ethics, especially David Rodin, Seumas Miller, and John Weckert; as well as to Terry Nardin and Melissa Williams. All cited Web sites were last accessed and checked on July 31, 2004.

1. The articles of Chapter VII of the U.N. Charter authorize the U.N. Security Council to take forceful action in response to any "threat to the peace, breach of the peace, or act of aggression" (Article 39, *cf.* Article 42).

2. Thomas Franck, "Legality and Legitimacy in Humanitarian Intervention," this volume, chap. 5, 143.

3. Ibid.

4. United States, "The National Security Strategy of the United States of America," September 2002, 6, 15–16. Available at www.whitehouse.gov/nsc/nss.pdf. National Security Presidential Directive 17 (NSPD 17), identical to Homeland Security Presidential Directive 4 (HSPD 4), 3. Available at www.fas.org/irp/offdocs/nspd/nspd-17.html. There is also a classified version of the latter document.

5. Kofi Annan, "Two Concepts of Sovereignty," *The Economist*, September 18, 1999.

6. Franck, "Legality and Legitimacy," 144.

7. Ibid., 145.

8. See Philip Gourevitch, *We Wish to Inform You That Tomorrow We Will Be Killed With Our Families* (New York: Picador, 1998); United Nations, *Report of the Independent Inquiry into the Actions of the United Nations during the 1994 Genocide in Rwanda*, December 15, 1999, also available at http://www.un.org/Docs/journal/asp/ws.asp?m=S/1999/1257; Alison Des Forges, *Leave None to Tell the Story: Genocide in Rwanda* (New York: Human Rights Watch, 1999), also available at http://www.hrw.org/reports/1999/rwanda/index.htm; OAU International Panel of Eminent Personalities, *Rwanda: The Preventable Genocide*, July 7, 2000, also available at http://www.visiontv.ca/RememberRwanda/Report.pdf; Samantha Power, "Bystander to Genocide," *Atlantic Monthly*, September 2001, also available at http://www.theatlantic.com/issues/2001/09/power.htm.

9. For the full text of this fax, see PBS Frontline, available at http://www.pbs.org/wgbh/pages/frontline/shows/evil/warning/cable.html. It is clear from the record that the governments of the United States, France, and the United Kingdom, as well as the U.N., had received abundant independent information about the planning and buildup toward genocide. This information was not made available either to Dallaire or to other members of the U.N. Security Council.

10. Security Council Resolution 872 (October 5, 1993), which initiates UNAMIR. The Kigali weapons-secure area had in fact been established on December 24, 1993. United Nations Department of Peacekeeping Operations, UNAMIR Background Document, n.d., available at http://www.un.org/Depts/dpko/dpko/co_mission/unamirS.htm.

11. The two cited messages were sent on January 10 and 11. See United Nations, *Report of the Independent Inquiry*, 11.

12. Des Forges, *Leave None to Tell,* under "Warnings," available at http://www.hrw.org/reports/1999/rwanda/Geno4-7-01.htm.

13. United Nations, *Report of the Independent Inquiry,* 19.

14. *Cf.* note 17.

15. These last two historical hypotheticals do not entail, and are not meant to suggest, that Annan's conduct was motivated by a desire to promote his career. The materials I have read do not, in my view, support a confident judgment of this question one way or the other.

16. United Nations, *Report of the Independent Inquiry,* 69.

17. Security Council Resolution 912, 21 April 1994. At this time, UNAMIR's actual troop strength was already down to 1,515. In accordance with the plan revealed by the informant, troops of the Rwandan Presidential Guard had beaten ten Belgian soldiers to death on April 7, 1994, and had thereby achieved their purpose of inducing Belgium to pull out its contingent (on April 14). Withdrawing toward the airport, the Belgians left behind about 2,000 civilians, who had found refuge in the Official Technical School (ETO) that the Belgian contingent was occupying in Kigali. Most of these civilians were murdered immediately after the Belgians abandoned the ETO on April 11. By April 25, UNAMIR's troop strength was down to 503 (Samantha Power, "Bystander to Genocide"). Dallaire nonetheless managed to protect some 25,000 Rwandans throughout the following weeks.

18. On the TV program *Nightline,* May 4, 1994: "Here you have a real genocide, in Kigali." Cited in United Nations, *Report of the Independent Inquiry,* 70.

19. Peter Ronayne, *Never Again? The United States and the Prevention and Punishment of Genocide since the Holocaust* (Lanham Md.: Rowman and Littlefield, 2001), 174–75. The *New York Times* reports, "One document, dated May 1, 1994, summarizes a meeting of several unidentified officials who were analyzing the Rwanda situation. The meeting ends with a warning against branding the massacres genocide. 'Be careful,' the document reads. 'Legal at State was worried about this yesterday. Genocide finding could commit U.S.G. to actually "do something."' 'Legal' refers to the legal adviser at the State Department and U.S.G. is the United States government." Neil A. Lewis, "Papers Show U.S. Knew of Genocide in Rwanda," *New York Times,* August 22, 2001, A5, also available at http://query.nytimes.com/gst/abstract.html?res=FA0915F63D550C718EDDA10894D9404482. The prohibition on using the word "genocide" is manifested in the contorted answers various spokespersons for the U.S. State Department provided to questions about the applicability of the word. Having evaded the question on April 28 and May 11, spokespersons later (May 25, June 10) said that they had been given "guidance" to speak of

"acts of genocide," prompting a reporter to ask, "How many acts of genocide does it take to make genocide?" See PBS Frontline, *The Triumph
of Evil* (online), "One Hundred Days of Slaughter: A Chronology of
U.S./U.N. Actions," 1999, available at http://www.pbs.org/wgbh/pages/
frontline/shows/evil/etc/slaughter.html.

20. *Cf.* U.S. Department of State, "Clinton Administration Policy on
Reforming Multilateral Peace Operations" (PDD 25), February 22, 1996,
available at http://www.fas.org/irp/offdocs/pdd25.htm. Even after the
catastrophe in Rwanda, the United States continued its battle to reduce
the U.N. budget and its own share thereof, targeting peacekeeping operations in particular. As part of this effort, it refused for years to pay its
dues and ended up owing the U.N. about $2 billion. The effort paid off.
Christmas 2000, the richest country on earth with 31.8 percent of global
GDP that year (United Nations Development Program [UNDP], *Human
Development Report 2002* [New York: Oxford University Press, 2002], 190–
93) had its share of the U.N. budget reduced from 25 percent to 22 percent and its share of the peacekeeping budget from 30.4 percent to 26
percent. The total savings for the United States: 58 cents annually per citizen. Pro-UN.org, "2000 Year in Review and Annual Awards," available at
http://www.pro-un.org/year2000.htm.

21. *Cf.* note 10 above. Also relevant is "Operational Directive No. 02:
Rules of Engagement" (Interim), File No. 4003.1, of November 19, 1993,
extensively cited in Des Forges, *Leave None to Tell.* She describes this document, which is not publicly available, as follows:

> The first paragraph of the document indicates that these Rules of
> Engagement "are drafted by the Force, but are approved by the U.N.
> and may only be changed with U.N. authority." . . . Although the
> document was marked "interim," it was accepted by U.N. headquar-
> ters in New York and was not amended by it. It was circulated to the
> member states that provided troops to UNAMIR and was in effect
> at the time of the genocide. (Ibid., under "Choosing War," available
> at http://www.hrw.org/reports/1999/rwanda/Geno1-3-11.htm)

> The UNAMIR mandate permitted the peacekeepers to use force in
> self-defense, which was defined as including "resistance to attempts
> by forceful means to prevent the Force from discharging its duties
> under the mandate of UNAMIR." They were allowed to use their
> weapons "to defend themselves, other U.N. lives, or persons under
> their protection against direct attack" and, even more broadly, they
> were directed to use armed force "when other lives are in mortal
> danger." In addition, the strong language of Paragraph 17 of the
> Rules of Engagement specified that the force was "morally and

legally obligated" to "use all available means" to halt "ethnically or politically motivated criminal acts" and that it "will take the necessary action to prevent any crime against humanity." (Ibid., under "Ignoring Genocide," available at http://www.hrw.org/reports/1999/rwanda/Geno15-8-01.htm)

22. In 1994, the U.N. Security Council consisted of Argentina, Brazil, China, the Czech Republic, Djibouti, France, New Zealand, Nigeria, Oman, Pakistan, Russia, Rwanda, Spain, the United Kingdom, and the United States. Three of these states—Djibouti, Nigeria, and Oman—were not parties to the Genocide Convention, and may therefore have been legally free to oppose U.N. action. Still, had the other twelve states done what they had committed themselves to doing, they would have declared the situation in Rwanda a threat to the peace (under Article 39 of the U.N. Charter) and would have stopped the genocide.

23. See note 19.

24. *Cf.* PBS Frontline, "One Hundred Days of Slaughter." After the vote was taken, on May 17, Albright testified on Capitol Hill: "Emotions can produce wonderful speeches and stirring op-ed pieces. But emotions alone cannot produce policies that will achieve what they promise. If we do not keep commitments in line with capabilities, we will only further undermine U.N. credibility and support. . . . [U]ltimately, the future of Rwanda is in Rwandan hands" (ibid.).

25. Years later, when Gourevitch's account of the genocide was making headlines, Clinton pretended he had no clue about it and wrote little notes to his advisers: "Is what he is saying true?" "How did this happen?" In March of 1998, speaking at Kigali airport to genocide survivors, he said, "We come here today partly in recognition of the fact that we in the United States and the world community did not do as much as we could have and should have done to try to limit what occurred" (Samantha Power, "Bystander to Genocide"). Kofi Annan apparently liked this formulation, saying on the ten-year anniversary of the start of the genocide, "I believed at that time that I was doing my best. But I realized after the genocide that there was more that I could and should have done to sound the alarm and rally support." (BBC News: "UN Chief's Rwanda Genocide Regret," March 26, 2004, available at http://news.bbc.co.uk/2/hi/africa/3573229.stm). Promoted to Secretary of State, Madeleine Albright said in response to the publication of OAU report, *Rwanda: The Preventable Genocide*: "I followed instructions because I was an Ambassador, but I screamed about the instructions that I got on this. I felt that they were wrong and I made that point, but I was an Ambassador under instructions." Interview on ABC's *This Week*, July 9, 2000, available at http://usinfo.org/wf-archive/2000/000710/epf101.htm.

26. Franck, "Legality and Legitimacy," 149.

27. Des Forges, *Leave None to Tell*, under "Chronology," available at http://www.hrw.org/reports/1999/rwanda/Geno4-7-01.htm, and under "French Support for Habyarimana," available at http://www.hrw.org/reports/1999/rwanda/Geno1-3-11.htm.

28. Des Forges, *Leave None to Tell*, available at http://www.hrw.org/reports/1999/rwanda/Geno15-8-02.htm; *cf.* PBS Frontline, "One Hundred Days of Slaughter."

29. See note 17.

30. "Perhaps there was no better reflection of the world's shabby treatment of post-genocide Rwanda than the matter of the debt burden incurred by the Habyarimana government. The major source of the unpaid debt was the weapons the regime had purchased for the war against the RPF, which had then been turned against innocent Tutsi during the genocide. . . . [I]ncredibly enough, the new government was deemed responsible for repaying to those multilateral and national lenders the debt accrued by its predecessors. The common-sense assumption that Rwanda deserved and could not recover without special treatment and, that the debt would have been wiped out more or less automatically, had no currency in the world of international finance. Instead of Rwanda receiving vast sums of money as reparations by those who had failed to stop the tragedy, it in fact owed those same sources a vast sum of money." OAU, *Rwanda: The Preventable Genocide*, sections 17.30 and 17.33. As the report recounts, the leading sellers of arms into Africa are the United States, Russia, China, and France. Weapons sales to the developing world at large for the 1994–2001 period (in 2001 dollars) amounted to $60 billion from the United States, $40 billion from Russia, $25 billion from France, $8 billion each from China and the United Kingdom, $5 billion from Germany, and $20 billion from the rest of Europe. Congressional Research Service, *Conventional Arms Transfers to Developing Nations*, August 6, 2002, 21. Also available at http://fpc.state.gov/documents/organization/12632.pdf.

31. This paragraph and the next summarize points made more elaborately in Thomas Pogge, *World Poverty and Human Rights: Cosmopolitan Responsibilities and Reforms* (Cambridge: Polity Press, 2002).

32. United States Department of Agriculture, *U.S. Action Plan on Food Security*, March 26, 1999, iii. Also available at http://www.fas.usda.gov/icd/summit/usactplan.pdf. The U.S. government mentions this fact whilst arguing that the developed countries should *not* follow the U.N. Food and Agriculture Organization's proposal to increase development assistance for agriculture by $6 billion annually, that $2.6 billion is ample. See ibid., Appendix A.

33. *Economist*, December 22, 2001, 82–83.

34. In 2002, these countries, with 15.6 percent of the world's population, had 80.6 percent of global income ($25,383.7 billion out of $31,483.9 billion). World Bank, *World Development Report 2004* (New York: Oxford University Press, 2004), 253.

35. The United States has led the decline by reducing ODA from 0.21 to 0.11 percent of GNP in a time of great prosperity culminating in enormous budget surpluses. *Cf.* UNDP, *Human Development Report 2003* (New York: Oxford University Press, 2003), 228 and 290. This report gives aggregate ODA for 2001 as $52.3 billion, down from $53.7 billion in 2000 and $56.4 billion in 1999. UNDP, *Report 2002*, 202; UNDP, *Human Development Report 2001* (New York: Oxford University Press, 2001), 190. All available at http://www.undp.org. After the invasions of Afghanistan and Iraq, ODA is now growing rapidly through disbursements to these and neighboring states (esp. Pakistan). ODA is reported to have been $58.3 billion for 2002 and $68.5 billion for 2003. OECD: "Table 1: Net Official Development Assistance in 2002," available at http://www.oecd.org/dataoecd/43/56/2507734.pdf; OECD: "Modest Increase in Development Aid in 2003," available at http://www.oecd.org/document/22/0,2340,en_2649_37413_31504022_1_1_1_37413,00.html.

36. As the USAID proclaimed on its Web site, "The principal beneficiary of America's foreign assistance programs has always been the United States. Close to 80 percent of the U.S. Agency for International Development's (USAID's) contracts and grants go directly to American firms. Foreign assistance programs have helped create major markets for agricultural goods, created new markets for American industrial exports and meant hundreds of thousands of jobs for Americans."

37. Down from 28 percent in 1990 (UNDP, *Report 2003*, 290). India, with more poor people than any other country, receives ODA of $1.50 annually for each of its citizens; the corresponding figures are $42.70 for the Czech Republic, $54.50 for Malta, $69.50 for Cyprus, $76.60 for Bahrain, and $132.40 for Israel (UNDP, *Report 2002*, 203–5). These countries' gross domestic products *per capita* are 12 to 37 times that of India (UNDP, *Report 2003*, 278–80). Still, even their citizens get much less aid than the 21 million cows within the EU, who receive subsidies of about $1,000 per year. Charlotte Denny and Andrew Clark, "Cows Can Fly Upper Class on Agricultural Fare," *The Guardian*, September 25, 2002, available at http://www.guardian.co.uk/country/article/0,2763,798597,00.html. Such subsidies—still permitted under the supposedly free-market rules of the WTO—greatly disadvantage farmers in the poor countries, who cannot compete against heavily subsidized milk powder, sugar, etc., exported from the EU.

38. OECD: "Table 1: Net Official Development Assistance in 2002," available at http://www.oecd.org/dataoecd/43/56/2507734.pdf.

39. "Implementation of the Declaration and the Programme of Action in developing countries, in particular in Africa and the least developed countries, will need additional financial resources and more effective development cooperation and assistance. This will require: . . . (c) Agreeing on a mutual commitment between interested developed and developing country partners to allocate, on average, 20 per cent of ODA and 20 per cent of the national budget, respectively, to basic social programmes." U.N. World Summit for Social Development, "Programme of Action," 1995, Article 88(c). Available at http://www.un.org/esa/socdev/wssd/agreements/poach5.htm.

40. After the end of the Cold War, the developed countries were able to reduce their military expenditures from 4.1 percent of their combined GDPs in 1985 to 2.2 percent in 1998. UNDP, *Human Development Report 1998* (New York: Oxford University Press, 1998), 197; UNDP, *Human Development Report 2000* (New York: Oxford University Press, 2000), 217. With their combined GDPs at $25,768 billion in the year 2002 (UNDP, *Human Development Report 2004* (New York: UNDP, 2004), 187), their peace dividend in 2002 came to about $490 billion.

41. In 2002, the high-income countries had an aggregate population of 941.2 million (UNDP, *Report 2004*, 155). These people also give aid through nongovernmental organizations. In 2001, such aid amounted to about $7 billion, or $8 per citizen. See UNDP, *Report 2003*, 290.

42. If U.S. leaders really cared about human rights and liberation, they would show some interest in Burma, whose population, twice that of Iraq, has long suffered under a brutal and widely hated military junta. Toppling the junta and letting Aung San Suu Kyi take power in Burma would be vastly easier and cheaper than the U.S. operation in Iraq. Aung San Suu Kyi won 82 percent of parliamentary seats in the 1990 national elections, which the junta permitted but then refused to recognize. Since that time, her movements have been tightly restricted by the junta.

43. Franck, "Legality and Legitimacy," 150–151.

44. Ibid., 145.

45. But see David Gauthier, *Morals by Agreement* (Cambridge: Cambridge University Press, 1987) for the opposite view of what fairness is.

46. Even domestic juries are hardly ideal. Significant distortions may be introduced by how much the contending parties spend on their legal teams, jury selection specialists, and expert witnesses.

47. Franck acknowledges that the U.N. has not "acted wisely" in this case. In mitigation, he points out, "That Vietnam's use of force violated the Charter text is beyond question." Thomas Franck, "When, If Ever,

May States Deploy Military Force without Prior Security Council Authorization?" *Journal of Law and Policy* 5 (2001): 65. I disagree. Preceding the invasion, the Khmer Rouge regime had made many significant military incursions into Vietnamese territory that it claimed as its own. So there is a self-defense argument here. For the assessment of this argument it may also be relevant that the Khmer Rouge had killed two million Cambodians, committing a genocide that no other country was willing to stop. The Vietnamese had compelling reason to believe that this regime constituted a very serious danger.

48. Ibid., 62. Readers will recall that this air strike was timed to coincide with Monica Lewinsky's second and final day of grand jury testimony. See *Houston Chronicle*: "Clinton: A Story Unfolds," available at http://www.chron.com/content/chronicle/special/clinton/testimony/lewdex.htm.

49. This was after a ten-minute discussion in the U.N. Security Council meeting of August 24, 1998, during which the United States claimed that the Sudanese might tamper with the evidence. *BBC News,* "No U.N. Action on Sudan missile attack," August 24, 1998, available at http://news.bbc.co.uk/1/hi/world/africa/157192.stm. The United States did not explain how the Sudanese could remove all chemical traces from a site that had been hit by thirteen cruise missiles and was continuously open to international journalists.

50. It is said that doing so would have compromised U.S. intelligence sources. However, proof of chemical or biological weapons production could have been obtained through an examination of the factory site after its destruction. Despite U.S. opposition to such an examination, soil samples from the site were examined by three European laboratories and the Manchester engineering firm Dames and Moore, under the overall supervision of Professor Thomas Tullius, chairman of Boston University's Department of Chemistry. No evidence of suspicious chemicals was found. Maureen Rouhi, "Analytical Credibility," *Science Insights* 77, 8 (1999): 37ff., available at http://osf1.gmu.edu/~sslayden/curr-chem/chem-war/7708scit3.htm. A 300-page report by Kroll Associates (January 1999, commissioned by Idris) reaches the same conclusion. Henry L. Stimson Centre, "U.S. Case for Al Shifa Disintegrates," *CBW Chronicle* 3 (February 2000). Available at http://www.stimson.org/cbw/?sn=cb2001121262. The fact that the United States blocked an official investigation of the site suggests that its intelligence services expected such a search to turn up nothing.

51. Franck, "Legality and Legitimacy," 152.

52. Ibid., 147.

53. *Cf.*, e.g., Ian Urbina, "U.N. Resolution: Dangerous Ambiguity," *Asian*

Times Online, November 12, 2002. Available at http://www.atimes.com/atimes/Middle_East/DK12Ak01.html.

54. Carola Hoyos and Alan Beattie, "Nations Ponder Whether They Can Afford to Oppose U.S. Stance," *Financial Times,* November 7, 2002, 7.

55. Franck, "Legality and Legitimacy," 152.

56. Foreign Policy Association/Princeton Town Hall Meeting, "Transcript of Remarks by Thomas Franck," May 9, 2003, available at http://www.fpa.org/topics_info2414/topics_info_show.htm?doc_id=175569.

57. *Cf.* Security Council Resolutions 1483, 1500, 1511, and 1546.

58. A public criterion for judging military interventions, if it itself is to be judged in part at least by its effects, requires a metacriterion in the background for assessing alternative candidate public criteria by how well each would work in the world as it is. This model is exemplified by Rawls, who proposes his two principles of justice as a public criterion of justice that is justified against other candidate public criteria by reference to its expected relative impact on the fulfillment of citizens' higher-order interests. *Cf.* John Rawls, *Justice as Fairness: A Restatement* (Cambridge: Harvard University Press, 2001), 18–19, 42–43, 192. This sort of instrumentalization could be carried one step further: a theorist may think that she should base her public advocacy not on the quality of the effects of the various candidate public criteria ("I should advocate whatever criterion is such that its general acceptance would have the best effects") but on the quality of the effects of her own advocacy. For example, if she believes that C_1 would be the best public criterion but that only C_2 and C_3 stand any chance of adoption, she would then throw her full support behind C_2 in order to defeat the even worse C_3, while ignoring C_1, which, if it came into the discussion, would only divide and dilute the political forces opposed to C_3.

59. Franck, "Legality and Legitimacy," 146.

60. As the United States did in 1986 when it withdrew its acceptance of compulsory jurisdiction of the International Court of Justice and, defying its verdict, continued to support the Nicaraguan contras.

61. No substantial loss of internal legitimacy seems to have occurred when the United States, in 1986, quit the compulsory jurisdiction of the International Court of Justice over the case brought by Nicaragua or when the United States enacted the American Servicemember's Protection Act (colloquially known as the "Hague Invasion Act"), under which "[t]he President is authorized to use all means necessary and appropriate to bring about the release of any [covered United States persons, covered allied persons, and individuals detained or imprisoned for official actions taken while the individual was a covered United States person or a covered allied person, and in the case of a covered allied person, upon the

request of such government] who is being detained or imprisoned by, on behalf of, or at the request of the International Criminal Court." Section 2008 of Public Law 107-201, 116 Stat. 899, 22 U.S.C. 7401 (2002). Available at http://www.wfa.org/issues/wicc/aspafinal/aspahome.html. U.S. citizens also strongly supported the latest invasion of Iraq, despite the fact that the United States and the United Kingdom failed (by a very large margin) to obtain U.N. Security Council authorization.

7

WHOSE PRINCIPLES?
WHOSE INSTITUTIONS?
LEGITIMACY CHALLENGES FOR
"HUMANITARIAN INTERVENTION"

CATHERINE LU

As flies to wanton boys, are we to th' gods,
They kill us for their sport.

—William Shakespeare[1]

1. INTRODUCTION

The end of the Cold War did not herald the end of human conflict, cruelty, and catastrophe. On the contrary, millions of people
have continued to suffer the fate of flies in insensitive, thought-
less, or reckless human hands. Scenes of depravity and misery in a
long list of places have generated pleas for the international community to uphold "the collective conscience of humanity" and to
act "in defense of our common humanity."[2] For theorists and
practitioners of international politics, the various political, social,
economic, and moral pathologies that culminate in humanitarian
catastrophe have reinvigorated debate about the ethics of "humanitarian intervention," a term commonly used to refer to military action, employed without consent by a target sovereign state,
to prevent or halt large-scale violence perpetrated or permitted by
its government.

Before embarking on the main theme of this essay, I should
declare my ambivalence about the term "humanitarian intervention" itself. Given that any use of force by states in world politics

typically produces much immediate suffering, death, and destruction, the adjective "humanitarian" hardly seems appropriate as a descriptive label. In the post–Cold War era, some state leaders in the West became increasingly open to using the term, partly as a way to convey a break with the Cold War past; the term "humanitarian" referred to their claim that the military action proposed was prompted by humanitarian concerns rather than geopolitical or self-aggrandizing aims. In addition to expressing intentions, however, the term also seemed at times to convey an entire evaluative judgment, so that labeling a proposed military action "humanitarian intervention" amounted to declaring that it was morally legitimate or justified.

The legitimacy of any kind of intervention in situations of humanitarian catastrophe, however, cannot be answered by labeling the action humanitarian. Even the legitimacy of *descriptively* humanitarian practices, such as the distribution of medical aid and food supplies, cannot be judged morally appropriate in all circumstances. As participants in humanitarian relief organizations have noticed, enacting the duty of humanity understood as an obligation to relieve suffering as an end in itself can generate morally perverse consequences, such as prolonging or exacerbating violent conflict by indirectly providing militants with resources.[3] "Humanitarian" therefore does not automatically equal "ethical" or "legitimate," and the use of the term to imply or declare this evaluative conclusion should be discouraged in the scholarship and practice of international relations. To avoid this rhetorical danger, it might be more appropriate to call the 1999 NATO action in the Kosovo crisis, for example, a military intervention; debates about whether or not it was a "humanitarian intervention" are, in fact, debates about whether or not the use of force in that specific situation, in that specific manner, and by those specific agents, was morally and legally justified.

There might, however, be a morally positive consequence to the use of the term "humanitarian intervention" in international political discourse. In highlighting the "humanitarian" in relation to "intervention" or the use of force by states against a sovereign authority, the term can make more explicit and present the evaluative standard by which the abrogation of state sovereignty and the use of force by states must be justified.

In this essay I explore three aspects of the legitimacy problem for "humanitarian intervention" understood as the use of military force by states for humanitarian purposes. First, I consider challenges to the legitimacy of such a concept and practice that derive from controversies about the idea of "common humanity" itself. In response I forward a conception of common humanity that is based on an account of humans as social agents with a capacity for moral agency. Although my inspiration for this account comes from a version of liberalism, I argue that it is not confined to liberal culture or philosophy.

Second, I examine legitimacy challenges that take as their starting point the twin normative pillars of international society: state sovereignty and nonintervention. I pay specific attention to two competing interpretations of state sovereignty—"sovereignty as privacy" and "sovereignty as responsibility"—and argue that promoting a conception of international society that affirms an agency-based view of common humanity commits us to understanding state sovereignty as the authority and responsibility of states to protect and maintain conditions for meaningful human (social and moral) agency.

Third, I deal with problems of legitimacy that relate specifically to the use of force as a means to promote this end. In particular, I address problems of law and community at the international level that affect the legitimacy of processes of adjudicating uses of force for humanitarian purposes, given current world political conditions and structures. The hard question I consider in the conclusion to this essay is whether "humanitarian intervention" can effectively serve to promote a conception of world order that affirms "our common humanity."

2. AN AGENCY-BASED ACCOUNT OF COMMON HUMANITY

History suggests that in contexts of intergroup political conflict, moral imperatives based on "our common humanity" will more often than not be honored in the breach. Indeed, the woeful fate of the Melians, who placed their trust "in the fortune that the gods will send" and "in the help of men" to save them from an imperial Athenian takeover, has served as a timeless and sobering warning to students of international politics against placing much faith in either divine or earthly intervention, even in the face of impending disaster.[4] Ironically, the conditions that lead to calls for "humanitarian intervention" expose the fragmented nature of human solidarity and the attendant frailty of notions of universal moral obligation based on the notion of common humanity.

Can the idea of "common humanity" be a practical motivating force in a divided world? Even in the Melian case, it was not universal humanity but their kin and allies that Melians meant when they referred to "the help of men." In modern times, as Martha Finnemore has shown, the "humanitarian interventions" practiced by nineteenth-century Europe were nonuniversal in that the only "humanity" considered worthy of protection was limited to Christians: "[T]here were no instances of European powers considering intervention to protect non-Christians."[5] More recently, nonuniversal "humanitarian intervention" was exemplified in the evacuation of foreign nationals by French and Belgian soldiers in the early days of the 1994 Rwandan genocide.[6] Rather than transcending or disciplining political, religious, economic, and social divides and conflicts, the claims of common humanity have historically been subordinated to them, or at least heavily mediated by them, so that entitlements based on the status of being human were rarely, reluctantly, or only instrumentally extended to the enemy, infidel, refugee, and stranger.

Part of the controversy surrounding "humanitarian intervention" as a concept and practice results from disputes about the claims of common humanity itself. Many are skeptical about the philosophical tenability of making universalist moral claims in a pluralistic world.[7] On what grounds can any framework of moral rights and obligations be considered common to all human beings? The moral legitimacy of "humanitarian intervention" partly depends on the intelligibility of making universalist moral claims. If cultural pluralism deprives such claims of their very intelligibility, it is hard to see how any practice founded on them can ever be legitimated.

My answer to this line of argument is to distinguish between cultural pluralism and cultural relativism. Although norms and ideas are inevitably contextualized, this does not negate the possibility or utility of constructing, from diverse philosophical, ethical, and religious foundations, moral claims or norms that are broadly universalizable in our contemporary world.[8] In addition, part of the contemporary context in which moral ideas and claims are generated and developed, contested and validated, and entrenched and enforced involves cross-cultural, international, and global initiative, debate, and action. It would therefore be misleading to hold a simplistically insular or atomistic view of the relations between ethical, philosophical, or religious perspectives and traditions that obscures the interactive sources of their development.

In the 1990s state representatives from a wide variety of cultures affirmed the notion of common humanity in their recognition of the intolerable *inhumanity* of certain situations. In supporting United Nations Security Council Resolution 794 authorizing the use of military force in Somalia in 1992, for example, the Zimbabwean ambassador declared, "[W]e cannot countenance this untold suffering of innocent men, women and children from starvation and famine." The Moroccan ambassador similarly talked of "the universal conscience" being aroused by the desperate plight of Somalis.[9] Although there are compelling reasons to question whether the use of force was a necessary or appropriate means of alleviating the humanitarian catastrophe in Somalia, few would deny the moral cogency of the claim that the situation constituted an affront to "our common humanity."

The idea of common humanity entails an account of what is common and distinctive about being a human agent. To capture this quality, consider Shakespeare's image of human beings being treated like flies in the hands of wanton schoolboys. What is so morally offensive or disturbing about this depiction? I believe such an image violates our common self-understandings of what it means to be a human agent. To treat people like flies is to deny their personhood. The fly is a metaphor for powerlessness; to be treated like a fly is to be treated like an object, without agency or significance. People who are placed in the position of a fly are deprived of effective social, political, or moral agency. Because they also lack social standing, their need to feel a sense of belonging and purpose in the world is similarly unacknowledged. Constant anxiety and alienation are thus the tragic universal hall-marks of being powerless.

An agency-based account of common humanity recognizes hu-man agency, and especially the capacity for social and moral agency, as common and distinctive to all human beings. What makes practices such as torture and structures such as slavery and Nazi concentration camps *inhuman* is that they deprive their human victims of the ability to engage in meaningful self-interpre-tation and moral evaluation.[10] According to Judith Shklar, fear of agency-depriving practices and conditions animates liberalism as a political doctrine, which aims to secure "the political conditions that are necessary for the exercise of personal freedom."[11] Shk-lar's "liberalism of fear" is a response to the tragic histories of human conflict and cruelty in which the institution of systematic fear annihilates the conditions for human agency and "the dignity of persons." From a liberal perspective, the remedy is to design social structures to guarantee the individual "enough equality of power to protect and assert one's rights." In liberal polities this insight is translated into individual legal equality as a check on "arbitrary, unexpected, unnecessary, and unlicensed" institution-alized violence; and into social pluralism and equity, or "the elimi-nation of such forms and degrees of social inequality as expose people to oppressive practices."[12] On this account, as a political doctrine that affirms an agency-based view of humanity, liberalism militates against great concentrations or disparities in social, polit-ical, and economic power that create structures and climates in which some people can count for nothing.

This agency-based account of common humanity draws its in-spiration from liberal political philosophy, but it does not seem unreasonable to assert that all human agents, whatever their cul-ture and history, depend on societies regulated by social and polit-ical authority and power, and all can fear abusive or neglectful agents and structures of power that obliterate personhood or reduce human agents "to mere reactive units of sensation."[13] The unfortunate reality is that it is not difficult for an ordinary person to imagine being treated like a fly, because all human beings share *natural* vulnerabilities, and without the shelter of socially acknowledged and enforced rules of protection, a human being is little more than a "poor, bare, forked animal."[14] A social structure, however, may impose different levels of *social* vulnerability, making some more susceptible to domination, coercion, or exploitation by others. Political, legal, and social institutions and norms can thus create and sustain unequal or distinct social vulnerabilities that may, at the extreme, deprive some people of protection from intentional and unintentional assaults against their natural vulnerabilities.

Starting from an agency-based account of humanity, we can view the development of humanitarian norms and practices in world politics as part of a process of establishing conditions for the exercise of accountable power and authority that support rather than undermine individual human (social and moral) agency, dignity, and responsibility. Oliver Ramsbotham and Tom Woodhouse have identified three expressions of humanitarianism at the international level: international humanitarian laws governing armed conflict, such as the Geneva Conventions; the work of international and nongovernmental organizations and structures that deliver international humanitarian assistance; and the international human rights regime.[15] All three dimensions of humanitarianism are primarily concerned to guarantee the security and dignity of the person, a fundamental condition for human moral agency and responsibility. The law of armed conflict, for example, reflects the significance of such concerns—especially of noncombatants, as well as of sick and wounded combatants, and prisoners of war—even in contexts of politically organized and legally sanctioned violence.[16] International humanitarian assistance promotes the security and dignity of persons by aiming "to prevent and alleviate human suffering wherever it may be found" through the provision of food, clothing, shelter, and medical assistance.[17] In a human rights framework, these concerns are expressed through conventions prohibiting torture, genocide, slavery, and racial discrimination.[18]

An agency-based account of common humanity legitimizes humanitarian laws of war, the practice of humanitarian assistance, and the doctrine of human rights. To evaluate the legitimacy of "humanitarian intervention" one must examine how the use of force without the consent of a target state serves to secure conditions for the exercise of power that affirms rather than subverts human agency, dignity, and responsibility.

3. "Sovereignty as Privacy" versus "Sovereignty as Responsibility"

Even if doubts about the idea of common humanity are satisfactorily answered, "humanitarian intervention" continues to generate moral and legal, not to mention political, controversy because it entails the abrogation of the twin normative pillars of international society—sovereignty and nonintervention. According to Robert Jackson, "humanitarian intervention" is morally problematic because the pluralist international society that these norms maintain is the most morally defensible political "arrangement to uphold human equality and human freedom around the world."[19] Like Michael Walzer, Jackson appeals to the liberalism of John Stuart Mill to argue that the political independence of states guaranteed by the norms of sovereignty and nonintervention is the condition for the exercise of human social and moral agency. His arguments suggest that an agency-based view of humanity can be the moral reason to *uphold* the international norms of state sovereignty and nonintervention. Although this argument has some validity, it must be admitted that such norms are imperfect instruments for vindicating an agency-based account of humanity, and sometimes they may serve as perverse instruments for the powerful to evade their moral duties to common humanity. This is particularly likely when the norms of state sovereignty and nonintervention translate into an entitlement of states to "privacy" or freedom from interference from international society.[20]

The status of sovereignty makes states the recognized agents of international society, with certain rights and duties under international law, and one of the rights they enjoy in that society is an entitlement to "privacy" or noninterference in their domestic affairs. Hilary Charlesworth has noted that while conventionally the state is known as the quintessentially public actor or realm, it acquires the status of a private sphere through a distinction drawn in the realm of public international law. Article 2(7) of the Charter of the United Nations distinguishes between matters of international (public) concern and issues belonging to a national or domestic (and private) jurisdiction: "Nothing contained in the present Charter shall authorize the United Nations to intervene in matters which are essentially within the domestic jurisdiction of any states or shall require the Members to submit such matters to settlement under the present Charter."[21] The state, in relation to its own citizens and society, may constitute the public realm, an emblem of the universal, but in relation to other states and international society, it constitutes a private realm, a repository of all that is particular to its members.

The depiction of "sovereignty as privacy" implies an analogy between the state and the individual; another collective unit—the family—has enjoyed a similar moral claim to privacy. Indeed, the state and the family share a strikingly similar conceptual history as "private spheres," with rights to privacy understood in terms of communal integrity and freedom from external interference.[22]

Just as those who study familial domestic violence find the "family ideal," encompassing "ideas about family privacy, conjugal and parental rights, and family stability,"[23] to be a consistent barrier to social reform, advocates of "humanitarian intervention" confront the "state ideal," involving a set of ideas about state privacy, sovereign rights, and the integrity of domestic and international societies. The historical reluctance of international society to intervene in areas considered to belong to the domestic jurisdiction of states parallels the past reluctance of domestic law, the police, and court systems in Western societies to intervene in what were perceived to be "private" family disputes.

One contemporary example of how the interpretation of "sovereignty as privacy" shields abusive sovereign conduct comes from the testimony of Roméo Dallaire, the Canadian commander of the United Nations peacekeeping mission in Rwanda during the 1994 genocide. According to Dallaire, not only did he find his request for more troops denied, but he was not even able to halt transmissions from the local radio station, Radio Télévision Libre des Mille Collines (RTLM), which was inciting genocide. As he explains, the United Nations lacked the equipment to halt the broadcasts, but the United States did possess deployable jamming aircraft:

> The issue was studied by the Pentagon, which in due course recommended against conducting the operation because of the cost—$8,500 an hour for a jamming aircraft over the country—and the legal dilemma. Bandwidth within a nation is owned by the nation,

and *jamming a national radio station would violate international convention on national sovereignty.* The Pentagon judged that the lives of the estimated 8,000–10,000 Rwandans being killed each day in the genocide were not worth the cost of the fuel or the violation of Rwandan airwaves.[24]

Whatever the actual motivations were behind this decision, it is clear that the legal problem of violating sovereignty was used as an independent normative argument against the proposed action.

Such a decision is consistent with judgments made during the Cold War era, when both the U.N. and its members interpreted the right of sovereignty and the duty of nonintervention in a way that protected domestically irresponsible sovereigns from formal international censure. Although some Cold War–era military interventions yielded positive humanitarian consequences for populations in crisis, humanitarian concern was not a legally recognized ground for abrogating sovereignty in international relations.[25] The legitimation criteria for the use of force between states therefore excluded the validity of humanitarian reasons, especially in contexts where there was no direct threat to international peace and security.[26] Domestic tyrants could feel at home in the world of public states and private humanity.

In recent years the consensus on interpreting "sovereignty as privacy" has undergone significant contestation and revision within the society of states itself.[27] Whereas "sovereignty as privacy" emphasizes the power of sovereigns to order their domestic realms and entails their right to noninterference in this respect, the alternative account of "sovereignty as responsibility" highlights the international accountability of sovereigns for how they exercise that power, especially with respect to the protection of the human rights and humanitarian interests of their members. Most significantly, as the International Commission on Intervention and State Sovereignty (ICISS) put it, "Where a population is suffering serious harm, as a result of internal wars, insurgency, repression, or state failure, and the state in question is unwilling or unable to halt or avert it, the *principle of nonintervention yields to the international responsibility to protect.*"[28] Under this view, the internal dimension of state sovereignty, authority and agency, is tied to certain international standards of accountability. Sovereignty so conceived still empowers states to order their internal affairs, but it also obligates them to exercise that power in ways that meet the basic human rights and humanitarian interests of their members.

Some theorists have been concerned that the development of a global order founded upon notions of common humanity necessarily undermines the very foundations of a society of states. Hedley Bull puts it rather provocatively: "Carried to its logical extreme, the doctrine of human rights and duties under international law is subversive of the whole principle that mankind should be organized as a society of sovereign states."[29] A global order that universally affirms the claims of common humanity, however, does not require the abolition of state agency and authority; it requires only that states exercise their domestic agency and authority in consistence with humanitarian principles. Indeed, the idea of the abuse of authority (sovereign or parental) implies the possibility of legitimate authority. Intervention to avert or halt sovereign abuses of power that produce humanitarian catastrophes clearly does not undermine in any way the legitimate use of that authority. In the case of the genocide-inciting radio station during the Rwandan genocide, an alternative interpretation of "sovereignty as responsibility" would have justified international action to abrogate Rwandan state sovereignty over airwaves because the state itself was either unable or unwilling to halt the broadcasts. The abrogation of state sovereignty in the case of abusive governments does not undermine the concept of the state as a political institution; rather, it serves to reinforce the moral foundations of the state and sovereign authority.

To gauge the impact of a reconceptualization of "sovereignty as responsibility" on international society, we might return to the family/state analogy and consider the fate of the family as a social institution in the West following changes in conceptions of family privacy and parental authority. The rise of liberal egalitarianism in Western domestic polities in the past century has led to the social demise of patriarchal families. Yet although the patriarchal conception of paternal authority within the family has fallen into disrepute in liberal times, the family as a social unit remains, and certain forms of family have gained a legitimacy that was denied to them in a patriarchal framework. Just as families as social institutions have changed but also survived the decline of absolutist conceptions of parental authority in the household, states as political institutions may also survive the decline of absolutist conceptions of internal sovereign authority. A society of states, then, may also change and remain.

The preceding argument in favor of qualifying and reconceptualizing rules of state sovereignty and nonintervention should not be read as one that justifies military action in all cases of abusive or negligent sovereign power. Indeed, we should be careful not to conflate the problem of intervention with the problem of the use of force. The interventionary aspect of an activity, the fact that it is done "in other people's countries," is distinguishable from the activity itself—in this case, the use of force. The conflation of these two issues in international theory and practice has meant that governments have been able to claim a much stronger social convention against all types of intervention than is supported even in international law. It is, however, a mistake to advance a general doctrine against intervention because of the problems associated with a specific and extreme type of intervention. Many situations may justify some kind of interventionary international response that violates or restricts some aspect of a state's sovereign authority while ruling out a full-scale military assault. Crucial opportunities to engage in preventive and nonmilitary interventions, before a crisis explodes or escalates to the level of mass atrocity, are missed when the concept of intervention and the use of force are conflated. When sovereigns fail to meet their responsibility to protect their members' basic humanitarian interests, the relevant normative question for international society is not whether or not to intervene, but *how*.

4. The Use of Force and Problems of Law and Community

Another important challenge to the legitimacy of "humanitarian intervention" has to do with the legitimacy of the use of force by states in an international context as a means to protect or promote humanitarian interests. Skepticism abounds from the apparent contradictions between humanitarian aims and the immediate outcomes of uses of military force. Indeed, the devastation wrought by two world wars made the scourge of war the greatest threat to the interests of common humanity. As Jutta Brunnée and Stephen Toope have argued, "One can read the history of 20th century international law primarily as an attempt to reduce the evil of war by codifying a restrictive doctrine of 'just war' that limits justifications for recourse to the use of force in international relations."[30] The U.N. Charter prohibits forcible military interventions under Article 2(4); exceptions to this prohibition are permitted only when the Security Council authorizes the use of force for the sake of international peace and security under Chapter VII, Article 42, or if a state or collective of states can claim reasons of self-defense under Article 51.

Thomas Franck, in this volume and elsewhere, shows that the legitimacy of "humanitarian intervention" cannot be determined simply by reference to the text of the U.N. Charter. This is because the text itself admits of various interpretations, and any application of the Charter inevitably involves interpretation in a broader normative, ideological, and political context. Against positivist accounts of law that seek to isolate it from morality, Franck asserts the interconnectedness of law with both morality and politics.[31] As he has argued, law among mortals is "a system of norms constantly engaged in a process of challenge, adaptation, and reformulation."[32] The content and function of law are thus inextricably wedded to issues of power and ideas about justice in any society, whether domestic, international, or global.

Franck argues that the debate between states about the legitimacy of "humanitarian intervention" is not necessarily over the moral cogency of humanitarian claims or even over the moral necessity of overriding sovereign rights to avert humanitarian disaster. Rather, disputes about the legitimacy of "humanitarian intervention" reside in arguments over the process by which state actions, especially the use of force, come to be legitimized. Even if a law of "humanitarian intervention" were to enjoy widespread moral endorsement, the validation of specific interventions that claim to be applications of that law would depend on the development of a credible jury that "makes the definitive decision as to how the law—or the exception—is to be applied in specific instances." Jurors are "those to whom is to be entrusted the crucial work of finding the facts, applying the law to them situationally, and, in doing so, narrowing, when necessary, the gaps between law's legality and legitimacy."[33]

In "anarchical" international society, the idea of judgment by a jury of peers has more obvious resonance than the more typical legal image of judgment dispensed by an overarching supreme judge. Some might dispute the use of domestic law as an analogy for international law as a misleadingly optimistic exercise, but this would be true only if one held an excessively idealized view of the operation of domestic law. I think the analogy is appropriate and especially useful in highlighting the potential problems that attend attempts, at either the domestic or the international level, to establish a credible jurying process in a pluralistic, unequal, and divided society. The acknowledgment of these problems does not constitute a rejection of the idea that an authoritative jurying process is necessary for legitimizing "humanitarian intervention," but it does reveal defects, deficiencies, and limitations in current international conditions that need to be addressed for any jurying process to achieve widespread authoritativeness.

The problem of the legitimacy of the jurying process through which the rightness of any military intervention for humanitarian purposes would be evaluated involves two related questions: who can be part of the jury, and to whom must a jurying process be credible? The idea of trial by jury involves the idea of judgment by one's peers. Jury members are typically disinterested or not personally involved with the victim or defendant, but they are not entirely uninvolved because to be a peer is to be connected, especially to the defendant, either through common membership in a community or through equal status. This is to ensure that judgments of the defendant's conduct or the complainant's claim occur with "a degree of contextual reasonableness."[34]

The question of who can be a juror is determined by one's view of the relevant community that can claim the right to judge the parties. International law has conceived the international community as a society of states because that law is made by states. In that society, as Franck suggests, it is states, in their capacity as members of regional and interstate organizations, such as the U.N. Security Council and the General Assembly, that decide when a situation has become a humanitarian crisis, "whether the crisis is truly one of extreme necessity," "whether the force deployed is appropriate and commensurate with the necessity," and "whether the motive of the intervener is humanitarian, as distinct from self-aggrandizing."[35] States are peers through their common membership in the society of states, and because states are the self-professed agents of military force in world politics, it would seem logical to conclude that the people who can determine the legitimacy of military action by a state or collectivity of states must be the representatives of states themselves. From this perspective, just as most national militaries have special courts, distinct from their civilian counterparts, to judge professional transgressions by military personnel, the society of states can claim a distinct and exclusive authority to judge the conduct of its members.

Even within this restrictive view of international community, however, there are significant issues that affect the establishment of a credible jurying process. These problems—power asymmetries, gross economic inequality, and ideological divides—point to the enduring problem of community in all societies, including international society. Historically, the society of states, although legally governed by the principle of sovereign equality, has been hierarchically ordered. What will motivate the powerful to encourage the development of an egalitarian jurying process? All states can claim common membership in the society of states, but the power asymmetries between them foster the development of different peer groups within that society. Since the concept of a jurying process depends on the idea of a community of peers, the existence of superpowers and great powers inhibits the likelihood of establishing an egalitarian jurying process that could hold the most powerful actors accountable to the wider society of states. At best, perhaps, great powers will endorse a process that requires them to submit to the judgment of a jury of other great powers, which may explain the structure of the Security Council that grants privileged authority to the five victorious powers of the Second World War.

At this time, the United States is the sole global military superpower, and it prefers to be its own judge. The Bush administration's rejection of the International Criminal Court (ICC) and other various forms of international cooperation, as well as its evasion of Security Council judgment in its war against Iraq in 2003, indicates that it views the United States as peerless, making the idea of a jury or judgment by one's peers inoperable. In this context, Michael Byers and Simon Chesterman worry that "the legal principle of sovereign equality is now, quietly but resolutely, under attack."[36]

Power asymmetries present another kind of problem for a credible jurying process when the powerful *are* involved in its establishment. Robust legal regimes that exist in a social context of extreme power disparities, whether their basis is economic, political, and/or social, often serve to perpetuate established tyrannies and servilities and thus suffer from limited moral authoritativeness. This is because law depends on political will for effectiveness in any society, and it is an unfortunate fact that in contexts where power and justice pull in opposing directions, law gains power or efficacy only by compromising on justice or moral legitimacy. Law by itself is not going to be able to create greater substantive equality between states, but it can at least resist becoming a legitimizing tool for great power and superpower domination by adhering to its moral function as a check on the arbitrary exercise of power. In the case of the ICC, for example, this would involve resisting U.S. demands for formal exemptions of U.S. personnel from the jurisdiction of the court.[37]

The establishment of a credible jurying process within the society of states is also complicated by the prevalence of the friend-enemy distinction as an organizing principle of international politics. Although the Cold War is over, the friend-enemy distinction underlying Cold War politics continues to animate other conflicts and divides in international society, especially the current "war on terror." Consider the decision of the United States, in the aftermath of 9/11, to justify its military intervention in Afghanistan by presenting its evidence of Taliban complicity with Al Qaeda to NATO. Franck argues that the "underlying rationale appears to be that . . . if a plea of extreme necessity is accepted by a multiplicity of governments, it is more likely to be believed than when asserted unilaterally by the government directly at interest."[38] The legitimacy obtained by demonstrating evidence only to one's friends or allies, however, is not likely to be authoritative with those who may have less reason or interest to grant one the benefit of the doubt. Being able to secure endorsements from a multiplicity of states may show only that one has more friends (or power), rather than that one's case is morally legitimate or credible.[39]

Even in the society of states, then, the authoritativeness of a jurying process for legitimizing "humanitarian interventions" will be hotly contested, given the power asymmetries, economic disparities, and ideological divides that mark the international arena. Law presupposes community, but as Judith Shklar has noted, "Law does not by itself generate institutions, cause wars to end, or states to behave as they should. It does not create a community."[40] Establishing a jurying process that would be credible to the wider society of states thus depends less on legal transformation than on significant political, social, and economic transformations within international society.

Franck suggests that there are actually three arenas where jurying of "humanitarian interventions" may occur: the International Court of Justice, international political forums such as the Security Council and General Assembly, and the court of public opinion.[41] His acknowledgment of the "court of public opinion" as another jurying arena exposes the limited nature of this discussion so far. My preceding arguments have assumed that the relevant community is the society of states; that society, however, does not exist in a vacuum but is embedded within a wider and more diverse cosmopolitan society encompassing all of humanity.

Indeed, since the 1990s one challenge to restrictive interpretations of international law that prohibit military interventions for humanitarian purposes has come from global civil society actors. As Adam Roberts has observed, the security problems encountered by nongovernmental humanitarian relief organizations attempting to deliver humanitarian assistance to populations in crisis have contributed to the development of a humanitarian rationale for military interventions.[42] This development shows that although the basis of legality in world politics may be located in the society of states, because states alone are the lawmakers of international society, the basis of moral legitimacy in world politics ultimately lies beyond that society, and this larger society is one source that provides direction and substance to changes in the legality and legitimacy of various state and interstate norms and practices.

Given the humanitarian justifications to be scrutinized, it would be reasonable to argue that it is not representatives of states but representatives of humanity that ought to form the jury. But where are these representatives? One might look for them in the emerging global nongovernmental organizations dedicated to the promotion of humanitarian and other aspects of a global "public interest."[43] There are, however, significant moral, and not just political, difficulties in designating nongovernmental organizations as potential jurors, given the uncertain character of their "public" status and authority and the lack of external accountability mechanisms for many such organizations. There is currently no institutional expression of global democracy that would support the idea of a global citizenry from which prospective nongovernmental jurors could be drawn.

Still, these problems are not insurmountable, nor are current institutional arrangements of global governance unalterable, and once one accepts the idea that states ought to answer not only to a select society of like units but to a wider cosmopolitan community, it becomes less clear why the jury for determining the legitimacy of "humanitarian interventions" must be restricted to current state representatives. The important point is that the jury, to be legally proper, must be legally defined, but like an ordinary jury in domestic trials, those who are legally appointed as jurors are drawn not from the ranks of government or the police but from the citizenry. The conduct of police officials is judged not only by internal review boards or other police organizations or members but also by civilian boards and courts, especially in circumstances involving the use of force. Police officers are not thought to be accountable only to other police officers; they are accountable to the wider society of citizens because it is on behalf of their moral interests and protection that police officers acquire the authority to use force. Similarly, states and their representatives are accountable to a wider community beyond the society of states because it is ultimately the moral interests and protection of the members of the wider community of humanity that ground the moral legitimacy of states' resort to force. If one accepts this interpretation of state accountability for the use of force, current jurying mechanisms that draw exclusively from the pool of current state representatives seem inherently biased.

The ICISS rigorously outlines key judgments that must be made in determining the legitimacy of any military action for humanitarian purposes. The jury must evaluate whether the "just cause threshold" ("large scale loss of life" or "large scale 'ethnic cleansing'") has been met; whether the intervener has the right intention ("to halt or avert human suffering"); whether the use of military force constitutes the last resort; and whether it is proportional to the scale of humanitarian catastrophe and can enjoy "a reasonable chance of success in halting or averting the suffering which has justified the intervention."[44] There is no principled reason why these issues cannot be adjudicated by a mixed group of past and current state and nongovernmental organizational and individual representatives. Just as arms control experts ought to be the recognized authorities on whether or not there are weapons of mass destruction in a given location, for example, a team of government and international organization representatives, along with experts on genocide and crimes against humanity, could constitute an authoritative adjudicative panel that determines whether a military intervention is necessary and justified in any particular case. Such an institutionalized mechanism of adjudicating international responses to humanitarian crises would make it less possible for states and international organizations to evade or distort their humanitarian responsibilities by obscuring or manipulating the facts of the case.

5. Conclusion

I have argued in this essay that the idea of common humanity underlying the concepts of humanitarianism and "humanitarian intervention" can be founded on a recognition of all human agents as social beings with the capacity for moral agency. It is plausible that a universal commitment to basic humanitarian norms that protect the security and dignity of persons can be forged from a convergence of diverse religious, philosophical, and cultural perspectives. A global order that affirms "our common humanity" must construct state sovereignty as the authority and responsibility of political agents and structures to protect the basic humanitarian interests of their members. An international society within such a global order acquires an obligation to confront and discipline irresponsible sovereigns that, through abuse or neglect, undermine the very conditions for human (social and moral) agency and responsibility. In some situations of humanitarian catastrophe, military action can be legitimately employed for humanitarian reasons, although the mechanisms of adjudication and legitimization of "humanitarian intervention" are contentious and underdeveloped in contemporary international society.

In the post–Cold War era military actions explicitly justified on humanitarian grounds gained legitimacy, but the mixed results of those interventions reveal the difficulty of matching consequences to intentions in the complicated political environments that generate humanitarian crises. The threat and use of force between states are well-worn, if not clearly effectual, roads to effecting desired political transformations. Even if one endorses the claims of common humanity, embraces the interpretation of "sovereignty as responsibility" to protect basic humanitarian interests, and deems authoritative current international mechanisms for adjudicating uses of force by states for humanitarian purposes, the question remains whether military force can ever be effectively employed in the name of common humanity. Pacifists are likely to answer in the negative, and it may be difficult to disagree with them when one views the inevitable record of sorrow, death, and destruction wrought by contemporary human warfare. Military intervention may be effective at changing the political status quo, but violence is an unpredictable teacher, and the indeterminacy of the lessons people learn from its use makes it a particularly risky and unreliable means of *directing* political transformation toward humanitarian ends. Nicholas Wheeler thus argues that the U.S. and U.N. intervention in Somalia in the early 1990s raises "the troubling question" of "whether the threat or use of force can ever promote conflict resolution in situations where societies are plunged into lawlessness as a consequence of civil war and the disintegration of state structures."[45]

The greatest challenge to the legitimacy of "humanitarian intervention," then, is a practical consideration. In the complicated and desperate political and social environments that culminate in humanitarian catastrophes, what are the prospects for a successful intervention? If success is measured in terms of stopping or averting the suffering that prompted the intervention, there are likely to be cases in which "humanitarian intervention" has a reasonable prospect of success. Dallaire, for example, has argued that a "humanitarian intervention" in the first weeks of April 1994 could have stopped the ensuing slaughter of 800,000 Rwandans; world leaders have since considered themselves blameworthy for this "failure of humanity in Rwanda."[46] Such an intervention, even if it did occur, however, might not have been enough to guarantee Rwandans security from future atrocities.

This is because the success of any "humanitarian intervention," measured in terms of its broader consequences for the establishment of accountable social structures that affirm the claims of common humanity, depends on international society's further commitment to meet "postintervention obligations" to rebuild the affected societies.[47] Without this commitment, "humanitarian interventions" are likely to become more necessary more often while being less and less effective in advancing humanitarian interests.[48] The tragic situation in Iraq shows that although military intervention may be successful in toppling domestic tyrants such as Saddam Hussein, it alone is unlikely to guarantee any progress toward a more humane or accountable political order. "Humanitarian interventions," even against abusive regimes, cannot be legitimate if they do not include a commitment of the required resources to meet postintervention obligations to help the affected population establish a better political alternative.

"Humanitarian intervention" as a concept and practice may thus involve a cruel set of ironies. The subject of "humanitarian intervention" enjoys moral salience only because the world in which we live is far removed from one that universally affirms the claims of common humanity. This is to say that "humanitarian intervention" illuminates the profoundly tragic contours of political and moral agency in a nonideal world of domestic and international political agents and structures that are morally limited, defective, and fallible. The effectiveness and hence legitimacy of "humanitarian interventions," however, depend on the extent to which the overall global order represents an accountable social structure that is morally responsive to the claims of common humanity. The conditions required to maximize the overall success and legitimacy of "humanitarian interventions" are also the conditions that would render them less necessary or in need of legitimization. Ironically, an increase in the number of legitimate "humanitarian interventions" therefore may not indicate progress toward a more humane and accountable world order founded on a respect for our common humanity; rather, it might actually signify moral regress and a decreasingly legitimate global order.

Furthermore, if the key to resolving humanitarian crises is to transform the contemporary global order toward a greater affirmation of our common humanity, "humanitarian intervention" cannot be the primary means of promoting such transformation. This is not only because military action produces inevitable humanity-depriving consequences; it is also because the use of force is largely irrelevant or inappropriate as a means to address the greatest assault on common humanity in contemporary times. As Thomas Pogge has observed, "Our present global economic order produces a stable pattern of widespread malnutrition and starvation among the poor, with some 18 million persons dying each year from poverty-related causes, and there are likely to be feasible alternative regimes that would not produce similarly severe deprivations."[49] A transformed world order founded upon a respect for our common humanity would be one in which such agency-depriving conditions were not tolerated as an acceptable or inevitable outcome of global economic structures. Commitment to our common humanity would require the world's politically and economically powerful to establish greater formal and substantive equality in the rules and institutions governing the society of states and the international economy, as well as to institutionalize a duty of assistance[50] to societies burdened by incompetent governance, toxic regimes, or the legacies of historical injustice.

Some might argue that global poverty is a problem distinct from the problem of violently abusive domestic tyrants, which typically generates calls for "humanitarian intervention," but the relation between these two faces of inhumanity may be deep. Because both constitute affronts to our common humanity, it is likely that the "change in moral consciousness"[51] required to mount legitimate "humanitarian interventions" is the same attitudinal change required to implement effective solutions to global poverty. More practically, if wealthier states and publics cannot bring themselves to make the material sacrifices required by a more equitable global economic order, it is difficult to see how they could be made to accept the burden of more significant sacrifices in terms of lives that would be required by any "humanitarian intervention."[52]

Some have also argued that ameliorating global economic disparities and their attendant human misery is key to preventing the kinds of political, social, and economic dysfunctions that degenerate into humanitarian crises. This line of argument understands the vindication of an agency-based view of common humanity to require the commitment of more attention and resources to preventive rather than ameliorative measures. As John Tirman has asked, "If obligations exist to ameliorate calamities underway, are there obligations to prevent calamities?"[53] The ICISS argues that prevention "is the single most important dimension of the responsibility to protect [and] more commitment and resources must be devoted to it."[54]

Focusing on preventive as opposed to reactive humanitarian measures raises contentious and complicated questions about causal and moral responsibility for humanitarian catastrophes. If one locates the causes of humanitarian crises in the global order itself, "humanitarian interventions" against irresponsible or negligent domestic tyrants can at best treat symptoms but not causes. At worst, a preoccupation with humanitarian crises and "humanitarian intervention" is actually a way for the rich and powerful to avoid their own culpability in constructing and maintaining a global order that consistently produces such tragedies. The focus on "humanitarian intervention" under this view betrays a faulty moral and causal assumption that humanitarian catastrophes "have everything to do with the dictator, the warlords, or the ethnic rivalries, and nothing to do with us in the Western democracies."[55]

I think it has to be admitted that the causes of humanitarian catastrophes are multiple and multilayered; in other words, there is usually enough blame to go around. For example, even though responsibility for the 1994 Rwandan genocide obviously lies with the individuals who planned, orchestrated, and conducted the mass slaughter, it would be difficult to explain how the genocide could have occurred without an account of nineteenth century European racial ideologies that informed Belgian colonial practices in Rwanda; the politics of resentment and exclusion following independence; the wedding of politics and violence in the post–Cold War democratization process; the context of civil war, started by exiled Tutsis of the Rwandan Patriotic Front in 1990, and the attendant social, political, and economic problems; the lack of moderating influences from external influential powers, such as the French, that could check extremist elements of the Habyarimana government; the decline of coffee prices and the implementation of World Bank structural adjustment policies that further exhausted the economy; as well as the weakness of international institutions such as the United Nations and the indifference of capable international agents such as the United States.[56]

Clearly, failures of humanity of the proportion of the Rwandan genocide require multiple failures at all levels of governance in practically every sphere of human relations. Moral condemnation of the direct perpetrators is not enough and constitutes only the first step toward preventing such failures from recurring. Effective prevention requires the institutionalization of a humane and accountable global order that is proactive rather than merely reactive in its vindication of the claims of common humanity. Meanwhile, in our nonideal world, reactive responses to unfolding humanitarian catastrophes are still necessary if largely inadequate; thus, sadly, the legitimacy of "humanitarian intervention" will likely remain a pertinent and important, if tortured, theme of normative inquiry in world politics.

NOTES

1. William Shakespeare, *The Tragedy of King Lear* (Scarborough, Ontario: New American Library of Canada, 1987), 4.1.36–37.

2. See United Nations Secretary-General Kofi Annan, Address to the 54th session of the UN General Assembly, 1999; and his Millennium Report to the General Assembly, 2000. Quoted in International Commission on Intervention and State Sovereignty (ICISS), *The Responsibility to Protect: Report of the International Commission on Intervention and State Sovereignty* (International Development Research Centre: Ottawa, December 2001), 2.

3. See Fiona Terry, *Condemned to Repeat? The Paradox of Humanitarian Action* (Ithaca: Cornell University Press, 2002).

4. Thucydides, *History of the Peloponnesian War*, trans. Rex Warner (Toronto: Penguin Canada, 1972), 407–8.

5. Martha Finnemore, "Constructing Norms of Humanitarian Intervention," in *The Culture of National Security: Norms and Identity in World Politics*, ed. Peter J. Katzenstein, 153–85 (New York: Columbia University Press, 1996), 163.

6. See Gérard Prunier, *The Rwanda Crisis: History of a Genocide* (New York: Columbia University Press, 1997), 234–36.

7. See the critiques in Martha Nussbaum, *For Love of Country: Debating the Limits of Patriotism*, ed. Joshua Cohen (Boston: Beacon Press, 1996).

8. See Charles Taylor, "Conditions of an Unforced Consensus on Human Rights," in *The East Asian Challenge for Human Rights*, ed. Joanne R. Bauer and Daniel A. Bell, 124–44 (Cambridge: Cambridge University Press, 1999).

9. Quoted in Nicholas J. Wheeler, *Saving Strangers: Humanitarian Intervention in International Society* (Oxford: Oxford University Press, 2000), 196.

10. Elaine Scarry has argued that torture, or a willful attack on bodily integrity and decisional agency, unmakes the individual self as well as the social world of which the individual was a part. Scarry, *The Body in Pain: The Making and Unmaking of the World* (Oxford: Oxford University Press, 1985), 45–51. On the agency-denying effects of totalitarian systems, see Primo Levi, *The Drowned and the Saved*, trans. Raymond Rosenthal (New York: Vintage International, 1989). On humans as self-interpreting agents, see Charles Taylor, "What Is Human Agency?" and "Self-interpreting Animals," in *Human Agency and Language: Philosophical Papers I* (Cambridge: Cambridge University Press, 1999), 15–76.

11. Judith N. Shklar, "The Liberalism of Fear," in *Liberalism and the Moral Life*, ed. Nancy Rosenblum, 21–38 (Cambridge: Harvard University Press, 1989), 21.

12. Ibid., 28–31.

13. Judith N. Shklar, *Ordinary Vices* (Cambridge: Harvard University Press, 1984), 5.

14. Shakespeare, *King Lear*, 3.4.107–8.

15. Oliver Ramsbotham and Tom Woodhouse, *Humanitarian Intervention in Contemporary Conflict: A Reconceptualization* (Cambridge: Polity Press, 1996), 9–10.

16. The mere existence of such rules reveals war to be an activity conducted by human agents with the capacity for moral agency and, therefore, for incurring moral responsibility.

17. The principle of humanity, so described, is found in *The Fundamental Principles of the International Red Cross and Red Crescent Movement* (proclaimed by the XXth International Conference of the Red Cross, Geneva, 1965). See Ramsbotham and Woodhouse, *Humanitarian Intervention in Contemporary Conflict*, 14–16.

18. In addition to the 1945 United Nations Charter and 1948 Universal Declaration of Human Rights, we can include the 1926 Covenant to Suppress the Slave Trade and Slavery; the 1948 Convention on the Prevention and Punishment of the Crime of Genocide; the 1966 International Convention on the Elimination of All Forms of Racial Discrimination; and the 1984 U.N. Convention against Torture and Other Cruel, Inhuman or Degrading Treatment.

19. Robert Jackson, *The Global Covenant: Human Conduct in a World of States* (Oxford: Oxford University Press, 2000), 43.

20. For a more elaborate discussion of "sovereignty as privacy," see Catherine Lu, "Intervention and the Public/Private Distinction in World Politics: A Normative Inquiry" (PhD diss., University of Toronto, 2000).

21. Quoted in Hilary Charlesworth, "Worlds Apart: Public/Private Distinctions in International Law," in *Public and Private: Feminist Legal Debates,* ed. Margaret Thornton (Melbourne, Australia: Oxford University Press, 1995), 244.

22. Writing in the sixteenth century, Jean Bodin asserted, "[T]he well-ordered family is a true image of the commonwealth, and domestic comparable with sovereign authority." See Bodin, *Six Books of the Commonwealth,* trans. M. J. Tooley (Oxford: Basil Blackwell, 1955), 6. More recently, Jackson has noted explicitly, "States, like houses, are human constructs: they are built on a piece of land to provide a home for certain people who become the resident population." Jackson, *The Global Covenant,* 29.

23. Elizabeth Pleck, *Domestic Tyranny: The Making of Social Policy against Family Violence from Colonial Times to the Present* (New York: Oxford University Press, 1987), 7.

24. Roméo Dallaire with Brent Beardsley, *Shake Hands With the Devil: The Failure of Humanity in Rwanda* (Toronto: Random House Canada, 2003), 375. Italics mine.

25. The usual cases cited include India's intervention in Pakistan in 1971 that led to the creation of Bangladesh; Vietnam's intervention in Cambodia in 1979 that overthrew the genocidal Pol Pot regime; and Tanzania's intervention in Uganda in 1979 that ousted the dictator Idi Amin. See Wheeler, *Saving Strangers;* and Michael Akehurst, "Humanitarian Intervention," in *Intervention in World Politics,* ed. Hedley Bull, 95–118 (Oxford: Clarendon Press, 1986), 95–99.

26. As Ramsbotham and Woodhouse have noted, "A general conclusion on state reaction to massive human rights violations during the Cold War era would have to be that the normal response was to do nothing. Not only were instances of forcible intervention rare, but even formal protest and the initiation of collective measures through recognized human rights procedures were seldom and, even then, only reluctantly invoked." Ramsbotham and Woodhouse, *Humanitarian Intervention in Contemporary Conflict*, 56.

27. In some ways, this shift does not constitute a dramatic discontinuity in the moral foundation of world order. Indeed, the Westphalian conception of sovereignty developed in a context of universals. For example, Bodin defined sovereignty as "that absolute and perpetual power vested in a commonwealth," but he stressed that if "we insist however that absolute power means exemption from all law whatsoever, there is no prince in the world who can be regarded as sovereign, since all the princes of the earth are subject to the laws of God and nature, and even to certain *human* laws common to all nations." Bodin, *Six Books of the Commonwealth*, 25 and 28.

28. ICISS, *Responsibility to Protect*, xi. Italics mine.

29. Hedley Bull, *The Anarchical Society: A Study of Order in World Politics* (New York: Columbia University Press, 1977), 152.

30. See Jutta Brunnée and Stephen Toope, "Slouching towards New 'Just' Wars: The Hegemon after September 11th," *International Relations* 18, no. 4 (2004): 405–23.

31. For a thorough critique of positivist and realist accounts of law, see Judith N. Shklar, *Legalism: Law, Morals and Political Trials* (Cambridge: Harvard University Press, 1986 [1964]).

32. See Thomas Franck, "Interpretation and Change in the Law of Humanitarian Intervention," in *Humanitarian Intervention: Ethical, Legal, and Political Dilemmas*, ed. J. L. Holzgrefe and Robert O. Keohane, 204–31 (Cambridge: Cambridge University Press, 2003), 204.

33. Thomas Franck, "Legality and Legitimacy in Humanitarian Intervention," this volume, chap. 5, 147.

34. Franck, "Interpretation and Change in the Law of Humanitarian Intervention," 205.

35. Franck, "Legality and Legitimacy in Humanitarian Intervention," 148.

36. Michael Byers and Simon Chesterman, "Changing the Rules about Rules? Unilateral Humanitarian Intervention and the Future of International Law," in *Humanitarian Intervention: Ethical, Legal, and Political Dilemmas*, 177–203 at 193.

37. Byers and Chesterman argue that "providing a formal exception

for a powerful state (or states) to violate rules that continue to apply to all other actors severely undermines respect for a particular rule and for international law more generally. It would probably also encourage violations of the law—at least insofar as the capacity to violate the law and get away with it was the benchmark of being a 'leading state.'" Ibid., 197.

38. Franck, "Legality and Legitimacy in Humanitarian Intervention," 154.

39. As Byers and Chesterman have noted, to secure enhanced legitimacy for Operation Desert Storm to repel Iraq's invasion of Kuwait, "the United States made various promises to resume normal trade relations, provide aid, support World Bank loans, and exclude certain states from international conferences in order to secure the adoption of Security Council Resolution 678 in November 1990 . . . It is [also] well known that Yemen lost US $70 million in annual aid from the United States because of its vote against Resolution 678." See Byers and Chesterman, "Changing the Rules about Rules?" 192.

40. Shklar, *Legalism,* 131.

41. Franck, "Interpretation and Change in the Law of Humanitarian Intervention," 228.

42. Adam Roberts, "Humanitarian Issues and Agencies as Triggers for International Military Action," in *Civilians in War,* ed. Simon Chesterman, 177–96 (Boulder: Lynne Rienner, 2001).

43. It is not that in a state-centric jury model, nongovernmental organizations would have no role; their representatives could be (and have been) called as expert witnesses. Decisional agency, however, is denied to them.

44. ICISS, *Responsibility to Protect,* xii.

45. Wheeler, *Saving Strangers,* 206.

46. Dallaire, *Shake Hands with the Devil,* 515–16. In a visit to Rwanda four years after the genocide, U.S. President Bill Clinton expressed his regret for the unresponsiveness of the international community. See Wheeler, *Saving Strangers,* 240.

47. See ICISS, *Responsibility to Protect,* 39–46.

48. Similarly, familial domestic violence cannot be resolved by repeated police interventions alone; changing the dynamics of such families requires a much wider social effort, including the assistance of teachers, doctors, social workers, and children's aid societies, and the support of friends, employers, and neighborhood associations.

49. See Thomas Pogge, *World Poverty and Human Rights* (Cambridge: Polity Press, 2002), 176.

50. See John Rawls, *The Law of Peoples* (Cambridge: Harvard University Press, 1999).

51. Wheeler, *Saving Strangers*, 310.

52. On the limits of sacrifice, see ibid., 299–310.

53. John Tirman, "The New Humanitarianism: How Military Intervention Became the Norm," *Boston Review* 28, no. 6 (December 2003/January 2004), available at http://bostonreview.net/BR28.6/tirman.html.

54. ICISS, *Responsibility to Protect*, xi.

55. Tirman, "The New Humanitarianism." As he puts this argument, "[H]umanitarianism itself is seen then as the superficial if pervasive policing (i.e., intervention) of the complex and often deteriorating situations that liberal economic and political governance (i.e., globalization) has been so intimately involved in creating."

56. See Prunier, *The Rwanda Crisis*; Dallaire, *Shake Hands with the Devil*; Mahmood Mamdani, *When Victims Become Killers: Colonialism, Nativism, and the Genocide in Rwanda* (Princeton: Princeton University Press, 2001); and Michael Barnett, *Eyewitness to a Genocide: The United Nations and Rwanda* (Ithaca: Cornell University Press, 2002).

8

JURYING HUMANITARIAN INTERVENTION AND THE ETHICAL PRINCIPLE OF OPEN-MINDED CONSULTATION

BRIAN D. LEPARD

[The General Assembly recommends] to the permanent members of the Security Council that . . . [t]hey meet and discuss, collectively or otherwise, and, if necessary, with other States concerned, all problems which are likely to threaten international peace and hamper the activities of the United Nations, with a view to their resolving fundamental differences and reaching agreement in accordance with the spirit and letter of the Charter.
—U.N. General Assembly, Uniting for Peace Resolution, 1950

[C]onsultation must have for its object the investigation of truth. He who expresses an opinion should not voice it as correct and right but set it forth as a contribution to the consensus of opinion. . . . Before expressing his own views he should carefully consider the views already advanced by others. If he finds that a previously expressed opinion is more true and worthy, he should accept it immediately and not willfully hold to an opinion of his own. By this excellent method he endeavors to arrive at unity and truth.
—The Bahá'í Sacred Writings[1]

Professor Thomas Franck has written in this volume a compelling essay on the legality and legitimacy of humanitarian intervention. In that essay he advocates the need for a credible "jurying" process to apply international rules relevant to humanitarian

217

intervention to particular cases and also to "close the gap" between the letter of the law and what he refers to as "common sense and morality." He suggests that a variety of international institutions, including the United Nations Security Council and certain regional organizations, such as the Economic Community of West African States (ECOWAS) and the North Atlantic Treaty Organization (NATO), are making strides toward fulfillment of a legitimate jurying function. And he highlights some of the characteristics he thinks a jurying procedure ought to exemplify in order to have widespread credibility. These include a jury whose members share a sense of social cohesion and are aware that they do, are willing to be detached and not to pursue "preordained outcomes," and have been chosen in a fair manner that does not give a disproportionate voice to members of any economic, social, or political group.[2]

In this essay, I would like to take Franck's astute analysis as a point of departure for an exploration of one feature of a jurying function regarding humanitarian intervention that I believe is particularly essential for such a process to lead to desirable decisions from an ethical perspective and for it to be perceived as legitimate. That feature is a process of decision making in which participants are willing to put aside self-interest in favor of an open-minded search for all relevant facts and for the best solution, morally, to the problems that give rise to the perceived possibility of military intervention—a search that includes the active solicitation of and learning from the views of others. I will refer to such a process as one of "open-minded consultation."

Open-minded consultation is particularly important in dealing with issues relating to humanitarian intervention because of the intense ethical conflicts that these issues arouse. These include, for example, conflicts between the norms of sovereignty and nonintervention and between the effective enforcement of international human rights standards and the preservation of peace. Only a full exploration of all angles of a problem, with a receptivity on the part of all relevant actors to new perspectives and information, can allow these conflicts to be mitigated and a decision best accommodating these competing norms and values to be reached.

In the following sections I will first describe open-minded consultation in more detail, explain its character as an ethical principle, and demonstrate that it finds support in both international law and many of the world's major religious and philosophical traditions. I will also show that we can understand open-minded consultation as the ideal form of decision making by juries and explore some elements of it based on theories about the ideals of jury deliberations.

I will then suggest ways in which the ethical principle of open-minded consultation ought to inform and affect decision making concerning humanitarian intervention. In particular, I will propose that it support respect for laws (including the U.N. Charter) relating to humanitarian intervention that have been drafted through such a process of full and open discussion. It also implies that we should give special deference to procedures that contemplate open-minded consultation among diverse states. The principle further requires bodies and institutions such as the U.N. Security Council, which have legal discretion to determine whether and how to intervene, to engage in a serious and open-minded dialogue about those issues, detached, insofar as realistically possible, from the self-oriented concerns of their members. It also is a counsel to institutions (again including the U.N. Security Council) charged with the interpretation or application of legal norms relating to humanitarian intervention. And, as experience has shown, existing laws must often be revised to address more effectively the needs of contemporary society. Again, any such revisions are best made through full and open-minded consultation. Finally, the principle of open-minded consultation requires that decision makers who have the power to determine when violations of the law ethically may be excused make these weighty decisions through that same process.

1. DEFINING THE ETHICAL PRINCIPLE OF OPEN-MINDED CONSULTATION

The ethical principle of open-minded consultation is a logical corollary, as I have argued in my previous writings,[3] of an ethical principle of "unity in diversity." According to that principle, all human beings ought morally to be viewed as members of one human family that is enriched by the diversity of individuals, communities, races, nationalities, classes, and creeds that compose it. Thus, diversity is desirable, but only when it is appreciated within a larger framework of global unity. The principle of open-minded consultation flows from this conception of human relationships. It requires that at all levels of society human beings welcome the opinions of others from diverse backgrounds, listen actively to their views, and strive together with them in a spirit of cooperation to ascertain solutions to the problems that they all face. It also requires that participants be willing to modify their original opinions and positions through this interactive, collaborative exchange of perspectives.

Importantly, open-minded consultation can result in decisions that are ethically sounder because they consciously take into account the perspectives of many different actors and address many different ethical views. Open-minded consultation represents, to borrow the words of psychologist Lawrence Kohlberg, a form of "moral musical chairs."[4] According to philosopher Jürgen Habermas, "Each of us must be able to place himself in the situation of all those who would be affected by the performance of the problematic action or the adoption of a questionable norm."[5] Furthermore, he emphasizes, in keeping with the concept of consultation as mutual dialogue, that such "ideal role taking cannot be performed privately by each individual but must be practiced by us *collectively* as participants in a public discourse."[6]

Although not all decisions arrived at through open-minded consultation are necessarily morally right according to a particular set of normative principles—and certainly some decisions on which agreement is reached can be blatantly morally wrong—if the participants in consultation are motivated by belief in a reasonably defensible set of moral principles, their consensus stands a better chance than the views of any single actor of best implementing those moral principles.[7] Moreover, open-minded consultation can assist in the more accurate ascertainment of objective facts as well as in the solution of moral problems. It does so by bringing to light many different perceptions of reality, all of which may incorporate some objective element of that reality. And moral decision making is enhanced to the extent that it is based on more accurate perceptions of the facts underlying the moral decisions involved.

Recognition of an ethical principle of open-minded consultation is implied in various key international legal documents. For example, the U.N. Charter explains that its purposes include to develop "friendly relations among nations" and to achieve "international co-operation in solving international problems." The Charter also describes the U.N. as "a centre for harmonizing the actions of nations in the attainment of these common ends."[8] These references to friendly relations, cooperation, and harmonization all support an ethical principle of open-minded consultation on global issues such as humanitarian intervention. Indeed, the Charter creates important organs—including the General Assembly and the Security Council—in which such open discussion and consultation are expected to take place.[9] These organs are designed to have a diverse membership representing many regions of the world and, implicitly, many different viewpoints. The General Assembly comprises representatives of all U.N. member states;[10] the Security Council currently has fifteen members drawn from five major regions of the world, and includes five permanent members (China, France, Russia, the United Kingdom, and the United States) that often themselves manifest differing perspectives.[11]

Although realists might view these organs as simply additional fora in which states are expected to pursue their narrow self-interest, many U.N. resolutions support the ideal of states engaging in open-minded consultation in these bodies with the purpose of reaching a common agreement on solutions to global dilemmas. For example, the Uniting for Peace Resolution, adopted by the General Assembly in 1950, emphasized "the importance of unanimity among the permanent members of the Security Council on all problems which are likely to threaten world peace." In that resolution, the General Assembly further recommended to the permanent members, as quoted in the epigraph of this essay, that they "meet and discuss, collectively or otherwise, and, if necessary, with other States concerned, all problems which are likely to threaten international peace and hamper the activities of the United Nations, with a view to their resolving fundamental differences and reaching agreement in accordance with the spirit and letter of the Charter."[12]

As already indicated, a number of philosophers have argued

in favor of practical discourse as a means of resolving ethical problems. For example, Jürgen Habermas has developed a theory of "discourse ethics" that incorporates many of the key features of the ethical principle of open-minded consultation I have described.[13]

If an ethical principle of open-minded consultation is emerging in international legal sources and has been articulated in the philosophical literature, so also can it find support in selected passages from the revered scriptures of various world religions. This support may provide the basis for practical agreement on the moral importance of the principle among adherents to multifarious religions and ideologies.[14] To offer just a few examples, the Torah of Judaism affirms that one should "not be partial in judgment" but, rather, "hear out low and high alike."[15] According to Buddhist scriptures, the Buddha encouraged his followers to be open to different points of view and to refrain from quarreling. One way he did so was through the parable of the blind men and the elephant, in which a number of blind men each felt a different part of an elephant—the head, the trunk, an ear—and argued that his perception alone of what an elephant is was correct, whereas in fact they all accurately perceived different elements of the reality of the elephant.[16] Confucius, in the Analects, consistently urged individuals to be humble about their own opinions, to learn from others, and constantly to seek to overcome their own shortcomings.[17] Likewise, according to the New Testament, Jesus counseled humility.[18] And there may be support for the concept of open-minded consultation in the following passage from the writings of Saint Paul:

> When you come together, each one has a hymn, a lesson, a revelation, a tongue, or an interpretation. . . . Let two or three prophets speak, and let the others weigh what is said. If a revelation is made to someone else sitting nearby, let the first person be silent. For you can all prophesy one by one, so that all may learn and all be encouraged.[19]

In Islam, the Qur'ān exhorts believers to consult with others: "[T]ake counsel with them in the affair; and when thou art resolved, put thy trust in God."[20] And a tradition recounts that Muhammad instructed his followers to resolve problems that might arise after his death through open-minded consultation: "Get together amongst my followers and place the matter before them for consultation. Do not make decisions on the opinions of any single person."[21] The Sacred Writings of the Bahá'í Faith likewise call for open-minded consultation as an organizing principle of social life, as indicated in the epigraph of this essay. In addition, the prophet-founder of the Bahá'í Faith, Bahá'u'lláh, affirmed, "Take ye counsel together in all matters, inasmuch as consultation is the lamp of guidance which leadeth the way, and is the bestower of understanding."[22]

2. OPEN-MINDED CONSULTATION AND THE IDEALS OF JURY DELIBERATION

The ideal of open-minded consultation also finds expression in domestic legal systems, including the American jury system. Franck's metaphor of a "jury" is particularly apt in describing and understanding the ethical principle of open-minded consultation because open-minded consultation is exactly the form of deliberation in which ideally we expect jurors to engage. That is, we expect jurors (1) to approach a trial with open minds and to be able to put aside their self-interest in arriving at a decision; (2) to be prejudice free; (3) to be open to receiving new information that may contradict their previous beliefs; (4) to express freely their opinions, while also being willing to learn from the opinions and perspectives of fellow jurors, and to adjust or even abandon their initial views as a result of the jury's deliberations rather than adhere arbitrarily to a position they formulated when they entered the jury room; (5) to have concern for accurately ascertaining relevant facts and for reaching a just decision based on those facts; and (6) to have significant regard for the need for the jury to reach a consensus on the facts and the appropriate judicial disposition of the case, and not arbitrarily to "hold out."

A number of academic commentators have elaborated on the ideal of open-minded consultation in jury deliberations. For example, psychologists Saul M. Kassin and Lawrence S. Wrightsman have identified three ideals of jury decision making.[23] First, jurors are to be independent and equal. Second, jurors have a responsibility to be open-minded and to consider the views of other jurors with a willingness to be persuaded. And third, jurors should not be pressured by other jurors.

Turning to the first ideal, one implication of the principle that all jurors are equal is that all jurors should have access to the same information through the trial. Furthermore, the typical prohibition on discussion among jurors during the trial phase helps to ensure that jurors develop their own unique perspectives on the case and fosters "the diversity of the group as a whole."[24]

According to the second ideal, jurors are expected to engage in open-minded deliberation and to be willing to revise their own initial opinions through dialogue with the other jurors. In the words of Kassin and Wrightsman:

> Once inside the jury room, jurors have a duty to interact and discuss the case. They should share information, exchange views, and debate the evidence. . . . Two essential characteristics of an ideal jury follow from the requirement of deliberation. One is that jurors maintain an open mind, that each juror withhold judgment until "an impartial consideration of the evidence with *his fellow jurors.*" . . . The second is that consensus should be achieved through an exchange of information. Jurors should scrutinize their own views, be receptive to others', and allow themselves to be persuaded by rational argument.[25]

The U.S. Supreme Court itself has upheld this ideal of open-minded deliberation. In the case of *Allen v. United States*, it stated:

> The very object of the jury system is to secure unanimity by a comparison of views, and by arguments among the jurors themselves. It certainly cannot be the law that each juror should not listen with deference to the arguments and with a distrust of his own judgment, if he finds a large majority of the jury taking a different view of the case from what he does himself. It cannot be that each juror should go to the jury-room with a blind determination that the verdict shall represent his opinion of the case at that moment; or, that he should close his ears to the arguments of men who are equally honest and intelligent as himself.[26]

One aspect of open-mindedness is that jurors must strive to be impartial and must leave their personal interests aside when they consult in the jury room. As stated by the Supreme Court in another case, impartiality "is a state of mind" that requires a "mental attitude of appropriate indifference."[27]

In a recent study of the American jury system, Randolph N. Jonakait emphasizes the process of open-minded deliberation and explains how it differs from the more common types of decision making used in American political life, including campaigning, bargaining, vote trading, and the like. He writes,

> [The] traditional requirement of jury unanimity produces a kind of consideration and debate unknown in other governmental bodies, a process that helps force a jury to assess thoroughly the information and its implications. . . . A juror has to try to persuade all jurors who disagree with him to his point of view. He cannot do this by offering some incentive unrelated to the case. He cannot offer a vote swap on some other matter. He cannot appeal to the jurors' past decisions. He cannot trot out concerns for upcoming elections. Although exceptions do occur, the juror's only legitimate path of persuasion centers on the presented evidence. Furthermore, since each juror has to be concerned about convincing others, the group's various perspectives and memories about the evidence are likely to emerge for all to consider.[28]

Jonakait also points out that jury deliberations constitute a dynamic process of listening and reevaluation of one's own views:

> A juror will not be persuasive unless he responds to what the others are saying. Within such a process, all views are likely to be truly considered by the entire body. Such give-and-take does even more. It undercuts rigid dogmatism, for by being forced to listen to others so that rational—hence, persuasive—responses can be made, the persuader puts himself in the position of also being persuaded.[29]

Melissa S. Williams makes similar points in her study of the right to fair legislative representation. Focusing on legislative decision-making rather than juries, she contrasts what she calls a "deliberative" model of legislative decision making with a "competitive" model, and classifies jury decision-making as an example of the deliberative model. Under the competitive model, "representatives act as aggressive advocates for the interests of their constituents against the interests that compete with them." By contrast, in a deliberative model, "representatives aim at reaching agreement through exchanging different perspectives on the common interest and the place of particular interests within it."[30]

The third ideal identified by Kassin and Wrightsman is that although "juries should strive for a consensus of opinion, it should *not* be achieved through heavy-handed normative pressure. Obviously, jurors who dissent from the majority position should not be beaten, bullied, or harangued into submission."[31] Each juror should vote based on his or her own conscience. However, each juror should also make an appropriate effort to reach a consensus with the other jurors. He or she should not arbitrarily "stonewall." This ideal is reflected in a charge that, in many federal circuits, can be given to a deadlocked jury. It is based on the instructions approved in *Allen*, and thus is often referred to as an *Allen* charge. In the *Allen* case, the Supreme Court explained that the instructions at issue were

> that in a large proportion of cases absolute certainty could not be expected; that although the verdict must be the verdict of each individual juror, and not a mere acquiescence in the conclusion of his fellows, yet they should examine the question submitted with candor and with a proper regard and deference to the opinions of each other; that it was their duty to decide the case if they could conscientiously do so; that they should listen, with a disposition to be convinced, to each other's arguments; that, if much the larger number were for conviction, a dissenting juror should consider whether his doubt was a reasonable one which made no impression upon the minds of so many men, equally honest, equally intelligent with himself. If, upon the other hand, the majority was for acquittal, the minority ought to ask themselves whether they might not reasonably doubt the correctness of a judgment which was not concurred in by the majority.[32]

With respect to the composition of juries, it is generally accepted that we can have more faith in the ethical soundness or justice of decisions of juries that represent a diverse cross-section of the community and that exemplify different racial and ethnic backgrounds, different social groups, and different age groups, and on which both men and women serve. This is often referred to as the "cross-sectional ideal."[33] We value this diversity in part because it ensures that a variety of perspectives will be brought to bear during the jury's deliberations, giving us greater confidence in the ethical justifiability of any consensual view arrived at through those deliberations. However, we can have such confidence only if the diverse participants pursue open-minded consultation, as just described, rather than engage in the type of competitive politics described by Williams that aims to promote the interests of oneself or the group with which one identifies. Franck touches on these points in his emphasis on the importance of how juries are constituted and on the need for confidence that they will apply the law fairly. Under the view presented here, the cross-sectional ideal and open-minded consultation are both essential elements of a credible jurying process and work hand-in-hand.

With respect to the cross-sectional ideal, political scientist Jeffrey Abramson, in a study of the jury system and democracy, has described a historical evolution in ideals of jury decision making from a classic model in which jurors adopt an impartial mind-set, even though they may have a homogenous social background (educated, male, and white), to a model that seeks out greater diversity of jurors but with the expectation that they will engage in open-minded deliberation (as advocated here), and finally, to a model in which a cross-sectional jury is intended "to give voice or representation to competing group loyalties."[34] He advocates a return to the "middle" model.[35] According to this model:

> The worthy vision was never one of the races and sexes voting their preconceived preferences through their juror representatives. Rather, the democratic aim of the cross-sectional jury was to enhance the quality of deliberation by bringing diverse insights to bear on the evidence, each newly evaluating the case in light of some neglected detail or fresh perspective that a juror from another background offered the group.[36]

This is the vision most in keeping with the ethical principle of open-minded consultation.

Of course, the American ideal of jury deliberations is by no means a perfect manifestation of the ethical principle of open-minded consultation. For example, jury deliberations usually take place in secret, and the U.S. legal system carefully regulates the way in which information is provided to jurors, rather than permitting them freely to ask questions and seek out all relevant information on their own. Furthermore, jurors are not "accountable": they do not have to explain in a well-reasoned way how they reached their collective decision or the grounds for that decision. And jurors' deliberations are episodic, rather than dynamic; jurors are brought together to decide a single case and then disband afterward. There is no opportunity for continuous learning through ongoing interaction and dialogue. Finally, jurors in many jurisdictions are required to make their decisions unanimously, but the principle of open-minded consultation would allow room for decisions by a majority or supermajority. Open-minded consultation certainly need not, and in many cases should not, be regulated by restrictions like these.

3. OPEN-MINDED CONSULTATION AND RESPECT FOR LAWS REGULATING HUMANITARIAN INTERVENTION

Otto von Bismarck is reputed to have said that laws are like sausage; it is better for our health (and sanity) not to know how they are made. The business of making laws, including international treaties like the U.N. Charter, is in fact often a messy one, involving the clash of differing political interests and "backroom" compromises having nothing to do with moral principles. And yet, like the intervention of the U.S. Department of Agriculture (USDA) in supervising the making of sausage, there are forces that try to clean up some of the more unhealthy aspects of the business.

One of those forces, which can coexist alongside the battle of competing self-interest, is that of open-minded consultation. Many deliberations, including debates on the drafting of treaties such as the U.N. Charter, in fact manifest a combination of the pursuit of self-interest and relatively open-minded consultation with a view to searching for consensus based on moral ideals. In the words of Williams, "[I]nstitutions that foster deliberation [such as juries] use a mix of appeals to higher principles and reliance on parties' narrow self-interest. Consequently it is as imprudent to be too pessimistic about the capacity of human beings to put aside partial and selfish interests in the name of a shared interest in justice as it is to be overly optimistic."[37] In this connection, there is evidence that juries are able to fulfill the ideal of open-minded consultation relatively successfully. According to jury experts Valerie P. Hans and Neil Vidmar, most often juries reach a verdict through "spirited and dedicated discussion among jurors with conflicting views [that] forges common ground with which they can all agree."[38] There is similar evidence with respect to the drafting of multilateral treaties like the U.N. Charter, as I will discuss below. And just as we can have more faith in the safety of USDA-inspected sausage, or jury verdicts resulting from intense and open-minded deliberations, we can have greater confidence in the ethical soundness of international treaties that have been drafted through full and open discussions among diverse participants. We can do so even if the views of those participants are always colored to some degree by their perceived self-interest.

As Franck points out, the U.N. Charter does in fact contain a number of rules that are relevant to humanitarian intervention, and they are relatively straightforward. Thus, Article 2(4) requires U.N. members to "refrain in their international relations from the threat or use of force against the territorial integrity or political independence of any state, or in any other manner inconsistent with the Purposes of the United Nations."[39]

There are two major exceptions to this blanket prohibition of the threat or use of force by a U.N. member state—a prohibition that Franck refers to as an "idiot" rule because of its simplicity. First, each state under Article 51 retains an "inherent right of individual or collective self-defense" if an armed attack occurs against it, but only until such time as "the Security Council has taken measures necessary to maintain international peace and security."[40] Second, the Security Council under Chapter VII of the Charter has the authority to determine that a situation constitutes a threat to the peace, a breach of the peace, or an act of aggression, and to recommend or decide on appropriate measures, including the use of armed force, in response to such a situation.[41] This was the authority invoked by the Council in authorizing humanitarian intervention missions in Somalia and Haiti, for example. In this connection, Chapter VIII of the Charter envisages enforcement action under regional arrangements or by regional agencies but provides in Article 53 that "no enforcement action shall be taken" under these arrangements or by these agencies "without the authorization of the Security Council."[42]

Taken together, these rules allow states to use force in emergency situations involving an armed attack against themselves or another state but otherwise require that any use of force by states individually or by regional agencies be authorized by the Security Council. This, in turn, requires some degree of discussion and debate (and perhaps even open-minded consultation) among Council members, who themselves represent diverse regions of the world.

A review of the debates during the drafting of the above-mentioned provisions of the U.N. Charter discloses that these provisions were not, at bottom, the dust and debris that results from an unregulated battle of state self-interest. They were instead, in large part, the product of considered, though often passionate, discussion among states representing a variety of points of view, many of whom took positions that apparently contradicted their self-interest. The debates on these provisions, including the foundational Articles 2(4) and 53, were extensive and protracted, and they covered many relevant aspects of the problem of whether and when the unilateral use of force by states or regional organizations ought to be legal. Although the delegates at San Francisco did not focus on the legality of humanitarian intervention as such, their discussions certainly touched on this issue.[43] In short, the debates at San Francisco reflected at least in part the ideal of open-minded consultation. Furthermore, the delegates represented many regions of the world, though obviously not the yet-to-be independent colonies of the great powers. Those debates thus fulfilled at least in large part a cross-sectional ideal similar to that which we recognize for juries.

Certain fundamental changes in the structure of international society have obviously taken place since 1945, but as emphasized by Franck, these changes have not significantly altered the political context of the ethical problem of whether and when humanitarian intervention ought to be allowed. Such intervention may occur in states that have now won their independence from the colonial powers that existed in 1945, and may be undertaken by states that have more or less military or economic power than they had in 1945 (or even by states that did not yet then exist). But the questions of whether unauthorized intervention by a state on behalf of human rights victims in another ought to be allowed, or of how the (admittedly larger) international community ought to decide when some form of collective intervention is warranted, are largely fraught with the same ethical dilemmas as in 1945. Massive human rights violations, as well as terrorism, were well known to the leaders of the postwar world.

For these reasons, the product of the thoughtful discussion that took place in 1945 and that was formalized in the rules of the Charter should not be cast aside as obsolete. Rather, as inhabitants of the twenty-first century, we ought to reflect on the factors that prompted our predecessors to adopt the Charter norms under which we now live and at least take them seriously, even if some of these norms may need revision.

Indeed, the rules that resulted from the consultations that took place in 1945—which were at least partially "open-minded"—reflect a balanced, reasoned, and nuanced approach to the problem of regulating military action by states. The rules, taken together, are, in Franck's lexicon, "sophist" rules. In general, they prohibit intervention, including on humanitarian grounds, by individual states or by regional organizations without prior approval of the Security Council because of the danger, as history has often poignantly shown, that humanitarian concerns may be invoked to justify military ventures that are not so purely motivated. However, the rules do not shut the door completely on humanitarian intervention; on the contrary, the Charter permits such intervention to occur, but only with the authorization of the U.N. Security Council. As Franck notes, the Security Council constitutes a nascent international "jury." It represents, as mentioned above, five broad regions of the world as well as five permanent members with diverse interests, thus fulfilling to a large extent (though not perfectly) a cross-sectional ideal. Such an authorization procedure is ethically defensible because it at least implicitly contemplates open-minded consultation among Council members representing a cross-section of U.N. member states, and thus increases the chances that humanitarian intervention will be undertaken when necessary.

This consultative decision procedure also increases the probability that intervention will be the product of an exchange of diverse perspectives, all of which may represent a glimpse of an angle of truth. It, in principle, allows "good sense" and even morality to prevail, and it permits the flexibility that Franck emphasizes is necessary to deal with the kinds of problems that could not have been contemplated by the Charter's framers. It is a way of "closing the gap" between law and the "prevalent sense of justice, morality and common sense" referred to by Franck. Franck notes that, in practice, the Security Council has sometimes been able to help close this gap. The Charter's prescribed procedure for the lawful use of force also constitutes a form of "safety valve," permitting intervention to take place so long as a sufficient number of Council members (including all five permanent members) believe that intervention is appropriate under the circumstances.

Of course, the permanent-member veto may often block action approved of by a majority of the Security Council's members, and this is morally problematic in light of the principle of open-minded consultation. But the system erected in 1945 is certainly not ethically irrelevant or unjustifiable.

Further, there are reasons to prefer the Security Council as a "jury," rather than individual regional organizations, such as NATO or ECOWAS, acting without Security Council approval. These regional organizations may be more or less representative of states in their respective regions but naturally do not reflect the views of states outside the region, which may have valuable perspectives to offer. This is another reason to give deference to the judgment made by the Charter's framers, reflected in Article 53, that the Council, as a body representing all major regions of the world, should have the final authority in determining whether and when the use of force by states or regional organizations is justified.

4. OPEN-MINDED CONSULTATION AND RESPECT FOR PROCEDURES REQUIRING MULTILATERAL DELIBERATION

In addition to giving significant weight to treaties drafted in large part through open-minded consultation, we ought to give greater deference to procedures requiring multilateral deliberation because these procedures at least potentially can manifest the ethical principle of open-minded consultation. This is one reason why the rules in the Charter for the authorization of the use of force by the Security Council deserve significant respect. Why should we give greater respect to rules that contemplate open-minded consultation among a variety of actors? As I have already argued, we should do so, most importantly, because open-minded consultation can result in ethically sounder decisions. Franck observes that the international rules implicated in humanitarian intervention are "fraught with tough calls and hard choices."[44] Likewise, Terry Nardin notes that decisions about humanitarian intervention must take into account the specific factual context of each case in which it is contemplated.[45] Open-minded consultation increases the probability that this context will be considered and that all relevant facts will be uncovered and evaluated from a variety of perspectives.

For these reasons, multilateral decision making about humanitarian intervention is ethically, and not merely pragmatically, preferable to unilateral decision making. As Harry Kalven has asserted in the parallel context of jury deliberations, which, as I have suggested, reflect in large part the ideal of open-minded consultation, "It is not merely that twelve heads may be better than one but that a verdict hammered out as a group product is likely to have important strengths."[46] Pratap Bhanu Mehta's contribution to this volume appears to be based on a similar line of argument, for he states that our moral thinking on humanitarian intervention cannot bypass the need for collective international institutions and that unilateral intervention runs the risk of allowing states to be judges in their own cause. And finally, Franck seems to adopt this view by affirming that any new rules governing when humanitarian intervention is legitimate should be linked to a specific commitment to employ force only "upon having convinced an appropriate, credible 'jury' that the criteria have been met in any particular instance."[47]

Ideally, consultation in multilateral fora about humanitarian intervention ought to occur *prior* to the deployment of any intervention force, rather than being relegated to an after-the-fact, "postmortem" role. This is because prior open-minded consultation can help to determine whether military intervention is the best response to human rights violations, to regulate how the intervention is conducted, and to allow for planning for postintervention rebuilding. Without the benefit of prior consultation and authorization by multilateral bodies such as the Security Council, unilateral or regional interventions may be undertaken hastily, without sufficient attention to all relevant ethical issues, and may use force in ways that are excessive. Certainly a strong case can be made that NATO's intervention in Kosovo exhibited some of these ethical weaknesses, which might have been mitigated had there been a more serious attempt at Council consultation and collaboration before the action.

Of course, as already noted, the veto can prevent the results of open-minded consultation among at least a large majority of the Council's members from being implemented. It is thus morally problematic and ought to be reformed. For example, during the 1994 Rwanda genocide, the United States sent out strong signals that it might veto any Security Council resolution that would increase or even hold constant the size of the U.N. force in Rwanda, UNAMIR. Under U.S. pressure, the Council instead reduced the force's size.[48] The tension between the veto and the ethical principle of open-minded consultation suggests that some instances of humanitarian intervention without Council authorization may be ethically warranted if the results of the Council's deliberations cannot be implemented because of a veto of a single member. This issue is discussed in more detail in my book.[49]

5. Open-Minded Consultation and the Exercise of Legal Discretion Relating to Humanitarian Intervention

Just as we ought to give greater normative weight to laws that have been drafted through a process of relatively open-minded consultation and to procedures calling for deliberation that may take the form of open-minded consultation, so we ought to insist that deliberative bodies given discretion under law exercise that discretion through such consultation. In particular, states that are members of multilateral bodies such as the U.N. Security Council that have the authority under their constitutive charters to decide on the use of force for humanitarian purposes ought to take these decisions only after seeking out diverse viewpoints. Further, they should do so only after thoughtfully examining the facts of a human rights crisis and possible solutions through determined, engaged, and open-minded dialogue with other members of those bodies. They should, in short, practice open-minded consultation and conceive of their task in the ways that jurors ideally should conceive of their functions, as explored at some length above.

Too often, of course, Security Council deliberations resemble the making of sausage without the effective supervision of the USDA. They are not "cleaned up" through open-minded dialogue and frequently involve highly politicized bargaining and horse trading that takes place behind closed doors and under the extraordinary political influence of one or more powerful member states.[50] Political horse trading will result in ethically defensible decisions only by accident, if at all. Thus, it is imperative that members of the Council be encouraged, particularly when they are debating the life-and-death issues associated with contemplated humanitarian intervention, to listen carefully to one another's arguments and to be willing to rethink their positions with an open mind. For example, the evidence seems clear, in hindsight, that the United States might have done well to listen more attentively to those voices at the U.N., particularly from Africa, urging that U.N. forces not be pulled out of Rwanda in the midst of the devastating genocide that unfolded there in early 1994.[51]

Fortunately, there is also evidence that at times Council members have been willing to revise their initial positions based on a thoughtful consideration of the views of other members, allowing a consensus to be reached. This appears to have been the case, for example, with respect to the Security Council's decision to authorize intervention in Haiti. We also saw signs of the possibility of states shifting their positions to achieve consensus in the Security Council's discussions leading up to the unanimous adoption of Resolution 1441 in November 2002, in which the members reached agreement that Iraq was in "material breach" of its obligations under relevant Security Council resolutions.[52] Indeed, as Franck observes, the Security Council has shown that it is capable at times of credibly discharging a "jurying function" and of "making quite sophisticated judgments that take into account the full panoply of specific circumstances in each case." He notes that the response of Council members to "crises in Bosnia, Sierra

Leone, and the fight against terrorism are recent instances of many members acting more as responsible 'jurors' than committed partisans."[53]

6. Open-Minded Consultation and the Interpretation and Application of Laws Relating to Humanitarian Intervention

Thomas Franck opens his essay with a profound quotation from Saint Paul: "The letter killeth but the spirit giveth life."[54] It is often the job of particular institutions like the U.N. Security Council to "give life" to the law so as to prevent its letter from suffocating the very people it was designed to protect. These institutions do so by interpreting and applying the letter of the law. I suggest, once again, that open-minded consultation ought to characterize these efforts at interpretation and application. Indeed, we are beginning to see evidence that the Security Council can effectively engage in open-minded consultation and reinterpret the Charter in accordance with a new consensus resulting from it. For example, over the course of the past forty years or so, the Council has effectively reinterpreted the term "threat to the peace" in Article 39 of the Charter to include widespread and severe human rights violations.[55] This reinterpretation has occurred in a thoughtful manner and through considered discussion among Council members. Thus, to take one instance of such discussion, and its conclusion, despite the Council's early failure to act effectively in response to the Rwanda crisis, it eventually reached a consensus in its Resolution 955 that the situation of "genocide and other systematic, widespread and flagrant violations of international humanitarian law . . . committed in Rwanda" constituted a threat to international peace and security.[56]

7. Open-Minded Consultation and the Revision of the U.N. Charter

To argue, as I have, that laws such as the U.N. Charter that have been crafted through some semblance of a process of open-minded consultation deserve significant respect is not to advocate a rigid textual approach to law. Indeed, an emphasis on open-minded consultation suggests that existing laws ought to be the subject of continual discussion and reflection, with revisions made as necessary to comport with contemporary requirements. Although the rules of the U.N. Charter relating to humanitarian intervention deserve ethical and legal respect and have many merits as sophist rules, for the reasons elaborated by Franck it would be helpful to commence a comprehensive, inclusive discussion of how to revise them to address the problem of humanitarian intervention explicitly and systematically. However, it is also true that the existing Charter rules could work reasonably well if we could have confidence that the Security Council, in exercising its discretion under the Charter, will engage in the type of open-minded consultative decision making I have described.[57]

Indeed, any revisions to the Charter should incorporate and promote the principle of open-minded consultation. How? First, it is important to remove the Security Council veto. The chances of the existing permanent members accepting this reform are slim, but this change is necessary if decisions arrived at after full consultation by a supermajority of Council members are not to be thwarted by a single permanent member. One intermediate reform moving closer to this ideal would be to amend the Charter to require at least two vetoes for a resolution to be defeated. Such a reform might have permitted the Security Council to endorse some form of military action in the case of Kosovo, or might even have increased the prospects for effective action against the unfolding genocide in Rwanda.

Second, the Charter should require that the Security Council consult with involved parties, including nongovernmental actors, as well as U.N. specialized agencies, before taking decisions concerning humanitarian intervention.[58] Obviously, there may be cases in which the exigencies of the situation preclude time for such consultation, but this type of consultation should be the general rule. Fortunately, the Council is already putting a greater priority on consultations with other involved actors. These types of consultations can improve the quality of the information and facts made available to the Security Council that form the basis for its decisions about humanitarian intervention. For example, had the Council had more effective access, on a timely basis, to information provided by the commander of the U.N. forces in Rwanda,

General Roméo Dallaire, it might have better perceived the scale and genocidal character of the tragedy as well as the possibility of averting it through the rapid interposition of a relatively modest-sized force.

Third, the Charter should be amended to require consultation between the Security Council and representatives of the General Assembly. It is important that the views of the General Assembly, which represents all U.N. member states, be carefully considered by Council members in an interactive, and not just a formal, process. This is particularly true in the case of interventions with humanitarian aims, which usually affect states not represented on the Council. It is important that these states be brought into the deliberative process and feel that they have a voice in portentous military decisions affecting them and their people.

Fourth, Chapter VIII and Article 53 of the Charter should be revised to create a mechanism for permanent communication between the Council and regional organizations. Such a mechanism would have been helpful, for example, in the case of Kosovo, to allow the Security Council to collaborate closely with NATO. And, finally, Articles 2(4), 51, and 53 ought to be revised explicitly to mention military intervention on purported humanitarian grounds and to indicate whether and when it should be allowed by states or regional organizations without prior Council authorization. In general, the ethical principle of open-minded consultation incorporating a variety of regional perspectives suggests that prior Council authorization should continue to be required—at least if the veto is eliminated or reformed as just suggested. The case of Kosovo demonstrates the need for greater clarity with respect to the legality of humanitarian intervention as well as the importance of international consensus on decisions to employ military force for humanitarian ends.

8. Open-Minded Consultation and Decision Making about When Illegal Humanitarian Intervention May Be Ethically Excused

Thomas Franck highlights the fact that in most national legal systems provisions are made for excusing violations of the law in extreme circumstances. But these provisions often require a decision maker, such as a jury, to determine, after the fact, that these circumstances existed and therefore excused the violation. He rightly points out that the Security Council has often played a "jurying" role, in effect excusing military interventions that violated the letter of Article 2(4) or Article 53 on the grounds that they were necessitated by humanitarian concerns. He offers as recent examples of these cases intervention by ECOWAS in the Liberian and Sierra Leonean civil wars and NATO's intervention in Kosovo.

In fact, there is always a need for such a "safety valve" in any legal system, and I would argue that ex post facto "jurying" of violations of Article 2(4) or Article 53 that are justified by the interveners on grounds of humanitarianism ought to take place, again, through a broadly consultative process. Certainly one element of this process ought to be a thoughtful determination of whether an "excuse," moral or political, should be generalized into a legal justification, thereby resulting in a reinterpretation of existing law or a decision explicitly to revise existing law. In its practice, the Security Council has often not been very clear about the law-interpreting or law-reforming impact of its ex post facto decisions. It is possible to view many of its decisions apparently "ratifying" past interventions, such as those in Liberia, Sierra Leone, or Kosovo, as decisions grounded in political expediency rather than as actions intended by Council members to reinterpret the law.[59] Its decision-making process in evaluating interventions after the fact also needs to be improved to move closer to the ideal of open-minded consultation. We can at least see sporadic evidence of a more serious consideration by the Council, in reviewing a past intervention, of ways in which the intervention ought to affect the Council's approach in the future. For example, following NATO's unauthorized intervention in Kosovo, one Council member expressed the hope that "a new inclination to find, within the Council, multilateral solutions to other serious problems affecting world security, will gradually emerge."[60]

9. CONCLUSION

In this essay I have sought to expand upon Franck's advocacy of a "jurying" process for humanitarian intervention, including through international bodies such as the Security Council, by identifying and explaining an ethical principle of open-minded consultation and by exploring how this principle should affect decision making about humanitarian intervention. We are still far from implementing this ethical ideal in fundamentally political bodies such as the Security Council, NATO, and ECOWAS. However, these bodies have, during the past decade, begun to develop a significant reservoir of experience in engaging in relatively open-minded consultation about the advantages and disadvantages of humanitarian intervention in particular cases, and the most effective means of undertaking such intervention. As world leaders continue to grapple with recurring humanitarian crises demanding a concerted global response, it is incumbent on them to continue to draw from that reservoir and to develop their knowledge and practice of open-minded consultation.

NOTES

1. In Abdu'l-Bahá, *The Promulgation of Universal Peace: Talks Delivered by Abdu'l-Bahá during His Visit to the United States and Canada in 1912* (Wilmette, Ill.: Bahá'í Publishing Trust, 1982), 72.

2. See Thomas Franck, "Legality and Legitimacy in Humanitarian Intervention," this volume, chap. 5, 153.

3. See Brian D. Lepard, *Rethinking Humanitarian Intervention: A Fresh Legal Approach Based on Fundamental Ethical Principles in International Law and World Religions* (University Park: Pennsylvania State University Press, 2002), 68–71.

4. Lawrence Kohlberg, "Justice as Reversibility," in *Philosophy, Politics and Society: Fifth Series,* ed. Peter Laslett and James Fishkin (New Haven: Yale University Press, 1979), 272.

5. Jürgen Habermas, *Justification and Application: Remarks on Discourse Ethics,* trans. Ciaran Cronin (Cambridge: MIT Press, 1993), 49.

6. Ibid. (emphasis in original).

7. In this connection, Habermas has advocated a process of reflective communication based on the "presupposition to the effect that all affected can in principle freely participate as equals in a cooperative search for the truth in which the force of the better argument alone can influence the outcome." He argues that this "explanation of the moral point of view privileges practical discourse as a form of communication

that secures the impartiality of moral judgment together with universal interchangeability of participant perspectives." Ibid., 49–50.

8. See U.N. Charter, Art. 1(2–4).

9. See, e.g., ibid., Art. 10 (General Assembly); Art. 24 (Security Council).

10. See ibid., Art. 9.

11. See ibid., Art. 23.

12. G.A. Res. 377C (V) (1950).

13. See generally, e.g., Habermas, *Justification and Application.*

14. For more examples of such support in religious scriptures, see Lepard, *Rethinking Humanitarian Intervention,* 69–71.

15. Deut. 1:17. This text is taken from the 1917 Jewish Publication Society's English translation of the Tanach, available at http://www.sacred-texts.com/bib/ps.

16. See *Udana* 6.4, in *Some Sayings of the Buddha According to the Pali Canon,* trans. F. L. Woodward (London: Oxford University Press, 1973), 190–92.

17. See, e.g., Confucius, *The Analects,* 7.22, 12.21, in *The Original Analects: Sayings of Confucius and His Successors,* trans. E. Bruce Brooks and A. Taeko Brooks (New York: Columbia University Press, 1998).

18. See, e.g., Matthew 7:1, 3 (NRSV).

19. 1 Cor. 14:26, 29–31 (NRSV).

20. The quotation from the Qur'ān (3:153) is from A. J. Arberry, trans., *The Koran Interpreted* (New York: Simon & Schuster, 1955). On the concept of open-minded consultation in Islam, see generally Fazlur Rahman, *Major Themes of the Qur'ān* (Minneapolis: Bibliotheca Islamica, 1980), 43–44.

21. Quoted in C. G. Weeramantry, *Islamic Jurisprudence: An International Perspective* (New York: St. Martin's Press, 1988), 92.

22. Bahá'u'lláh, *Tablets of Bahá'u'lláh Revealed after the Kitáb-i-Aqdas,* trans. Habib Taherzadeh (Haifa: Bahá'í World Centre, 1978), 168.

23. See generally Saul M. Kassin and Lawrence S. Wrightsman, *The American Jury on Trial: Psychological Perspectives* (New York: Hemisphere Publishing, 1988), 172–73.

24. Ibid., 172.

25. Ibid., 173 (quoting American Bar Association Project on Minimum Standards for Criminal Justice (1968), Standards relating to trial by jury, Section 5.4; emphasis in original).

26. *Allen v. United States* 164 U.S. 492 (1896), 501–2.

27. *United States v. Wood,* 299 U.S. 123 (1936), 145–46.

28. Randolph N. Jonakait, *The American Jury System* (New Haven: Yale University Press, 2003), 62–63.

29. Ibid., 63.

30. Melissa S. Williams, *Voice, Trust, and Memory: Marginalized Groups and the Failings of Liberal Representation* (Princeton: Princeton University Press, 1998), 221; see also 222.

31. Kassin and Wrightsman, *The American Jury on Trial,* 173 (emphasis in original).

32. *Allen v. United States,* 501.

33. See Jeffrey Abramson, *We, the Jury: The Jury System and the Ideal of Democracy* (New York: Basic Books, 1994), 99–141.

34. Ibid., 102. See generally ibid., 100–102.

35. See, e.g., ibid., 126–27.

36. Ibid., 101.

37. Williams, *Voice, Trust, and Memory,* 222.

38. Valerie P. Hans and Neil Vidmar, *Judging the Jury* (New York: Plenum Press, 1986), 111.

39. U.N. Charter, Art. 2(4).

40. Ibid., Art. 51.

41. See ibid., Arts. 39, 42.

42. Ibid., Art. 53(1).

43. See, e.g., the statements of the Australian delegate, H. V. Evatt, in Doc. 969, I/1/39, *UNCIO Docs.* (1945), 6:436, 438–40 (contending that if a treaty were to make the protection of minorities a matter of international concern, nothing would prohibit the U.N. from intervening to protect such minorities).

44. Franck, "Legality and Legitimacy," 148.

45. See Terry Nardin, "The Moral Basis of Humanitarian Intervention," *Ethics and International Affairs* 16, no. 1 (2001): 57–70. ("Decisions about whether and how to intervene will always involve a wide range of contingencies" [69].)

46. Harry Kalven Jr., "The Jury, the Law, and the Personal Injury Damage Award," *Ohio State Law Journal* 19 (1958): 176.

47. Franck, "Legality and Legitimacy," 155.

48. See, e.g., Samantha Power, *"A Problem from Hell": America and the Age of Genocide* (New York: Basic Books, 2002), 366–70.

49. See generally Lepard, *Rethinking Humanitarian Intervention,* 326–29, 353–70.

50. Sydney D. Bailey and Sam Daws, *The Procedure of the UN Security Council,* 3d ed. (Oxford: Clarendon Press, 1998), 53–75, describe the Council's frequent habit of meeting in private and in informal consultations.

51. On the opposition of African nations to a troop withdrawal, see Power, *"A Problem from Hell,"* 369.

52. See S.C. Res. 1441 (2002), par. 1.

53. Franck, "Legality and Legitimacy," 151–52.

54. 2 Cor. 3:6 (NRSV).

55. See generally the discussion in Lepard, *Rethinking Humanitarian Intervention*, 149–78.

56. S.C. Res. 955 (1994), preamble.

57. See Lepard, *Rethinking Humanitarian Intervention*, 319–22, 324–26.

58. See ibid., 322–24.

59. See my discussion of this point, ibid., 353.

60. U.N. Doc. S/PV.4011 (1999), 17 (statement of Mr. Fonseca of Brazil).

9

THE JURY, THE LAW, AND THE
PRIMACY OF POLITICS

MELISSA S. WILLIAMS

[I]nternational law is itself a policy, depending for its success and
failure on other political developments and ideologies.

—Judith Shklar[1]

"The law's self-interest," Thomas Franck writes in his essay in this
volume, ". . . demands that a way be found to bridge any gap
between its own institutional commitment to the consistent application of formal rules and the public sense that order should not
be achieved at too high a cost to widely shared moral values."[2]
Whether in the realm of domestic law or in the international legal
order, the gap that may sometimes open up between legality and
legitimacy must be filled; otherwise the law itself loses its claim to
respect and authority and hence its capacity to guide and limit
action. In Anglo-American legal systems, this gap is sometimes
filled through the institution of the jury. By representing and
embodying the "widely shared moral values" that undergird the
law's claim to legitimacy, the jury's judgment may soften the blow
of the law's application to cases where the law imperfectly reflects
the full range of the community's moral sensibilities. In rare cases,
the gap between the law's strict requirements and the community's moral sense may be so great that the jury effectively excuses
actions that clearly violate the law's letter.

Acknowledging that there is no perfect analog of the jury in
the international legal system, Franck argues that in recent years
international actors and bodies (particularly the United Nations
Security Council) have functioned like juries in cases of humani-

tarian intervention. Although the strict letter of international law (in particular Article 2(4) of the U.N. Charter) prohibits intervention on humanitarian grounds, this prohibition conflicts with a growing moral consensus that stopping and preventing gross human rights violations can be legitimate reasons for the use of force across international boundaries. Citing a range of cases throughout the 1990s, Franck makes the case that the post hoc actions and resolutions of the Security Council express a judgment that these interventions, even though strictly illegal, were excusable breaches of the law, justified by the "extreme necessity" of ending human rights violations. In this way, as in the famous "lifeboat cases" in which Anglo-American juries effectively excused defendants who had committed murder under dire circumstances, these judgments leave the letter of the law intact while softening its application in the particular case. As Franck puts it, the "juries" here construe the law "in such a way that the case would not tear a large hole in the fabric of the prohibition, while yet accommodating what was seen as a highly exceptional circumstance of a kind not within the contemplation of society in fashioning the legal prohibition on killing" (pp. 145–146). In effect, he suggests, such judgments transform the law from a strict prohibition into a "rebuttable presumption" against the action in question.

Professor Franck's invitation to view judgments concerning humanitarian intervention as a practice of "jurying" is a welcome innovation. It encourages us to narrow the distance between those who would tend to debate the legality of humanitarian intervention and those who focus on its moral justifiability; "legitimacy," in this light, may be understood as a halfway house between legality and morality. Yet it is worth noting that how one understands the role and activity of the jury depends importantly on how one understands the nature of the law itself. In particular, an account of the jury reflects, whether implicitly or explicitly, an understanding of the relationship between customary practice, ideas of moral community, and positive law.

As Marianne Constable demonstrates in *The Law of the Other*, the jury is an institution whose historical development is tightly interlinked with the historical transformation of customary law into a system where a positivist understanding of the legal order has taken hold. This transformation, she argues, does not consist primarily in the difference between informal norms and codified rules but, rather, in the contrast between understanding law as constituted by a shared *practical knowledge*—a knowledge of how to act in general and in particular circumstances—and the positivist assumption that "rules are *graspable as propositions.*"[3] Positivism's claim that rules express propositional knowledge gives it a standpoint from which to criticize customary norms as lacking the rationality and coherence of a well-ordered system of rules.

Grounded as it was in a system of customary law, Constable shows, the early English jury comprised the "*senioribus et legalioribus*" of the community, its local leading men who were choice worthy as jurors because of their reputation for knowing and acting in accordance with the embedded norms of the community. For such juries, the facts of a case and the law that governed it were not sharply distinguished in practice. "Their task," Constable writes, "was to speak the truth ('ver-dict') at a time before truth referred to propositions of 'fact' and before law was relegated to a question of 'values.'"[4] Ideally, then, the early jury embodied the moral truth as it was understood by the community. On this reading of the jury, the moral judgment of the community is the measure both of the general requirements of law and its application in a particular case; what distinguishes the role of the juror is the practical wisdom that mediates between the general and the particular.

In contrast, under modern systems of positive law, the formal role of the jury is to decide questions of fact. The task of interpreting the law belongs to the judge alone, who instructs the jurors in the legal parameters within which they are to reach their judgment. Whereas jurors in the early jury brought their prior knowledge of both facts and norms to bear on their collective judgment, the positivist jury is forbidden to rely on factual knowledge that is independent of the evidence produced at trial.[5] We see this supposition played out in highly publicized cases, such as the O. J. Simpson trial, where the venue of a trial is changed because of the assumption that local citizens will have imbibed too many reports of the facts in news media and that such information will bias their judgment of the facts presented in evidence. Within this model, the "moral sense of the community" has no proper place in mediating between the formal law and its application. Certainly the role of the jury is not to represent such a common moral sense *as against* the strict letter of the law. Instead, the content of the law is fully provided by its letter and judicial interpretation thereof, and the jury is narrowly confined to the work of judging the facts as presented by defending and prosecuting attorneys. The community's moral sense, if it exists at all, bears no direct relationship to law's legitimacy.

What are we to make of legal positivism's claim that custom, while immature as a legal system, can nonetheless form a basis of positive law? To oversimplify, there is an evolutionary process through which customary practice becomes transformed into positive law through the creation of a common law system whose authority derives from the sovereign, who invests the judiciary with the power to say what the law is. On a positivist account, then, common law stands alongside statutory law as grounded in sovereign authority. The direct connection between the law's legitimacy and the embedded norms of the community is replaced by the formal legitimacy of the magistrates' authority to interpret the law.[6] This transformation opens up a potential gap between community norms and the formal requirements of law that did not exist in (the idealized form of) customary law and its jury system. In the positivist reading of a fully mature legal system, then, customary law gives way to a combination of common law and statutory (codified) law.

Against the background of this admittedly oversimplified contrast between customary and positive law jury systems, how are we to make sense of the jury that effectively excuses breaches of the law under circumstances of "extreme necessity"? As Franck notes (citing positivism's champion, H. L. A. Hart), sometimes the idea that a legal prohibition constitutes a "rebuttable presumption" of the impermissibility of an act is codified into the law itself and therefore becomes an element of positive law.[7] But no such codified exceptions were available in the lifeboat cases, and none are available in relation to Article 2(4) of the U.N. Charter. The latter is, as Franck notes, an "idiot rule" akin to a stoplight: the law's command is clear, and you are either in compliance or you are not.[8] For the jury to interpose "widely shared moral values" between the written text of the law and its application, then, signals a departure from a strictly positivist understanding of the law itself. It signals, indeed, the reintroduction of an element of customary law into a system where positive law predominates. Viewed in this light, the jury's action in "excusable breach" cases is continuous with the action of the nullifying jury, which acquits a defendant altogether in the face of facts that clearly show a violation of law. A nullifying jury indicts the legitimacy of the law itself and not only its application in the particular case. Although a nullifying jury does not leave the law intact, the logic of its substitution of the community's moral sense for the letter of the law renders it indistinguishable from a breach-excusing jury. Both cases make sense only within a hybrid legal system in which the defects of positive law are rectified through recourse to community norms, a possibility that a strict positivist would find it difficult to stomach.

It is a commonplace, of course, that there are two primary sources of international law: formal treaties and customary international law. The distinction between customary and treaty-based international law may be somewhat confusing, insofar as both are commonly understood as forms of positive law. Both, that is to say, have well-developed criteria establishing "rules of recognition" according to which those subject to law acknowledge its existence and authority. For treaties, the rule of recognition is straightforward: if an international agreement meets the criteria customarily acknowledged as determining its validity—criteria now codified in the Vienna Convention on the Law of Treaties—it is a valid treaty and its provisions are legally binding. In customary international law, the rule of recognition is less clear. Norms must be observed in practice over a length of time that cannot be specified in advance, and parties must explicitly acknowledge the norms as binding authority for their action (*opinio juris sive necessitatis*). Once a norm meets these standards, it becomes "graspable as a proposition" and is potentially codifiable in a treaty.

Yet it is important to note that the transformation of customary norms into positive international law is a trickier matter than in domestic legal systems, for the obvious reason that there is no sovereign power with direct or delegable authority to declare what the law is and hence to render law determinate. Thus, although the distinction between common law (as a fully developed form of positive law) and customary law (as grounded in community norms) is plausible in domestic legal systems, it is blurred in the international legal order by the absence of a sovereign authority. The creation of an international court system, with a judiciary that takes upon itself the task of interpreting and applying international customary norms as law, can be construed as an attempt to jerry-rig an international common law in the absence of a sovereign authority. But the true test of law so arrived at is whether international actors actually acknowledge and observe it; the process through which it was generated does not by itself establish its authority and legitimacy.

I will leave it to international law scholars to debate whether the advent of the United Nations and its Charter effectively eclipsed custom as a significant source of international law.[9] Instead, I wish to proceed from the supposition that something like a customary law understanding is implicit within Franck's account of "jurying" in cases of humanitarian intervention. If this is the case, then to gain an understanding of the evolution of customary norms concerning humanitarian intervention, we should look not only to the cases in which strictly illegal interventions were more or less forgiven by the "jury" of the Security Council but also to cases where the same body authorized interventions that were motivated largely, if not entirely, by humanitarian concerns.[10] That is to say, if the "breach-excusing" judgments reflect an emerging moral consensus about the justifiability of humanitarian intervention in certain cases, then we have reason to suppose that the same moral consensus is at work in authorizing interventions. Taking these cases together, we might even go so far as to say that through its repeated practice, the Security Council is effectively "nullifying" the rule of sovereignty understood as a perfect right against cross-border military force except in the name of self-defense.

In other words, the existence of more than a few authorized and unauthorized humanitarian interventions in recent decades suggests that Franck's characterization of intervention as extraordinary and rare is overstated. Contrary to his argument that humanitarian interventions are acts of "extreme necessity" that leave the core of the law untouched, the recurrent practice of intervention signals that the circumstances that occasion humanitarian intervention are not so extraordinary after all. They have arisen in the past and will continue to arise in the future so long as there are states that have the power to inflict atrocities on their citizens or lack the power to stop nonstate actors from doing so. And the moral impulse to act in response to such abuses—however unreliably it actually produces humanitarian action—also seems unlikely to abate. Therefore the dilemma of humanitarian intervention is not extraordinary but endemic to the current international system.

Taking authorized and unauthorized cases of humanitarian intervention together, what (if anything) do they reveal about a changing moral consensus about the justifiability of humanitarian intervention? To set the scene for such an inquiry, we must first notice that decisions about humanitarian intervention constitute a broad field upon which the classic contest between peace and justice as the ends of political order is played out. Should we follow Hobbes in holding that peace is the *sine qua non* of all other human ends and must take first priority in all political decisions? Or shall we follow what Kant called a "true, but boastful" dictum: *fiat iustitia, pereat mundus*—"let justice prevail, though all the world perish"?[11] Such a policy would give primacy to the claims of justice (here read as fundamental human rights) over the claims of peace (read as the absence of transborder violence).

The bargain that created the U.N. system clearly refuses the latter option. "International peace and security" is the mantra of that international order. This is unambiguous in the language of the Charter, which nowhere establishes human rights protection as a valid basis for the use of force. Even on this reading of the ends of international society, though, it is important to recognize that the justification of sovereignty-as-noninterference is not a first principle of international order. Rather, the normative justification of Article 2(4)'s guarantee of noninterference is *derivative from* the claims of security: that violent conflict will be contained and reduced if the rules for the use of force are clear and determinate and if states are deprived of gains seeking as a motive or justification for aggressive action.

Of course, the rejection of any view that gives primacy to justice over peace as the first principle of international society does not entail that justice (again, read as basic human rights) has no place at all. As Kofi Annan and others have repeatedly stressed, international society rests on the dual pillars of security and human rights. The Universal Declaration of Human Rights, the Genocide Convention, the Convention to Eliminate All Forms of Discrimination against Women, the Convention on the Rights of the Child —these are just a few of the treaties that express an international moral commitment to human rights. Moreover, human rights are not a mere afterthought appended to a security-based U.N. system. Article 1(3) of the Charter, for example, commits the U.N. to "promoting and encouraging respect for human rights and for fundamental freedoms for all."

From the outset, then, the claims of peace and the claims of justice have both had a place in the normative rhetoric of the U.N. system, but peace is undeniably the senior partner in this arrangement. For the most part, the two principles have been worked out as *separate logics*: the agreed-upon meaning of "international peace and security" and the terms on which force may be used legitimately have developed on one track, and the content of human rights on another. Human rights conventions tend not to address security concerns, and discussions of security tend to treat human rights concerns as an afterthought, if at all, a garnish on the main dish. This two-track development of the logics of human rights and security, however, becomes unworkable once humanitarian intervention arises as a possibility. Here, the two tracks converge: a principled engagement with one necessarily entails a principled engagement with the other.

The cases where intervention occurred were exceptional not because they posed extraordinary threats to human rights that could or did override principles of security or sovereignty-as-inviolability. Rather, what makes the cases exceptional is that there were actors on the world stage who were willing to put soldiers and treasure at risk in order to find a proper balance between security and rights, between peace and justice, in the particular and inevitably messy contexts that generate egregious human rights abuses. If we look to the many cases where humanitarian intervention did not occur—in Rwanda, in Chechnya, and more recently in Darfur, for example—we may be tempted to conclude (with Thomas Pogge in this volume) that there is no meaningful "moral sense of the community" to guide international responses to gross human rights abuses. Instead, there is only an international system governed, as realists argue, by the strategic self-interest of the most powerful states.

But this conclusion cannot make sense of the cases where intervention did occur, with the approval or eventual acquiescence of the broader international community.[12] Still, the irregular quality of decisions about intervention raises difficult questions. Do cases of authorized and unauthorized intervention add up to a principled account of the proper balance between international security and human rights? Do they constitute an international moral community capable of legitimizing or delegitimizing a particular intervention?

To address these questions, it is useful once again to return to the idea of the customary law jury. Here, however, I have in mind a particular permutation of the early jury: the jury *de medietate linguae*—literally, "of the half-tongue"—in which two distinct communities are represented. As Constable relates, these medieval and early modern English juries emerged against the background condition of minority communities—notably Jews—who lived on English soil but were internally governed by the customary norms specific to their communities. This was a system of personal law, where the rules for an individual's conduct derived from the community of which he or she was a member: English laws for Englishmen, "foreign" laws for "foreigners." Within the English legal system, as we have seen, cases were decided by a jury that embodied and represented the constitutive norms of the community. But English and "foreign" communities were not wholly insulated from one another, and cases also arose as a by-product of the interactions between them. In these cases, a mixed jury was constituted: half of the jurors were Englishmen, and half were from the "foreign" community.[13]

The mixed jury makes for a fascinating study in the emergence of new normative orders. Against the background idea that law is grounded in the situated morality of a community rather than in either a universal morality or a positivist understanding of legitimacy, it is difficult to conceive how a law-governed relationship could arise between two distinct situated communities. The easy solution would be to impose the substantive norms of the strong upon the weak. But the practice of the mixed jury rejected this solution. It did not simply impose English laws on "foreigners" but constituted a *legal* body in which two normative communities were equally represented. The task of such a jury was to arrive at a judgment that could be recognized as just and impartial by members of both situated communities. Yet there was no system of norms upon which these communities could be said to agree *ex ante*. In light of this absence of moral agreement, the practice of the mixed jury presents an intriguing possibility, that of reaching shared moral judgment across the boundaries of situated moral communities *without being able to specify in advance what the content of such moral agreement might be*. In doing so, it expresses a will for a shared, if limited-purpose, moral community between Englishmen and "foreigners," a desire to live together under a system of norms that are recognizably legitimate within both communities. Thus the practice of jurying both *presupposes* the possibility of a norm-governed relationship and partially *constitutes* such a relationship through its judgment. Although I do not want to make strong historical claims about the emergence of shared norms between English and "foreign" communities, the logic of mixed juries opens up a new prospect: that through the iterated judgments of mixed juries over time, a body of shared normative principles for governing intercommunal relations could emerge.

In this light, we can read the train of cases of both authorized and unauthorized humanitarian intervention as an iterated practice that seeks to discover a balance between the claims of security and the claims of human rights. As a repeated practice among members of international society, this effort expresses the possibility of a principled balance without being able to specify in advance what the content of such a balance might be. It thus also presupposes the possibility of a norm-governed relationship between states *in advance* of any explicit agreement between them. An optimistic reading of these cases is that they are efforts at constructing a community of shared moral judgment within a moral and political vacuum. In such a vacuum, the codification of norms *ex ante* is not an available option, for several reasons. As Jane Stromseth has recently argued, no set of codified norms is likely to meet all the complexities of the situations in which the need for humanitarian intervention arises. Beyond this, a premature attempt at codification assumes agreement where none has been established, and so short-circuits the repeated activity through which a genuine community of judgment could emerge.[14]

In the rhetoric of these cases, the priority of security to human rights is clear.[15] But these cases involve circumstances where the two principles do not necessarily conflict. Sometimes there is a good argument to be made that an intervention will serve both security and human rights. In some cases, the harmony of security and human rights is achieved through a gradual stretching of the concept of security such that it encompasses some human rights concerns. Human rights abuses tend to create refugees, and in several cases—including Bosnia, Rwanda, and Kosovo—cross-border refugee flows were recognized as threats to regional security even by the Security Council. Sometimes an intervention promises positive benefits for human rights but looks neutral in its effect on security. Whether security concerns leave space for the claims of human rights is a highly contextual judgment involving many considerations: the identity of the intervening states and the history of their relationship to the target state and its region; the interveners' capacity to claim credibly that they seek to promote stability and human rights rather than narrow self-interest; the adequacy of the intervention force; and so on.

Reading past interventions as an iterated practice of international "jurying" suggests an optimistic view of the possibility of a norm-governed international regime of humanitarian intervention. The impression, however, is misleading because this outcome depends on a shared will among states to constitute themselves as a norm-governed community. The effort to arrive at agreement constitutes a *political* choice for law, rather than force or power, as the basis of relationship. This choice depends not only on the normative commitments of the various parties but also on their strategic interests, which may lead them to stray from their own confessed commitments or to believe that they are more likely to realize those commitments by force than by cooperation. Finally, the substance of participants' judgments about morality and interests is reflected not only—not even primarily—in their principled statements but, above all, through their actions.

What, then, are the chief obstacles to a principled practice of humanitarian intervention? The case record leaves ambiguous whether the fear of a Security Council veto is really a deterrent to justifiable interventions. Where the argument can be mustered that *both* security and human rights protection will be advanced through an intervention, it is sometimes possible to garner Security Council approval. Even in cases where a dual rationale is available, however, intervention is the exception rather than the norm. Why so? In part, it is for the same reason that threatens Security Council vetoes: the fear that humanitarian reasons will be used as a pretext for aggression by states seeking to advance their strategic or material interests. But perhaps more important is the chill of domestic politics on leaders' propensities to intervene. It is well established that fear of domestic political losses led the Clinton administration to withdraw American forces from Somalia after the brutal killing of U.S. servicemen in Mogadishu, with graphic images of their abused corpses shown on television screens worldwide. This fear was clearly at work in the U.S. refusal to support intervention in Rwanda. Nor have governments been punished at the polls for their failures to intervene. For all of Bill Clinton's subsequent self-lashing for his administration's failure to stop the Rwanda genocide, the fact remains that this failure did not damage his bid for reelection. And it has become a political truism that democratic publics will not tolerate the loss of life or bear substantial economic costs for interventions that do not clearly advance the national interest.

Nonetheless, evidence on the resistance of democratic publics to humanitarian intervention is mixed. American public opinion polls suggest that most people are willing to put troops and resources at risk in order to protect human rights, at least in some circumstances. One year after the Rwanda genocide, for example, 70 percent of Americans surveyed thought that the United States should "have gone in with a large military force to occupy [Rwanda] and stop the killings."[16] The withdrawal of U.S. troops from Somalia was driven more by congressional reaction to the loss of American lives than by popular outrage; public opinion polls taken shortly after the failed operation in Mogadishu showed that more than 60 percent of Americans continued to support the humanitarian mission.[17] More recently, 69 percent of respondents to a survey on the humanitarian crisis in western Sudan thought that, if the U.N. determined that human rights abuses in Darfur constitute a genocide, the United States should participate in an intervention, even if doing so required the use of military force.[18] This suggests that where there is strong political leadership to make sense of the moral duties of humanitarian intervention to democratic citizenries, there is a foundation of already-existing public opinion to appeal to. If the international community fails to undertake humanitarian interventions when such interventions could support human rights without threatening security, we should understand nonintervention as a failure of political and moral leadership, not the nation-centered choice of democratic publics.

The conclusion of these reflections is simple, almost self-evident: there can be no international normative community around issues of humanitarian intervention without a sustained *practice* in which the sometimes-competing aims of security and human rights are balanced against one another. There can be no international law of humanitarian intervention where there are not sufficient numbers of relatively powerful international actors prepared not only to endorse it but also to enforce it. Unlikely as this seems in the context of the war on Iraq, which so many have regarded as a flagrant demonstration of the Bush administration's disregard for international law, there are reasons to believe that it is not impossible. The United States might eventually recognize the costs of unilateralism and seek to restore damaged relationships through greater efforts at international cooperation. Widespread condemnation of the failure to intervene in Rwanda might strengthen the will to take action at least in cases of genocide, a proposition that finds its test in the crisis in Darfur. If the United States refuses leadership in developing a practice of shared judgment about humanitarian intervention, perhaps, as Thomas Pogge and Alan Buchanan suggest, it will be possible to circumvent the Security Council in institutionalizing a capacity for humanitarian intervention even without the participation of the United States, just as the creation of the International Criminal Court bypassed U.S. opposition.[19] In that case, the emergence of a norm-governed regime of humanitarian intervention will depend upon the military ability of participating states to enforce emerging norms, a capability that does not now exist among the states that most enthusiastically endorse a shared international "responsibility to protect."

All of these paths make clear that humanitarian intervention presupposes a normative community that is the outcome of political choices. The point is not to moralize. Rather, the point is simply to stress that there can be no law where powerful actors do not choose to be governed by it. There is no way of generating a law of humanitarian intervention, whether customary or codified, without the engaged political will of a significant number of states, including those who have the military power to intervene when it is justified and choose to exercise that power when and only when it is justified. Such a will can be mobilized only through political action, based not only on moral suasion (essential though that is) but also on the chastening of power, so that the powerful come to the conclusion that their interests in living under a norm-governed system outweigh the benefits of going it alone.

NOTES

I am grateful to Terry Nardin for encouraging me to write this essay and for his very helpful critical feedback, and to Rosemary Nagy for her excellent editing.

1. Judith N. Shklar, *Legalism: Law, Morals, and Political Trials* (Cambridge: Harvard University Press, 1986), 134.

2. Thomas Franck, "Legality and Legitimacy in Humanitarian Intervention," this volume, chap. 5, 145.

3. Marianne Constable, *The Law of the Other: The Mixed Jury and Changing Conceptions of Citizenship, Law, and Knowledge* (Chicago: University of Chicago Press, 1994), 88 (emphasis added); see 87–89 generally.

4. Ibid., 16.

5. Ibid., 132–33; see also 149–50.

6. "Till the courts apply them in particular cases [customary] rules are mere customs, in no sense law. When the courts use them, and make orders in accordance with them which are enforced, then for the first time these rules receive legal recognition. The sovereign who might have interfered has tacitly ordered his subjects to obey the judges' orders 'fashioned' on pre-existing custom." H. L. A. Hart, *The Concept of Law* (Oxford: Clarendon Press, 1961), 45.

7. Franck, "Legality and Legitimacy," this volume, chap. 5, 146.

8. Ibid., 149.

9. See J. L. Holzgrefe, "The Humanitarian Intervention Debate," in

Humanitarian Intervention: Ethical, Legal, and Political Dilemmas, ed. J. L. Holzgrefe and Robert O. Keohane (Cambridge: Cambridge University Press, 2003), 45–46.

10. These authorized interventions include Somalia (1992–93), Haiti (1994–97), Sierra Leone (1997–), and East Timor (1999–).

11. Immanuel Kant, "Perpetual Peace," in *Perpetual Peace and Other Essays* (Indianapolis: Hackett, 1983 [1795]), 133.

12. As in Northern Iraq, Liberia, Somalia, Sierra Leone, and Kosovo.

13. See generally Constable, *The Law of the Other*, chap. 1.

14. Jane Stromseth, "Rethinking Humanitarian Intervention: The Case for Incremental Change," in *Humanitarian Intervention*, ed. Holzgrefe and Keohane, 256, 258–61.

15. For a helpful case-by-case overview of humanitarian interventions during and after the Cold War, see Thomas G. Weiss, Don Hubert, et al., *The Responsibility to Protect: Research, Bibliography, Background: Supplementary Volume to the Report of the International Commission on Intervention and State Sovereignty* (Ottawa: International Development Research Centre, 2001), Section B: Past Humanitarian Interventions.

16. In contrast, at about the same time only 18 percent of the foreign policy elite would have supported the use of U.S. military forces if the threat of genocide reemerged. Donald Rothchild and Nikolas Emmanuel, "U.S. Public Opinion and Intervention in Africa's Ethnic Conflicts" (unpub. MS, on file with author), 26–27.

17. Ibid., 30.

18. Steven Kull, *Americans on the Crisis in Sudan* (Program on International Policy Attitudes, 2004), 3, available at http://www.pipa.org/OnlineReports/Africa/Report07_20_04.pdf. The same survey shows that 56 percent of Americans believe that a genocide was occurring in Darfur in July 2004; among those who considered themselves well informed about the crisis, 87 percent believed a genocide was taking place.

19. Thomas Pogge, "Moralizing Humanitarian Intervention: Why Jurying Fails and How Law Can Work," this volume, chap. 6; Allen Buchanan, *Justice, Legitimacy, and Self-Determination: Moral Foundations for International Law* (Oxford: Oxford University Press, 2004), 450–56.

10

FROM STATE SOVEREIGNTY
TO HUMAN SECURITY
(VIA INSTITUTIONS?)

PRATAP BHANU MEHTA

The debate over the relationship between sovereignty and human rights has acquired new vigor in the context of debates over armed humanitarian intervention. Do the emerging norms of humanitarian intervention imply that human rights trump the claims of sovereignty? Is the discourse on sovereignty being supplanted by other discourses, such as those on human security? Is sovereignty itself undergoing transformation? Do the new practices of humanitarian intervention in cases ranging from Haiti to East Timor, from Kosovo to Afghanistan, entail the emergence of new norms of humanitarian intervention? Is humanitarian intervention increasingly occasioned not just by a combination of war and poverty, or the possibility of genocide caused by the disintegration of multinational states, or by civil war, or by continuing human rights abuses by oppressive and brutal regimes but also by the anarchy that results from weakly institutionalized or failed states? Are failed states being seen not just as a humanitarian but also a security challenge? Are the traditional lines between humanitarian interventions and preemptive security operations becoming increasingly thin?[1] Arguably powerful states, such as the United States, may be motivated to intervene more often to preempt the possibility that others might become security threats.

Normative debate over humanitarian intervention is saddled with the immense baggage of state practice. There is a straightforward challenge that any normative account has to meet. It is the paradox that humanitarian intervention is almost always an action of strong states with respect to relatively weaker states. Any general criteria for determining which occasions warrant intervention, like violations of human rights, are often difficult to enforce against states that can make the costs of intervention high because of their military capabilities. The only question is whether the selectivity is an outcome of prudential considerations ("We cannot really do anything about Russia") or simply indifference (as in the case of Rwanda). Organized hypocrisy, to borrow Stephen Krasner's phrase, is almost inevitable when it comes to humanitarian intervention, but it seems at least better than an alternative world in which dominant powers were either immune to the suffering that called for humanitarian intervention or imprudent enough to jeopardize world peace by recklessly threatening other major powers.

This paper does not aim to specify the moral and legal basis for humanitarian intervention.[2] It attempts instead to make the following arguments. First, I argue that the main issue arising out of humanitarian intervention is not the conflict between state sovereignty on the one hand and human rights on the other. The principal issue is whether states can *unilaterally* intervene. Unilateral here does not refer simply to the number of nations participating in or supporting intervention. Any typical intervention will be made by an alliance of states. Rather, the challenge is to think of what might constitute due *authorization*. I suggest that the compelling moral reasons usually given to justify intervention do not suffice to ground a right to intervene. I argue that states have no such right, though I leave it an open question whether it might still be justified for them to intervene in exceptional circumstances, even in the absence of such a right. I argue that even states that have acted seemingly unilaterally have been reluctant to "institutionalize" the "right to intervene" for good reasons.

In the second half of the paper I turn to a discussion of whether the fact that NATO intervened in Kosovo suggests the onset of a new cosmopolitan international law, as thinkers such as Habermas have suggested. I argue that unilateralism, combined with the actual practice of intervention, enacts the very particularisms that "cosmopolitan" law or a concern for human rights is supposed to overcome. And I suggest that there is a dangerous tendency to think of humanitarian war as an enforcement mechanism for rights that might undermine the very values at stake in the defense of human rights. In the end, I conclude that there is no way to coherently ground our moral thinking in these matters in a manner that bypasses the need for collective international institutions. I say all this mindful of Stanley Hoffmann's warning against too much abstraction in international ethics. The study of international ethics, Hoffmann argues, "is not the province of the ethical philosopher"; it is the "province of the international relations scholar."[3] Although this claim is, strictly speaking, an exaggeration, it does call on us to think of situating ethical arguments in the context of institutions and politics more seriously.

1. NONINTERVENTION

The idea that individual states or the international community should stand idly by while immeasurable human suffering unfolds within the boundaries of some state simply because it is unfolding *within those* boundaries seems morally problematic. This idea seems at first glance to deny that the international community has any positive obligations, or even a right to protect the weak, mitigate suffering, and enforce human rights. On this view, the main obligation of the international community is to respect the territorial integrity and sovereignty of states. Such a conception would allow the innocent to be victims of anarchy, civil war, or genocide, and suggests an appalling lack of conscience, an absence of solidarity with others qua human beings, perhaps even a denial of common humanity. Yet humanitarian intervention, especially military intervention, seems a complicated moral issue. The logistics of humanitarian intervention involve delicate and often uncertain calculations of costs and benefits, and sometimes restraint is not a sign of indifference but a counsel of prudence. Sometimes the means employed by states in the position to carry out humanitarian intervention cast moral suspicion on the enterprise itself.

But the main resistance to justifying and legitimizing the idea of humanitarian interventions comes from the fact that such interventions put at risk one of the principal axioms of the international community: the nonintervention principle. Very briefly, the nonintervention principle argues that states are forbidden to exercise their authority and to use force within the territorial jurisdiction of other states. The United Nations Charter permits a state to defend itself from attack but prohibits the use of armed force against the political independence and territorial integrity of another state. And under the U.N. Charter, any use of force against a state has to be authorized by the United Nations itself, acting as a representative of the international community.

The debate between those who take the principle of nonintervention to be sacrosanct and, hence, armed humanitarian intervention to be illegitimate, on the one hand, and defenders of human rights, on the other, is often cast as a debate between those who defend the claims of particular communities and those who advocate a more universal morality, premised on the idea that there are some moral or legal norms, such as human rights, that the international community has a right to enforce or facilitate, irrespective of the sovereignty claims of a particular state. The debate is viewed as also being premised on two different conceptions of world order: (1) what is described as a "solidaristic" conception of world order in which human beings show solidarity with others qua human beings, and (2) a pluralistic world order in which sovereignty remains the lodestar of identity in many crucial respects. The principle of nonintervention is, on this view, thought to be antisolidaristic because it does not allow people in particular states to think about and act upon the suffering and predicament of people elsewhere; it almost morally enjoins them not to do so. It provides states with a convenient legal excuse for ignoring considerations of justice within other states. Cast in this way, the debate between advocates of nonintervention, on the one hand, and advocates of humanitarian intervention, on the other, is often quite misleading. It is misleading because, first, as Martin Wight suggested, "[A]dherents of every political belief will regard intervention as justified under certain circumstances."[4] To that extent, it is doubtful that anyone really is causally or morally immune from considerations pertaining to the well-being of citizens in other states.

The second reason that viewing nonintervention as a kind of

antiuniversal principle is something of a mistake is this: the historical origins of the principle suggest that it was seen just as the best expression of a healthy internationalism. Nonintervention gave weak states protection against the strong, implicitly sought to pacify the use of force by insisting that force be collectively authorized, and allowed a diversity of political and social forms to flourish. The nonintervention principle was a way for states mutually to recognize one another within the framework of a pluralistic international order. It placed a high premium on peace. And it was the international community that *collectively* created this semblance of order. Accordingly, to construe the debate between those who appear to be stricter noninterventionists and those who defend humanitarian intervention as a debate between those who defend cosmopolitan law or universal values, on the one hand, and those who defend the claims of particularity, on the other, can be misleading. Even noninterventionists are concerned about universal values such as peace and protecting weak states.

But the principle of nonintervention often seems to grant undue moral privilege to the claims of sovereignty. State sovereignty, whether seen as a juridical ideal or an empirical reality, is of course a complicated idea. But, at its core, it refers to the thought that there are matters in which each state is permitted by international law to decide and act without intrusion and undue interference from other states. Such matters could include choice of economic and political systems, foreign policy, and so on. Of course, substantial de jure and de facto limits on the exercise of sovereignty have always existed. The real question for humanitarian intervention is this: under what conditions can the claims of sovereignty be abrogated? If sovereignty is seen as a conditional grant, the challenge is specifying the conditions under which the claims of sovereignty may be forfeited.

An answer to the real question, then, turns on the subsequent question: what is the underlying basis of sovereignty? Proponents of intervention argue that the difficulty with the principle of nonintervention is that, in effect, it allows states with some degree of coercive control over their territory to themselves define the terms of their own legitimacy. Although in principle there is no contradiction between the principle of sovereignty and the principle of nonintervention, if one views sovereignty as a conditional

grant and the aim of intervention as the creation and mainte-
nance of a sovereign order that can more justly and effectively
preserve the underlying aims of society, the principle of nonintervention in practice gives carte blanche to states to define the
terms of their own legitimacy. The difficulty with the principle of
nonintervention is that it ignores the external and internal bases
of sovereignty: that legitimate sovereignty is in some measure
derived from the will of the people and that states that grossly violate human rights cannot be said to possess sovereignty in this
sense. And the principle of nonintervention ignores as well the
fact that there is no such thing as "sovereignty as such." It is international recognition that partly constitutes the state and confers
upon it the characteristic rights and immunities of a state. And,
therefore, the international community would be well within its
rights to insist on certain rules for recognition, which could
include things such as the observance of human rights.

Sovereignty is a complicated idea. But the chief worry about it
is that it is statist in orientation. It often preserves the rights of
states even at the expense of the rights of the people. Kofi Annan,
in an article that launched a fierce debate on humanitarian intervention, argued this:

> State sovereignty, in its most basic sense, is being redefined—not
> least by forces of globalization and international cooperation.
> States are now widely understood to be instruments at the service
> of their peoples, and not vice versa. At the same time individual
> sovereignty—by which I mean the fundamental freedom of each
> individual enshrined in the Charter of the U.N. and subsequent
> international treaties—has been enhanced by a renewed and
> spreading consciousness of individual rights. When we read the
> Charter today, we are more than ever conscious that its aim is to
> protect individual human beings, not to protect those who abuse
> them.[5]

Annan's statement captures much about an emerging international normative climate. Since the end of the Cold War, human
rights norms have been more widely accepted as norms. After
the "third wave" democratizations, there is a greater recognition
that although the international system will be composed of states
with a diversity of political forms, some measure of democracy is

going to limit the diversity of legitimate forms of government that the international community is going to countenance. Although "nondemocratic" states will continue to be recognized and act as major players on the international scene, there is an increasing trend toward thinking of democracy as something of a universal entitlement. Most important, however, sovereignty entails certain obligations. States that oppress their own citizens, put them at risk, and expose large numbers of them to serious harm lose moral standing. No state may do to its people as it pleases. The international community will continue to acknowledge that stable sovereign states, capable of securing internal order, are a necessary condition for securing rights within territories. Some argue that the point of intervention will be to enable societies caught in the perverse equilibriums of anarchy, civil war, or oppression to move toward the creation of stable states that can effectively provide internal security and act as instruments for the protection of basic rights. Sovereignty will no longer provide a shield against claims that the international community has responsibilities and duties to protect the vulnerable. To many, these claims, at least at a fairly high level of abstraction, seem morally unassailable. Even states that contest the universality of democracy or human rights recognize certain violations of human rights as being serious enough to merit international attention.

The difficulty lies in giving greater moral and legal specificity to these desirable goals. Even though these norms may be widely shared, there are legitimate questions about whether they can be *enforced* militarily. Indeed, the structure of the U.N. Charter and many other international treaties suggests that the international community recognizes many rights without providing for mechanisms to enforce them. Whether we like it or not, there are a number of rights that are recognized but often lack appropriate remedy. At least some who oppose armed humanitarian intervention can consistently maintain both that preventing human suffering on a large scale is desirable and that it is wrong to use force to do it. This may be because of prudential considerations but also because of moral considerations. For instance, you might hold the view, as some do in relation to domestic society, that the use of violence as a means requires proper *authorization*, and no matter what the aims, it is wrong to engage in violence without that authorization. Often, disputes about authorization seem to many to be legalistic nit-picking in the face of obvious human catastrophe; to others, authorization is the essence of morality. On this view, it is more important that collective modes for properly authorizing violence are created and maintained, even if these modes of collective authorization do not allow for intervention in particular cases where we think we ought to intervene.

But the more serious difficulty lies in the fact that the conclusions entailed by taking the norms of democracy, human rights, and security seriously are too broad. It would entail that there be in the international order two categories of states. First, we would have a privileged category of states that more or less approximate the ideals of democracy and human rights. These states would enjoy all the privileges and characteristics of sovereignty and the immunities it entails. The second class—of lesser states—would be, let us call them, nondemocracies. These would be standing candidates for intervention if prudence and the possibility of success permitted. Even those who have no doubt about the moral desirability of democracy and human rights balk at the prospect of giving a small group of states, usually former colonial powers, the moral authority to create a society of states in their own image, one in which nonliberal peoples have subordinate or no standing. On this view, even though human rights and democracy may be good things, to use them as sufficient warrant to interfere in the affairs of other states would be not only to risk peace and concentrate power and authority in a few states. It would also be to arrogate to a group of states the moral authority that could not possibly be justified to participants in the international community.[6]

So, using "human rights," "democracy," or "people's sovereignty" as a justification for intervention is too broad because it seems unduly to narrow the range of regimes that might be thought of as having a legitimate place in the international order. And it runs the risk of giving legitimacy to a few powers to shape societies in light of their own values and images, in a word, a form of colonialism.[7]

But for those who do not share these worries, there is a different worry: are these values that supposedly justify humanitarian intervention actually taken seriously by those who profess them?

Once we argue for the importance of shared values and common humanity, why are these in evidence only in moments of severe crisis of a particular kind? Humanitarian intervention seems to focus excessively on catastrophes caused by state failure in some form: breakdown of states or oppression by states. Crushing social injustice, deprivation, or inequality seem to merit less attention. As Bhikhu Parekh has argued, for those who take universal values and common solidarities seriously, "humanitarian intervention ceases to be a form of crisis management nervously operating at the periphery of international relations and becomes an important part of a much larger project of creating a just economic and political order."[8]

Indeed, if we accepted the duties entailed in taking human security, human rights, and democracy seriously, we could not consistently limit ourselves to humanitarian intervention in times of acute crisis. There is a whole range of state behavior that taking such duties seriously would prohibit: the prejudicial sustaining of authoritarian regimes, the dissemination of the means of violence, the destabilizing of regimes, the investment in grossly unfair economic arrangements, and so on. There is little evidence that states, even those that support humanitarian intervention, actually even attempt to live up to these obligations. The desire of some states for "humanitarian intervention" cannot, in the absence of those other measures, be itself taken as evidence that the norms that the intervening states are supposedly protecting command their genuine allegiance. Indeed, given that those powers likely to intervene are enormously complicit in producing some of the conditions that occasion humanitarian intervention in the first place, the profession of claims to carry out duties based on solidarity with the victims cannot be taken at face value. The very breadth of the values that underwrite humanitarian intervention impugns the credibility of those who invoke them. These values, then, cannot be taken as norms that set authoritative constraints on the behavior of states. At best, they are more like directive principles that guide us toward what a more just world order might look like, but they are, on their own, insufficient to justify interventions by particular states on particular occasions.

Two conclusions are usually drawn from the above argument.

The first is that because the intervening states themselves do not live up to the values they claim to enforce, their *authority* to be enforcers of universal values cannot be taken for granted. The second is that interventions should be undertaken not to promote broad values but only to prevent such unambiguously horrific possibilities as genocide. A justification of intervention that is narrower, that based itself on a criterion such as "extreme necessity" —to use Thomas Franck's phrase—is more likely to elicit support from the international community and is more likely to be credible than general talk about human rights, democracy, and new conceptions of sovereignty.

2. A JUDGE IN ONE'S OWN CAUSE?

It would be hasty to think that opposition to humanitarian intervention is driven only by a realist conception of national interest. Humanitarian intervention is the occasion in which not only the normative considerations pertinent to solving the suffering of particular people are thought to be at stake but also in which the rules that govern relations between states in general are thought to be at stake. When countries—usually a majority—oppose humanitarian intervention on grounds of sovereignty, they are using the contest over humanitarian intervention to insist on the *norms* that ought to govern relations between states. In particular, these countries are insisting that the prevention of *unilateral* and *unauthorized* acts of force and the preservation of the authority of collective institutions takes moral precedence over humanitarian intervention.

Even if one accepts the premise of the argument that the international order should be construed as based on the protection of individuals and people rather than states, the conclusion that therefore some states have the right to take countermeasures against violations of these rights does not automatically follow. The well-being of human beings as individuals might be better served by rejecting a unilateral right to intervention because states would, in using such a right, act upon their own moral principles—be a judge in their own cause—and jeopardize a peaceful international order.[9] Indeed, the debates during the 1990s in the United Nations seem to suggest that for most nations the primary tension with respect to humanitarian intervention is not the tension between human rights and sovereignty. Nor have the principal failures to intervene, most notably Rwanda, resulted from U.N. inaction. In many cases, the will of individual member states was lacking.[10]

There is after all, far less opposition to a right of humanitarian intervention by the U.N. than there is to giving individual states such a right. The power of the Security Council to intervene in times of humanitarian crisis has found broad acceptance. Sovereignty is, therefore, not the main issue. The proper authorization of force and the proper relationship between protecting human rights and not jeopardizing peace, are the main issues.

This long prologue is a roundabout way of saying that there are some difficulties inherent in talking of "humanitarian intervention" in terms of the moral language of "rights" and "duties." This is in part because its practice will be so subject to exceptions, disclaimers, and inconsistent state practice that it will be difficult to "constitutionalize" it. The existence of some general considerations in favor of intervention are either too broad or their interpretation too underspecified for them to be able to underwrite some *right* to humanitarian intervention. Those considerations provide, at best, general guidelines that should guide the basic architecture of the world system.

Further argument and specification are needed to get a *right* to intervene out of those considerations, for it is not clear that because an outcome is desirable anyone or everyone can claim the *right* to bring it about. It could be argued that when there are no settled procedures to determine who has the right to intervene, anybody who can do so effectively can exercise that right. Such is, for example, Michael Walzer's position on intervention in Kosovo. The difficulty with this argument is that there are other states and international institutions that actively deny the existence of any such unilateral right to intervene. They argue that there are some settled, albeit imperfect, procedures or institutions that authorize the use of force. Any right to intervene derives from the authority of those institutions, not directly from general moral considerations. Those institutions may find general moral considerations based on human rights compelling, and arguably they ought to find them compelling, but those considerations unmediated through institutions cannot form the basis of a right to intervene.

In order to avoid the discord that arises from unclear delimitation of morally defined rights, states are under an obligation to subject their behavior to the authority of international institutions. The dilemma is that when institutions are incapable of acting, actions undertaken outside their authority might actually help strengthen a norm that they cannot themselves enforce. But such actions might weaken those institutions themselves. I think this dilemma can be overstated. After all, it is the states with power in the international system that are most likely to intervene. And these states are often responsible for strengthening or weakening international institutions in the first place.

3. Law and Morality

We can see the force of the foregoing argument with greater specificity by examining the arguments of proponents of what might be called the "no divergence thesis" in international law. These scholars argue that that there is, in fact, no divergence between positive international law and the requirements of morality; a right to intervene can be derived from elements of international law itself. On this view, it is true that Article 2(4) of the U.N. Charter requires that "all Members shall refrain in their international relations from the threat or use of force against the territorial integrity of political independence of any state, or in any manner inconsistent with the purposes of the United Nations." The Security Council under Chapter VII and the right of individual and collective self-defense authorize the exceptions to this provision. The "nonintervention" norm has been subsequently clarified by, for instance, the U.N. General Assembly Declaration of 1970 that states:

> No State or group of States has the right to intervene, directly or indirectly, *for any reason whatever*, in the internal or external affairs of any other State. Consequently armed intervention and all other forms of interference or attempted threats against the personality of the State or against its political, economic or cultural elements are in violation of international law.[11]

Although many concede that there has been a clear delegation of authority in the area of the use of force to the United Nations, many argue that there has also developed in international law an independent right of military intervention in the affairs of another state for the purposes of protecting individuals from grave violations of human rights. After all, even the U.N. Charter itself, as well as other multilateral treaties, including those prohibiting genocide, indicate that human rights have almost acquired the status of an authoritative constraint on state action. This argument draws on the fact that there has been a gradual shift in international public opinion, which suggests the ascendancy of human rights norms. There is a normative climate in which the horrendous costs of state-building and consolidation of national identities that were taken to be an inevitable part of the process of nineteenth-century state formation in Europe are no longer held to be acceptable. But how widespread is the acceptance of human rights norms? And how do they find expression in international law?

That some such norms may be found in international law is beyond dispute. But there is a difficulty in using the existence of "human rights norms" in international law as an unproblematic ally leading to a right of humanitarian intervention. On the one hand, there is the rather curious phenomenon that many of the states that have engaged in what might be called humanitarian intervention seem not to acknowledge that humanitarian intervention was the legal obligation under which they were acting. Many of these states denounced the violation of humanitarian principles by the states in which they intervened, but the arguments were seldom explicitly made part of their justification for recourse to armed force. Indeed, Adam Roberts has argued that even in the case of Kosovo, NATO governments did not support their actions by suggesting that there was a long-standing international practice that justified such intervention.[12] At a minimum, this suggests that states are at least hesitant to recognize a legal right to humanitarian intervention. There is still a legal gap between the ascendancy of human rights and related doctrines and the *right* to humanitarian intervention.

On the other hand, even if one were to accept the argument that there is something in international law that one could point to as underwriting a right of intervention, the relationship of that legal right to the U.N. Charter would still have to be clarified. I take it to be the case that, at the moment, there is no hierarchy of the sources of international law that would suggest that the peremptory norms of human rights automatically trump the treaty obligations of noninterference that arise from the U.N. Charter. It has become more common to acknowledge that how a state behaves toward its own citizens, or how a government governs are not simply matters for that state or government alone to determine. But even if it is the case that the norms of decency and good governance are becoming global responsibilities, recognized by international law, and monitored by international institutions, the precise relationship between these norms and the doctrine of noninterference embodied in the U.N. Charter remains unclear and deeply contested. Indeed, the fact that both the legality and morality of these interventions are disputed shows the fragility of emerging human rights norms, at least in relation to other aspects of the U.N. Charter. In cases where there are multiple sources of norms and conflicting norms, the privileging of one set over another cannot escape the suspicion that the choice of which norms to privilege is not determined by any legally authoritative criteria but by the moral or political preferences of those who make this determination. At the very least, appealing to "emerging norms," which do not yet have the status in international law that, say, treaties have, is an exercise whose results will be uncertain and whose authority will be strongly challenged. This is a contest that can be settled only by properly *authorized* institutions.

Many argue that the Security Council and other international institutions that are empowered to approve and sanction the use of force are usually unable to respond effectively to situations that demand humanitarian intervention, particularly the possibility of serious human rights violations. Michael Reisman, in his defense of the Kosovo intervention, for example, argues that

> [a]ssigning a nearly exclusive right to use force to a Security Council, on which the five most powerful states of the world sit as permanent members, is a workable idea if the responsibility of that Council is restricted to restricting threats to and breaches of peace and acts of aggression. . . . But the assignment of exclusive power to

the Council ceases to be workable if the writ of the United Nations is also extended to the protection of human rights, the international control of the essential techniques by which governments manage and control their people internally. On these matters, there are profound, possibly unbridgeable divides between the permanent members.[13]

Reisman's criticism of the Security Council is widely shared and is, in some respects, exactly right. But the argument presented here is too quick. It seems to suggest that the distinction between "breaches of peace and acts of aggression," on the one hand, and the protection of human rights issues, on the other, is an easy one to make. According to this argument, because the Security Council is a workable institution on matters pertaining to breaches of security but not on matters pertaining to human rights, its authority is not particularly relevant. No matter what one thinks of the morality of particular interventions, surely the distinction between threats to peace and protection of human rights is not entirely clear. After all, for the state that is the target of intervention, and for states that oppose intervention, interventions to protect human rights are seen simply as possible breaches of peace and security.

If the Security Council is empowered to do anything, it is to determine when an act of force constitutes an act of aggression or a threat to peace, and, its functional deficiencies notwithstanding, one cannot simply and straightforwardly argue that interventions occasioned by the violations of human rights do not involve security issues and hence that the Security Council's authority does not need to be acknowledged. The constitutive indeterminacy of the moral norm of human rights in relation to "security" goes all the way down and itself is something that institutions such as the Security Council may need to discuss. Indeed, rather than being dysfunctional, the Security Council's decision not to endorse intervention in cases such as Kosovo is evidence of its success. It is working as a body that by giving or withholding consent is signaling that certain kinds of intervention *may* constitute a threat to peace and security. Even if one finds the particular results morally problematic, it is too quick a move to rubbish the authority of international institutions in these areas altogether.

As an aside, it may be the case that those countries that did not sanction intervention and those that supported intervention in Kosovo both have interests in impeding the emergence of norms governing unilateral humanitarian intervention. Even states that engage in intervention are more comfortable that intervention is not a threat to peace and security so long as they are the ones doing it. I doubt NATO signatories would be very enthusiastic about the prospect of the Russians, or the Chinese, engaging in "humanitarian" intervention in their zones of influence and believe it is best to leave the precedent somewhat ambiguous in its applications rather than to codify it into law.[14]

Even though there may be *realpolitik* considerations behind the reluctance to codify norms on humanitarian intervention, the reluctance might also be an acknowledgment of an underlying moral reality. The moral reality is that recourse to international law and norms notwithstanding, the most that states want to be able to say when they unilaterally intervene is that they did so because of exceptional circumstances. By not insisting on the codification of humanitarian intervention, states try to walk the thin line between accepting that they acted under some moral obligation and implying that all the rules of the international system should be configured in light of those moral obligations irrespective of the opposition of other states.

That stance raises a fascinating question. Would it be a good thing if the legitimacy of humanitarian intervention were allowed to follow a case-by-case logic, improvised as the occasion demands? Arguably, if one recognizes that the use of force ought to be sanctioned only by particular international bodies acting as representatives of the international community, the need to codify norms would be less urgent; the rules governing intervention would emerge as part of the deliberations of such an organization as the Security Council. Madeline Albright, for instance, argued during the Kosovo crisis,

> As for the use of force, Kosovo tells us only what we should have already known. Yes, in confronting evil and otherwise protecting our interests, force is sometimes required. No, as before Kosovo, it is not wise to formulate assumptions based on any single experience about exactly when and how force should be applied. In cop-

ing with future crisis, the accumulated wisdom of the past will have to be weighed against factors unique to that place and time.[15]

Reference to "unique" factors can often be a cover for *realpolitik*. But there is clearly a worry that turning occasions like Kosovo into settled norms might undermine the whole collective security structure outlined in the U.N. Charter and is unlikely to elicit support. But there is also the tacit acknowledgement that it will be difficult to outline the necessary and sufficient conditions when intervention is called for in advance of any crisis. Such a characterization will be too general, and it will leave unspecified the relationship between the obligation to intervene and other possible obligations, such as not jeopardizing peace. Codifications would preempt the relevant factors in each case. What is more important is the availability of institutions in which a discursive process leading to authorization can be carried out. Although the United States is rightly accused of undermining just such institutions, Albright's reluctance to use the Kosovo intervention to force open international law at least tacitly acknowledges the authority of those institutions. It does seem to suggest that the recourse to "unlawful" practices, without proper authorization, must be considered an *extrema ratio*, and, formally, the authority of the Security Council must not be impugned.

Michael Glennon, in contrast, frankly acknowledges that humanitarian intervention in Kosovo was a breach of the U.N. Charter if not of international law, yet he urges us to use this opportunity to rethink international norms.[16] While defending intervention, some scholars press for the promotion of a new legal system with general norms validating the use of force by international institutions every time the protection of human rights demands it. These norms would also specify the conditions under which states could engage in humanitarian intervention without Security Council authorization. The worry here is that the recognition of an exception to the prohibition on the use of force would open the door to a good deal of abuse. To follow a logic of case-by-case improvisation would run the risk of producing greater uncertainty and destabilizing the international system. This worry is somewhat overstated. The real issue is not whether jurists can specify the conditions under which a new legal regime

providing for possibilities for the legitimate use of force can be
created—arguably international institutions already allow such
possibilities. The actual danger is that an increasing number of
international actors, both "public" and "private," will claim the
legitimate right to wage war without submitting themselves to the
authority of international institutions, and it is doubtful whether
codification will matter either way.

We may be in a world where, speaking optimistically, there is
the emergence of a *modus vivendi* between different competing
principles and conceptions of world order: the claims of sovereignty, claims of human rights, the authority of collective institutions such as the U.N., and unilateral action by states are all
competing with one another for greater acceptance. The priori-
ties among them are not settled as yet by any principle, nor are
the internal relations among them fully specified. Which values
command allegiance is therefore a function of balancing acts and
compromises. Such a *modus vivendi* does not, of course, amount to
clarity in law, and, like all *modi vivendi*, it will be subject to the
vagaries of power within the international system. It may be the
only possible answer to the dilemma John Vincent articulated
almost two decades ago: "In the present case, it is not yet clear
that a middle course of humanitarian intervention has been
traced between a virginal doctrine of nonintervention that would
allow nothing to be done and a promiscuous doctrine of intervention that would make a trollop of the law."[17] The solution lies not
so much in the evolution of law as in the evolution of institutions.

4. How Not to Talk about Intervention

In this section, I want to argue that there are substantial fallacies
and moral dangers inherent in thinking that humanitarian intervention signals, as some argue in the case of Kosovo, the onset of
some kind of cosmopolitan law. It is held that because these interventions stake out a higher moral ground, they signal a new institutionalization of cosmopolitan concerns. They show that in the
international order, appeals to morality beyond positive law can
work. I want to argue that even justified interventions should not
be seen as evidence of the growing salience of human rights concerns. Indeed, I argue that there is something deeply problematic

about seeing humanitarian intervention, especially war, as some kind of enforcement mechanism of morality or human rights.

There is great difficulty in appealing to a morality beyond positive law. It is founded on a radical skepticism toward the moral content of international law, toward the efficacy of international institutions, and arguably even rests on a naive faith in the capacity of war to result in consequences that are, on balance, overwhelmingly preferable. The recourse to ethics as a sign of skepticism about the existing international legal order is a perfectly respectable position to take; it is candid in its acknowledgment that international law and the authority of international institutions do not amount to much in the face of impending moral catastrophe. But appeals to morality may have the unintended effect of furthering the cause of unilateralism.

Jürgen Habermas argues that certain kinds of humanitarian intervention, such as those in Kosovo, should be seen as attempts to transform international law in a cosmopolitan direction.[18] This cosmopolitanism has three components. First, its objective is to put an end to murderous ethnic nationalism; second, this form of humanitarian intervention exemplifies the fact that states can "transcend" the reason of state doctrines and act on behalf of universal principles; and third, and most important, it seeks to transcend existing international law and transform it into a legal system with a new basis. A humanitarian intervention such as the one in Kosovo should not be judged by existing standards of international law, according to which it would be considered interference in the internal affairs of a sovereign state. In addition, intervention may have violated a prohibition on the use of military force, not to mention a prohibition on the *threat* to use force. Habermas argues that until international institutions are configured on new lines that more deeply institutionalize and entrench human rights, the borderline between law and morals will be inevitably blurred, as it was, in fact, in the war for Kosovo. Faced with a blocked Security Council, NATO could not help appealing to the moral validity of international law, that is, to norms that are not actually applied and upheld within the international community. In fact, Habermas argues, NATO acted successfully precisely because it acted without legitimization.

I am less interested in the empirical accuracy of Habermas's characterization of the motives of Western powers than in the structure of his argument. It amounts to saying simply this: because international political institutions are normatively weak and politically ineffective, international positive law does not have much standing. Morality comes into play precisely because "authority" lies in ruins. Because there is no duly constituted authority that can carry out the requirements of morality, particular nations, in this case NATO, led by the United States, can be legitimately seen as carriers of universal morality that current international law only weakly institutionalizes; a humanitarian war is itself one step toward the creation of a new order.

Again, for the moment, I am not dwelling directly on the all-things-considered justifiability of NATO action but on the curiousness of this argument. This argument is paradoxical, first, in that the domain of cosmopolitan universality again turns out be much more bounded than Habermas realizes. It has no way of seeing the opposition to such intervention, particularly outside the West, as anything but a morally obtuse response. Russia's, China's, India's, or the world's opposition to the intervention can have no moral standing, in this view, because they are in the grip of particularistic principles, ethnocentric in their orientation, or prisoners of their interests in such a way that they are kept from perceiving the universal appeal of a cosmopolitan law based on human rights. In the very act of creating a space for a cosmopolitan conception of law, Habermas *enacts* a polarity between the West and the Rest. One could argue that the view of these states does not represent the views of their people in this matter, a proposition as empirically dubious as it is legally suspect. And to argue that these states' views do not have moral standing simply is to beg the question of whose views do. Yet, if they have moral standing, then cosmopolitan morality has a much thinner sociological basis than Habermas acknowledges; using Habermas's terminology, our lifeworlds do not quite meet our morality halfway. To dismiss the standing of other states and to suppose that human rights can be universalized without the consensus of states is more likely to destroy the international order than it is to strengthen human rights.

Second, the argument is paradoxical in that appealing to morality loosens the connection between law and morality in another context. There is danger in the skepticism about international institutions on which this argument rests. Is not the appeal to "ethics" over and above the rough-and-tumble of international institutions and the prevalence of international law such as it exists simply a license to circumvent the provisions that subject the use of force to suitable restraints agreed upon by the human community? Is it morally permissible to kill innocents to prevent a massacre? Is the killing of innocents acceptable so long as their deaths are simply "collateral damage" by military action? How is the distinction between willed action, foreseen effects, and unforeseen consequences to be made? Can there be international norms governing the requirements of proportionality of force? In the process of creating a new cosmopolitan norm, is not a new discrimination being institutionalized? Were not the lives of combatants of intervening countries ranked higher than the principle of noncombatant immunity? Is combatant immunity a greater principle than noncombatant immunity?[19] One should not readily assume that these questions have easy answers.[20] After all, countries are often willing to intervene only if their own casualties are minimized. But surely any claim that humanitarian intervention is evidence of the emergence of new legal or moral norms, of a new cosmopolitan sensibility, cannot dismiss the moral weight of these questions lightly.

A genuine cosmopolitanism of concern can emerge only if there is an attenuation of the asymmetrical valuing of human life. The *practices* of intervention, rather than the doctrine, enact the very contradiction between universal values and particularistic solidarities that intervention supposedly overcomes. Intervention exemplifies rather than overcomes the asymmetrical valuing of life on which the moral valences of sovereignty depend. The rhetoric of cosmopolitan solidarity, even the language of human rights, can often provide what Michael Ignatieff calls a "powerful new rhetoric of abstract justification."[21] The practices of war are so fraught that mere availability of abstract justification for intervention can disguise the polarities being enacted in practice.

Habermas's position on Kosovo mitigates these worries in two ways, both empirically contestable. On the one hand, with some qualifications, he does not take the toll on innocents to be morally significant in the case of Kosovo. On the other hand, he places a great deal of emphasis on the good intentions of those engaging in humanitarian action. Rather than concentrating on the concrete effects of war, he emphasizes too much the intention of participants—always a dubious move when it comes to judging the conduct of any war in its full effects. It is often tempting to consider humanitarian intervention as different from war because the motives are different, because there seems to be a good-faith, altruistic component behind it. Yet, too much emphasis on intention, a common Kantian failing, can occlude the moral issues at stake. Arguably, in the conduct of wars in the twenty-first century, restraints on the use of force will be at least as important a measure of the advance of cosmopolitan law as the international community's willingness to take occasional humanitarian action. There is a significant danger that humanitarian war does not help to achieve the pacifying functions of international law and may even discredit the cosmopolitan ideal of universal citizenship.

5. WAR AND ENFORCEMENT

Can war be used as a legal instrument to defend human rights? Is there any essential difference between just war doctrines and humanitarian intervention? Hans Kelsen gave currency to the idea that war can be viewed as a "legal sanction" when states use it in response to violations of international law.[22] In such cases, Kelsen argued, the state using force can be seen as vested with penal functions. Kelsen acknowledged that his theory had two problems. First, in the absence of a superior neutral authority that has the power to characterize acts of war as crimes, the description of just war as penal sanction makes little sense. Second, describing some wars as a sort of penal sanction flounders on the same paradox that it is a sanction that only the strong can use against the weak. But many writers come perilously close to thinking that humanitarian intervention is a form of penal sanction. Terry Nardin, for instance, wants to revive early modern ideas about using force to protect the innocent, which include the thought that every state has a right to enforce natural law.[23] Michael Walzer has argued that when the crimes being committed are serious, "an insult to human conscience," no one in particular has the moral obligation to intervene but all have the *right* to do so.[24] In other words, individual states or a group of states have executive authority to "enforce" natural laws or the laws of common morality. David Luban provides the clearest articulation of the view that nations are entitled to "wage war to enforce human rights."[25]

The troubling feature of this account is that it makes war an instrument of international morality; war is the sanction attached to "international morality" or norms. The reason this is troubling is that modern war, even when conducted with the utmost restraint, imposes heavy costs on innocent victims, to put it somewhat euphemistically. If terrorism involves the use of force against innocent victims to cause panic, most wars, including wars of humanitarian intervention, come perilously close to creating just such a panic. Can one therefore properly speak of "enforcing" the law or moral norms in the same way in which we think of punishment as a kind of enforcement? And claiming a general right to enforce the common or natural laws raises a different question: why do only states or international organizations have this right? After all, this is not merely a rhetorical question but a ground that many "terrorist" groups wish to occupy.

It is a bit optimistic to think that any rules can govern wars in a way in which rules govern punishment. Just as in domestic law, where it would be unjust to inflict serious costs of detention, property loss, injury, or death on innocents in order to "enforce" the law, it is very odd to describe intervention as a kind of enforcement regime when disproportionate numbers of victims are likely to be innocent. War, in that sense, is the antithesis of both morality and law. It could still be "justified" on grounds of dire consequences, but to describe it as an international enforcement mechanism is a travesty of the very human rights it claims to enforce. War, even one waged with the best of intentions, is at best a dubious instrument with which to advance the interests of law. There is something to the thought that in modern societies war—even humanitarian war—will remain the antithesis of justice and morality. There are only necessary wars, no just ones.

The emergence of "humanitarian interventions," especially in light of Kosovo, I have been suggesting, even if carried out with the purest of motives, does not augur the onset of new forms of human solidarity or the emergence of a new cosmopolitan thinking. Indeed, the fact that there is a real danger of unilateralism; the fact that there seems to many to be an asymmetrical valuing of human life enacted in these wars; and the fact that war itself risks undermining the individualistic basis of human rights should all urge caution upon us.

There are still serious disagreements on the proper conception of morality and who is best in a position to enforce it, but such disagreements are best handled within global institutions rather than through unilateral acts of force. Although Habermas has argued for a "fully institutionalized cosmopolitan order" more persuasively than anyone else, the quick recourse to ethical unilateralism undermines rather than furthers the move toward greater international institutionalization. Humanitarian intervention will be justified under certain circumstances, but better evidence for cosmopolitanism and solidarity will not be the fact that some states ostensibly act to protect human rights. Rather, it will be whether states will submit themselves to common international institutions. That will be genuine pacifism, in the Kantian sense.

6. Conclusion

Thomas Franck has argued that the confusions and hesitations of international institutions can be interpreted in a more benign way. These institutions, rather than being completely paralyzed by unbridgeable differences and strict fidelity to the principle of nonintervention, have in fact been reworking the Charter to conform to less rigid principles and are seeking "to apply this adapted version of the applicable principle on a case by case basis, informed by the contexts and the facts as much as by abstract normative concepts."[26] Thus, the false choice that is posed between intolerably passive and incapable institutions not allowing action in cases that clearly demand it, on the one hand, and the alternative, on the other hand, of jettisoning the authority of those institutions altogether can be somewhat mitigated. These international institutions and the Security Council in particular have responded to cases of intervention on a continuum ranging from condemnation to reluctant and mild censure to acceptance.

The international community's moral and legal response to intervention, if not its political will, has shown more discrimination than it is given credit for by those who would simply dismiss international institutions. This story of a nuanced evolution is important for many reasons. First, it rightly reminds us that international institutions have not always failed and that they still contain immense possibilities. And it bears repeating, as Wheeler notes, that "governments are notoriously unreliable as rescuers."[27] Second, a focus on political institutions would clarify the fact that the need for action in a humanitarian emergency does not permit the conclusion that *any* state or group of states has a right to intervene but, rather, that international organizations have duties. Third, a better measure of the emergence of "cosmopolitan" law would not be individual states selectively taking recourse to ethical values but the emergence of more robust and just international institutions. The willingness of states to strengthen these institutions and reform them will be a better signal of their willingness to transcend "reason of state" doctrines, and it will be a better test of how enduring norms of solidarity are.

It is perhaps with these considerations in mind that the Report of the International Commission on Intervention and State Sovereignty rightly suggests that the focus of the debate on humanitarian intervention should be on the obligations of the *international* community. The report rightly avoids thinking of humanitarian intervention in terms of the "rights" of particular states. Rather, it focuses on the responsibilities of the international community toward peoples and individuals let down, or abused, or put at risk by their own states. The concept of "human security," including a concern for human rights, lacks proper analytical precision.[28] And for that very reason, more attention will need to be paid to the issue of the proper authority to delimit the scope of the concept. But it at least picks out that human security is indivisible in one significant sense. There is no such thing as a "humanitarian crisis" happening *elsewhere*. As states realize this more, and as national security concerns and humanitarian concerns become increasingly conjoint, institutions that knit sovereign states into more enduring webs of interdependence ought to become more, not less, important. As we know, paradoxically, such institutions can be created solely by sovereign states. But only through such institutions can the aims of the pacification of violence and the protection of human rights be reconciled.

NOTES

I would like to thank Anne-Marie Slaughter, Terry Nardin, Melissa Williams, and participants at the ASPLP panel for very helpful comments on this paper. Terry Nardin is owed extra gratitude for his detailed editorial comments and reconstruction. And Rosemary Nagy for her superb editing.

1. As Michael Ignatieff argues in "Intervention and State Failure," *Dissent* 49, no. 1 (Winter 2002): 115–23.

2. For some helpful suggestions, see Gene Lyons and Michael Mastanduno, *Beyond Westphalia? State Sovereignty and International Intervention* (Baltimore: Johns Hopkins University Press, 1995); Simon Chesterman, *Just War or Just Peace? Humanitarian Intervention and International Law* (Oxford: Oxford University Press, 2001); N. K. Tsagourias, *Jurisprudence of International Law* (Manchester: Manchester University Press, 2000); Nicholas Wheeler, *Saving Strangers* (Cambridge: Cambridge University Press, 2000); Terry Nardin, "The Moral Basis for Humanitarian Intervention," *Ethics and International Affairs* 16, no. 1 (2002): 57–70; and older works by Stanley Hoffmann and Hedley Bull.

3. Stanley Hoffmann, *Duties Beyond Borders* (Syracuse: Syracuse University Press, 1983), 183.

4. Martin Wight, *Power Politics* (Harmondsworth: Penguin Books, 1979), 191.

5. Kofi Annan, "Two Concepts of Sovereignty," *The Economist*, September 18, 1999, 50.

6. A liberal conception that is more tolerant of nondemocracies is, of course, that of John Rawls in *The Law of Peoples* (Cambridge: Harvard University Press, 1999) and the voluminous literature that followed.

7. Robert Jackson, *The Global Covenant: Human Conduct in a World of States* (Oxford: Oxford University Press, 2000), 367.

8. Bhikhu Parekh, "Rethinking Humanitarian Intervention," *International Political Science Review* 18, no. 1 (1997): 59.

9. Hedley Bull, "Conclusion," in *Intervention in World Politics*, ed. Hedley Bull, 182–94 (Oxford: Clarendon Press, 1984), 193.

10. The most powerful argument in this regard is Samantha Power, *A Problem from Hell: America and the Age of Genocide* (New York: Alfred A. Knopf, 2002).

11. Declaration on Principles of International Law Concerning Friendly Relations and Cooperation among States in Accordance with the Charter of the United Nations, General Assembly Resolution 2625 (1970).

12. See Adam Roberts, "NATO's 'Humanitarian War' over Kosovo," *Survival* 41, no. 3 (1999): 104.

13. Michael Reisman, "Kosovo's Antinomies," *American Journal of International Law* 93 (1999): 860–61.

14. Jane Stromseth reaches a similar conclusion. See "Rethinking Humanitarian Intervention: A Case for Incremental Change," in *Humanitarian Intervention*, ed. J. L. Holzgrefe and Robert Keohane, 232–73 (Cambridge: Cambridge University Press, 2002).

15. Madeline Albright, "To Win the Peace," *Wall Street Journal*, July 14, 1999.

16. Michael J. Glennon, *Limits of Law, Prerogatives of Power: Interventionism after Kosovo* (New York: Palgrave, 2001).

17. John Vincent, *Nonintervention and International Order* (Princeton: Princeton University Press, 1974), 349.

18. I am relying mainly on Habermas's now-famous essay "Bestaliatät und Humanität," first published in *Die Zeit* 18 (1999). Habermas seems more disillusioned after U.S. intervention in Iraq. See his "The Fall of the Monument," *Hindu*, June 5, 2003.

19. For powerful moral and legal reflections on this, see Anne-Marie Slaughter and William Burke-White, "An International Constitutional Moment," *Harvard International Law Journal* 43 (Winter 2002).

20. On a possible justification for targeting civilians in war, see Jonathan Glover, *Humanity: A Moral History of the Twentieth Century* (New Haven: Yale University Press, 2001).

21. Michael Ignatieff, *Virtual War: Kosovo and Beyond* (New York: Picador, 2001), 3.

22. Hans Kelsen, *The Pure Theory of Law* (Berkeley: University of California Press, 1967).

23. Nardin, "The Moral Basis of Humanitarian Intervention." To be fair to Nardin, although he uses the language of "enforcement," he is far from advocating *unilateral* enforcement.

24. Michael Walzer, "The Lone Ranger," *New Republic*, April 27, 1998.

25. David Luban, "Just War and Human Rights," *Philosophy and Public Affairs* 9 (1990): 160–81.

26. Thomas Franck, "When, If Ever, May States Deploy Military Force without Prior Security Council Authorization?" *Washington University Journal of Law and Policy* 5 (2001): 64.

27. Wheeler, *Saving Strangers*, 310.

28. For the best discussion, see David Baldwin, "The Concept of Security," *Review of International Studies* 23 (1997): 5–26.

11

THE UNAVOIDABILITY OF MORALITY: A COMMENTARY ON MEHTA

KOK-CHOR TAN

1.

Pratap Mehta's historically sensitive paper reminds us of the great difficulties, both conceptual and practical, surrounding humanitarian intervention.[1] In particular, given that moral arguments have often been used to rationalize self-serving strategic interventions, Mehta argues that we need to pay more attention to the rules of international institutions when determining the permissibility of intervention. Ethical arguments, to the extent that they can be invoked, are to be situated "in the context of institutions and politics" (p. 261).

I agree with many of the observations Mehta makes in his instructive paper and with many of his concerns. In my role as commentator, however, I want to focus on, and tease out, two points of disagreement. The first concerns Mehta's primary thesis: that we should turn to the rules of international law and the procedures of international institutions, rather than to morality as such, when determining the permissibility of intervention. This is, Mehta worries, because allowing intervention to be justified on purely moral grounds will open the way for unilateral intervention. This prioritization of institutions over morality constitutes the philosophical core of Mehta's paper, and it speaks to the important question of the relationship between morality and institutions. Mehta is rightly suspicious of unilateral intervention, but I will contend that it is not moral reasoning as such that motivates unilateralism in intervention. I will suggest, to the contrary, that ignoring the demands of morality is more likely to lead to unilateralism in intervention than is respecting these demands.

The second point concerns Mehta's opposition to "institutionalizing" intervention, meaning by this the clarification and codification of intervention by international law. Mehta argues that clarifying the rules of intervention can lead to their abuse. However, I suggest that this concern over the potential abuse of an institutionalized practice is overstated. Moreover, the problem of selective intervention, which Mehta identifies as central in the contemporary practice of intervention, supports the case for greater clarity and specification in international law on intervention, not the case for its continuing vagueness.

2.

Mehta writes that there is "no way to coherently ground our moral thinking in these matters in a manner that bypasses the need for collective international institutions" (p. 261). Appealing to morality without reference to institutions, Mehta worries, allows certain powerful countries to decide and act unilaterally. As he writes, "[A]ppeals to morality may have the unintended effect of furthering the cause of unilateralism" (p. 277).

I take it that by "morality" Mehta means, rather incontrovertibly, the class of preinstitutional rules and principles that need not be identical to the established rules of positive international law. For Mehta, there is a distinction between morality and positive law, and a unilateral intervention is one that is not sanctioned by positive law even if moral arguments are advanced in its favor. The worry, apparently, is that allowing actors to appeal to principles outside the framework of existing international law will present a convenient avenue for unilateral intervention.

Mehta's worry about unilateralism is not to be lightly dismissed, given the dismal history of armed intervention. But most commentators who defend the relevance of moral consideration in intervention, and in international practice in general, do not deny the significance of international institutions in moral decision making and action. They recognize that institutional accountability is important, and that with collective institutional support, an intervention acquires legal authorization and legitimacy. In addition, institutions have the additional function of coordinating and mediating collective action, thereby enhancing efficiency in moral action. So "international idealists," as we can call them, do not downplay the importance of multilateral decision making and authorization. They emphatically deny that there is a necessary connection between endorsing moral reasoning in international practice and endorsing unilateralism. After all, a morally justified intervention may well also be one that is multilaterally endorsed (as in the U.N. authorized intervention to restore democracy in Haiti in 1993). The claim that moral arguments will lead to unilateral action is, therefore, based on a false antinomy between morality and institutional decision making. In fact, it is more likely that most cases of unilateral intervention (though, of course, not all) are also indefensible on moral grounds. Opponents of unilateralism, it seems, should want to encourage moral thinking in international relations, not question its relevance.

One reason why moral appeals are thought to encourage unilateral action is that moral reasoning is often distorted and misused to rationalize narrowly self-interested ends. Indeed, this worry about the abuse of morality is one source of the political realist's skepticism about moral thinking in international affairs generally. For realists, any talk of morality, including, in particular, cosmopolitan morality, is at bottom a guise for promoting narrowly defined national or strategic interests (see Mehta, pp. 275–76).

But even though this realist concern rightly warns us against taking any moral claim at face value, it does not repudiate the importance of moral reasoning in international practice. Moral claims may be misused, and indefensible moral arguments may be advanced to justify an intervention. Even so, the fact that such abuses of moral reasoning are possible does not alone disprove the relevance or validity of moral reasoning. On the contrary, that self-serving actors appeal to moral claims to rationalize their actions shows that moral claims are taken seriously and are regarded to have persuasive force. That the abusers of morality take advantage of moral claims to give their actions a cloak of legitimacy attests to the recognized force of moral arguments.

Indeed, Mehta's criticism of morality seems to run together what we can strictly call "morality" and what we should call, for want of a better term, *ideology*. By ideological claims, I mean those claims that reflect narrow political or national interests. Thus, unlike moral claims, ideological claims fail what many philosophers take to be the central requirement of any valid moral claim —that of universalizability. Kant's first formulation of the categorical imperative, the Formula of Universal Law, captures this universalistic character of moral reasoning well: "Act only on that maxim through which you can at the same time will that it should become a universal law."[2] Or, one may hold that moral claims are universalizable in the sense that they are based on principles that reasonable persons cannot reasonably reject, to adapt T. M. Scanlon's formulation.[3] The identification of morality with ideology distorts this common understanding of the nature of moral reasoning by treating it as a form of reasoning that need not be *universally shared.* It seems to me that this failure to distinguish morality, commonly understood, from ideology underlies and mistakenly motivates Mehta's skepticism about morality in international relations.[4]

We would do well, therefore, to distinguish between interventions carried out on ideological grounds—call them "ideological interventions"—and interventions carried out on moral grounds. The crucial feature of a moral intervention is that it is justified by reference to principles that could be universally assented to (or that all reasonable persons could reasonably agree on), whereas ideological interventions are based on reasons that need not be universally shared. Interventions performed on ideological grounds are unilateral in a pernicious way because they serve narrow interests rather than the demands of common morality; morally justified interventions are not unilateral in this way.

So moral arguments, properly understood, do not necessarily support unilateral intervention. Ideological interests may motivate unilateral action, and moral claims can be advanced to rationalize what is, at bottom, a self-interested intervention. But these observations about unilateral intervention do not repudiate the validity of moral reasoning as such. Indeed, one might even say that a properly justified moral intervention can never be *unilateral* in the strict sense of the term because it would be an intervention based on reasons that all reasonable persons could assent to, even if international law as it stands does not authorize the intervention.

To be sure, Mehta understands unilateralism legalistically, as it is commonly understood in international relations. That is, he means by unilateralism the absence of international legal authorization. So a morally justified intervention, meaning by this an intervention to which all reasonable persons could agree, could still be unilateral in this specific sense, if actual international authorization is not forthcoming. And it is unilateralism in this common understanding with which Mehta takes issue.

But why should unilateralism in the legalistic sense be a worry or, indeed, the principal issue, as Mehta puts it? If we should be wary about unilateral intervention so understood, it is not because unilateral interventions are appeals to morality as such *and* that we should be skeptical about moral claims (as Mehta suggests). Rather, it is because unilateral intervention, that is, an intervention that lacks international institutional support, more often than not stands on very weak moral grounds, if any at all. That is, we ought to be suspicious about unilateral intervention *not* because it is an intervention based on *moral arguments* but precisely because unilateral interventions are usually not morally defensible. Unilateral intervention serves only as an indicator, and an often reliable one at that, of an intervention's illegitimacy—an indicator that it is *not* an intervention based on universally binding principles. So, unilateralism is not in itself morally problematic; it is what unilateralism generally stands for that worries us.

So, although the international idealist does not discount the importance of international authorization, she will claim that institutions *as they are* do not necessarily define the moral limits of intervention. If, on due consideration and deliberation, we find that existing institutions do not meet certain moral standards, we have a duty—what John Rawls calls a "natural duty" of justice—to reform or replace these institutions.[5] Idealists, then, do not necessarily want to bypass institutions, but they do want their actions to be mediated by institutions as they should be—by "laws as they might be" (to borrow Rousseau's phrase)—not by institutions as they are. Existing institutional rules are to be judged against moral standards, not the other way around.[6] Accordingly, contra Mehta, idealists do not necessarily want to "rubbish the authority of international institutions in these areas all together" (p. 273). What idealists oppose is the acceptance of the authority of existing institutions as final and absolute.

If these conclusions are sound, what this means, ultimately, is that it is not unilateralism itself that is the principal issue but the *moral justification* of a unilateral intervention. If morality requires acting in a manner that existing rules of institutions prohibit, it is not straightforwardly the case that such action should be avoided. For example, should positive international law stand in the way of an intervention that has incontrovertible moral support, intervening without the sanction of positive international law (that is, intervening unilaterally, as Tanzania did in Uganda, Vietnam in Cambodia, India in the former East Pakistan, and NATO in Kosovo) is not necessarily morally problematic. At the very least, that an intervention is unilateral does not necessarily mean that it is morally objectionable. If anything, the need for unilateral action in this case might be evidence that our existing laws are not laws as they should be. Ruling a unilateral intervention to be morally objectionable just because it is unilateral is to confuse a means for an end by mistakenly giving moral significance to a method of evaluation.

Importantly, there is the prospect that a morally legitimate unilateral intervention can have the effect of revising positive international law. As Anne-Marie Slaughter argues with regard to the (illegal) NATO intervention in Kosovo, the intervention, though enacted without U.N. authorization and hence illegal in the strict sense, was morally legitimate. And this "illegal but legitimate" intervention, as Slaughter calls it, has motivated a new international legal thinking concerning the limits and even obligation of intervention.[7] In a similar vein, Allen Buchanan argues that illegal but morally justified interventions provide the avenue for what he calls "illegal legal reforms." Given the "heavy reliance on customary law, absence of a sovereign universal legislature, and the obvious limitation of the treaty process" in the international legal system, Buchanan notes, reform in international law without "illegality" is difficult to achieve.[8] I need not defend Buchanan's stronger thesis here; all I am asserting is that disallowing unilateralism in international action will have the effect of cutting off one source of international legal reform.

If I have understood him correctly, Mehta's moral skepticism is ultimately premised on his belief that there can be no institutionally independent method of arriving at moral agreement. The problem with making moral arguments, Mehta contends, is that there appears to be a diversity of moral points of view, and hence to advance one moral point of view over others is more likely to "destroy the international order" than to promote humanitarian cause (p. 278). But this argument about actual disagreement, at best, shows the difficulty of achieving moral consensus in our diverse world, not that moral reasoning and the search for moral agreement are to be abandoned altogether. It is too quick to reach conclusions about the impossibility of moral agreement (and of moral reasoning) from observations about actual disagreements. As a matter of fact, if this skeptical argument is taken seriously, moral reasoning in general becomes impossible, and not just international moral reasoning, for actual disagreements about moral matters are common in the domestic sphere as well. That is, the argument from disagreement, if granted, will support moral skepticism across the board, a position that I doubt Mehta would want to defend.

As evidence of the irreconcilability of different moral points of view, Mehta points out that defenders of universalist morality can treat opposing views as only "morally obtuse" (p. 278). But just as the failure to distinguish morality and ideology provides one source of the realist's skepticism, the failure to distinguish moral reasoning from what we might call "moral posturing" is responsible for another. There may be self-described defenders of humanitarian values who treat opposing views with contempt, in the way Mehta describes, but this is not how proper moral deliberation and discourse ought to proceed. In particular, constructive moral discussion across cultures, as Charles Taylor argues, must begin from "a presumption of equal worth," the presumption that "cultures that have provided the horizon of meaning for large numbers of human beings, of diverse characters and temperaments . . . are almost certain to have something that deserves our admiration and respect even if accompanied by much of what we have to abhor or reject."[9] Cosmopolitans, say, may reject views antithetical to the ethical universalism they endorse, but they do so not simply because these opposing views are seen as "obtuse" but because these views do not withstand scrutiny. And nothing about defending cosmopolitan ideals exempts cosmopolitans from recognizing that their own position might be mistaken. Cosmopolitans should critically examine their own commitments and assess them against opposing views. It is one thing to dismiss opposing views out of court as obtuse, another thing to reject them after critical evaluation.[10]

With all due respect to Mehta (p. 275–76), then, moral arguments, properly advanced, need not have the effect of destroying international order. Moral dialogue does not mean moral relativism or contempt for other moral points of view. At any rate, even if taking a moral stance risks some disorder, order is not the sole moral concern. As Charles Beitz writes, "From the moral point of view, many things matter. The things that matter include peace and stability . . . [but] they also include human rights and social justice."[11] To say that moral arguments ought not to be made just because they threaten international order curiously misses the very purpose of making moral arguments, namely that of criticizing and judging existing norms and practices.

Mehta does not deny that moral disagreements can be resolved, but he thinks that they are to be settled by reference to institutional rules, not independently of these rules. But preinstitutional moral reasoning remains unavoidable even here. If institutions are to serve the function of adjudicating competing moral claims, we are still faced with the question as to the *appropriate* institutional standards for mediating such conflicts. And this is, unavoidably, a moral question that precedes institutional norms. Institutions can serve the proper function of adjudicating competing claims, including that of deciding whether there is a right or duty to intervene, only if these are institutions that have satisfied certain moral conditions. Such conditions may include the ideals of impartiality or reciprocity, accountability, publicity, and respect for basic human rights.[12] The problem with granting absolute priority to institutions over morality in our world *as it is* is that our current institutional standards may not satisfy these and other moral conditions of institutional appropriateness.

To summarize, although I share some of Mehta's concern

about unilateral intervention, I do not share the basis of this concern. It is not moral reasoning per se that is responsible for unilateral action in international practice. Rather, more often than not, it is the failure to respect the constraints of proper moral reasoning that prompts unilateral action. Moreover, it is important not to misplace the real objection against unilateralism. Unilateralism is a worry, not because unilateralism is morally objectionable in itself but because unilateralism is often a sign that an action lacks moral support. Ultimately, it is the underlying moral basis of an intervention that should be of interest, not the actual international support that it receives.

The relationship between morality, on the one side, and institutions and law, on the other, is complex, and I do not pretend to have elucidated this complexity here. My claim is only that it is too quick to give priority to the dictates of institutions when the demands of morality and the rules of institutions conflict.

3.

Mehta is not only skeptical of moral arguments in defense of intervention, he is also reluctant to codify the conditions of permissible intervention. One difficulty with institutionalizing intervention that Mehta identifies is that it would be difficult to come to any agreement on the specifics of permissible intervention. Now, it is true that the conditions and limits of a just intervention are controversial, but this means that we need more and continued international *moral* deliberation on the precise terms of intervention, not its avoidance.

A worry might be that institutionalizing intervention would set the international community dangerously on a slippery slope toward excessive intervention—countries might then appeal to the legalized principles of intervention to lend legitimacy to their strategic incursions into other countries. But this worry is overstated: institutionalization with proper institutional safeguards can provide a way of regulating and controlling intervention while minimizing abuse. One such safeguard is the international "jurying" process discussed by Thomas Franck—an impartial decision-making procedure whose function is to determine whether the conditions for a permissible intervention have been met. Such a "jurying" mechanism provides a way of limiting potential abuses of an institutionalized right to intervene.[13]

Given that morally questionable interventions already take place in the absence of clear guidelines, it is not clear why anyone would think that the problem of abuse is unique to codification. Indeed, the problem of unjustified intervention stems not from the fact that laws permitting intervention lend themselves to abuse (for there are no such laws at present), but from the lack of *clear rules* regulating and restricting intervention, thereby affording international actors wide scope to interpret unilaterally the conditions of justified intervention. More explicit standards for intervention can provide a firmer and less disputable control on the practice of intervention and do not necessarily exacerbate it. By contrast, leaving the legal norms of intervention vague means that the practice of intervention cannot be properly regulated and controlled, thus making it more liable to misuse and abuse. In short, unjustifiable interventions take place because of, rather than in spite of, the lack of clear institutional guidelines and rules on the conditions and limits of intervention.

The importance of normative and legal clarity concerning intervention does not deny Franck's thesis that there has to be a credible international "jurying" process. First, the process of jurying, as Franck describes it, presupposes morally clear and sound principles; second, a jurying procedure is still needed even in the context of clear legal norms to ascertain whether the facts do justify the application of these norms.

There is another important reason why we need to institutionalize intervention. This reason recalls Mehta's own observation, namely, that the practice of intervention is plagued by hypocrisy. Powerful countries choose to intervene only when national interests are involved, voicing humanitarian sentiments to ennoble their military excursions. But they often refrain from acting when there are no compelling national interests at stake, even though the humanitarian stakes in these cases are high. Or, when they do act, they do so only when the costs to themselves are minimized, sometimes to the point of compromising the success of the intervention.[14]

Yet, such inconsistency in action calls for greater institutional clarification concerning intervention, not its continuing vagueness. The problem of selective intervention points to a relatively unexplored but pressing question: is a permissible intervention also an obligatory intervention? The widespread public criticism of international inaction in the face of genocide in Rwanda, for example, suggests poignantly that intervention is sometimes thought to be not only permissible but also obligatory.

But can there be a duty to intervene? Some would point out that the duty to intervene cannot be morally demanded of anyone because no one has been assigned that duty. It might be granted that the international community as a whole has the obligation to intervene to combat severe cases of human rights violations, but it is not clear which particular member of the international community is morally obliged to carry out the intervention. So no one can be morally bound to act.

But if the duty to intervene cannot be morally demanded of anyone because it is left unassigned, this is clearly a problem with the institutionalization and codification of duties. It is the absence of institutional precision that leaves duties unassigned and correspondingly makes the rights corresponding to these duties unclaimable.[15] The problem of selective intervention can, therefore, be assuaged if the duties of intervention are specified and institutionalized. The hypocrisy or inconsistency in action with respect to intervention requires, therefore, greater institutional clarity, not less. Codification can include, in addition to clarifying the conditions of permissible intervention, assigning and allocating responsibilities to particular international bodies and agencies, and establishing new agents of intervention such as an international humanitarian defense force with clearly defined duties and mandate.

Other issues may arise regarding the codification of intervention, and I do not want to underestimate the challenges that they do raise.[16] What I am suggesting is that the potential for abuse alone does not tell against institutionalization, and, more important, that the problem that exercises Mehta, that of selective intervention, is due in large part to the vagueness of existing international norms concerning the rights and obligations of intervention. Clarifying the moral and legal norms of intervention, which can include institutionalizing the duty to intervene, is a necessary step toward addressing Mehta's own concern.

To conclude, Mehta's stimulating essay reminds us of the common misgivings international realists have about the place of morality in international relations. Still, while real political constraints may limit the effectiveness of moral reasoning in international practice, such concerns do not themselves disprove the appropriateness of moral thinking in the international arena. It seems to me that many of the problems that rightly command Mehta's attention arise not from taking morality too seriously in international practice but from not taking morality seriously enough.

NOTES

I thank my fellow panelists at the ASPLP meeting in Boston, August 2002 —Pratap Mehta, Melissa Williams, and Ann-Marie Slaughter—for their thoughtful contributions and remarks; members of the audience for their helpful questions; Karen Detlefsen for several helpful discussions; and Terry Nardin and Melissa Williams for their editorial advice and guidance. I want especially to thank Terry for his careful and detailed comments on successive drafts of this commentary.

1. Pratap Bhanu Mehta, "From State Sovereignty to Human Security (Via Institutions?)," this volume, chap. 10. References to this work will henceforth be made parenthetically in the text.

2. Emmanuel Kant, *Groundwork of the Metaphysics of Morals*, trans. H. J. Paton (New York: Harper and Row, 1964 [1785]), 88.

3. As Scanlon puts it, "[T]hinking about right and wrong is, at the most basic level, thinking about what could be justified to others on grounds that they, if appropriately motivated, could not reasonably reject." T. M. Scanlon, *What We Owe to Each Other* (Cambridge: Harvard University Press, 1997), 4.

4. See, for example, Marshall Cohen, "Moral Skepticism and International Relations," in *International Ethics*, ed. Charles Beitz et al., 3–50 (Princeton: Princeton University Press, 1985).

5. John Rawls, *A Theory of Justice* (Cambridge: Harvard University Press, 1971), 115.

6. See Terry Nardin, "The Moral Basis of Humanitarian Intervention," *Ethics and International Affairs* 16, no. 1 (2002): 57–71; also Joseph Boyle, "Traditional Just War Theory and Humanitarian Intervention," this volume, chap. 1.

7. Anne-Marie Slaughter, "Good Reasons for Going Around the U.N.," *New York Times*, March 18, 2003.

8. Allen Buchanan, "Reforming the Law of Humanitarian Intervention," in *Humanitarian Intervention: Ethical, Legal, and Political Dilemmas*, ed. J. L. Holzgrefe and Robert O. Keohane (Cambridge: Cambridge University Press, 2003), 136.

9. Charles Taylor, "The Politics of Recognition," in *Multiculturalism: Examining the Politics of Recognition*, ed. Amy Gutmann (Princeton: Princeton University Press, 1994), 72–73. For more on moral dialogue across cultures, see Michele Moody-Adams, *Fieldwork in Familiar Places* (Cambridge: Harvard University Press, 1997).

10. I discuss this in Kok-Chor Tan, *Toleration, Diversity, and Global Justice* (University Park: Pennsylvania State University Press, 2000), chap. 8.

11. Charles Beitz, "The Reagan Doctrine in Nicaragua," in *Problems in International Justice*, ed. Stephen Luper-Foy, 182–95 (Boulder: Westview Press, 1988).

12. I adapt here the discussion by Amy Gutmann and Dennis Thompson, *Democracy and Disagreement* (Cambridge: Harvard University Press, 1996).

13. Thomas Franck, "Legality and Legitimacy in Humanitarian Intervention," this volume, chap. 5.

14. See, for example, Henry Shue, "Bombing to Rescue," in *Ethics and Foreign Intervention*, ed. Deen Chatterjee and Don Scheid, 97–117 (Cambridge: Cambridge University Press, 2003).

15. The importance of "institutionalizing duties" has been defended in various places by Onora O'Neill. See, for example, O'Neill, *Bounds of Justice* (Cambridge: Cambridge University Press, 2000), chap. 6.

16. Jane Stromseth, for example, argues that codification would be premature, given the current state of international practice. Stromseth's point is that any consensus on international law should be developed out of, and built around, international practice. See Stromseth, "Humanitarian Intervention: Incremental Change versus Codification," in *Humanitarian Intervention*, ed. Holzgrefe and Keohane. For some discussion mitigating Stromseth's concern, see the chapter in that volume by Allen Buchanan, "Reforming the International Law of Humanitarian Intervention," 140ff.

INDEX

Abramson, Jeffrey, 227

Adelman, Howard, 32

Afghanistan, 203. *See also* United States

Agency: agency-based account of humanity, 190–194, 195, 206–207, 210–211; as characteristic of humanity, 212n. 10, 212n. 16; as condition of duty, 15, 16, 27n. 11, 86, 94–96, 97–102; and sovereignty, 198. *See also* Duty; Humanitarian intervention; Humanity

Aggression: aggressor-defender distinction in just war tradition, 63–64; versus intervention, 32; just v. unjust, 33–34, 40, 63–64

Albright, Madeleine: on Kosovo, 274–275; and Rwanda, 161, 181n. 24, 181n. 25. *See also* Kosovo; Rwanda

Annan, Kofi: and Rwanda, 143–144, 159–167, 179n. 15, 181n. 24; on sovereignty, 264. *See also* Rwanda; United Nations Secretary General

Aquinas, Thomas: on just war, 10, 35–44, 46, 55n. 7, 65–66, 74; on right intention v. just cause, 10; and universalism, 69; on virtue and just war, 74. *See also* Just war tradition

Aristotle, 51, 65–66

Augustine, 31, 35, 38

Authority: and community, 22; domestic v. international, 132–136; and humanitarian intervention, 8, 19, 21–24, 25, 118, 121, 124, 130–136, 198, 253–254, 260, 265–269, 269–270; of institutions in humanitarian intervention, 269–270, 272–273, 275–276; and international law, 21–24; and legitimacy, 62–63;

moral, 48–53, 57n. 21; and moral duty of intervention, 118, 121, 124, 130–136; proper authority as condition of just war, 25, 35–38, 48–53, 56n. 10; and right of intervention, 269–270; and sovereignty, 35–38, 269. *See also* Humanitarian intervention; International law; Just war; Just war tradition; United Nations Charter; United Nations Security Council

Beneficence, principle of, 27n. 4; as ground for intervention, 17; imperfect duty as, 13, 15–16, 17, 121–122, 125, 126; and love as principle in law, 12. *See also* Duty

Bodin, Jean, 213n. 22, 214n. 27

Boutros-Ghali, Boutros, 161–162

Buchanan, Allen, 291–292

Cambodia, 170, 173, 184–185n. 47

Catholicism: and just war tradition, 31–54, 55–56n. 9, 56–57n. 16; Second Vatican Council's Constitution on the Church and the Modern World (*Gaudiem et Spes*), 39, 55–56n. 9, 127. *See also* Just war tradition

Cold War, 85, 197, 203

Colonialism: 97, 266

Community: and authority, 22; in cosmopolitanism, 69–73; diversity in, 219–220; international, 37, 94–95, 99, 133–136, 137n. 9, 244–257; and law, 190, 199–206; moral, 70–73, 74–79, 82–83n. 41, 125–126, 129–130, 133–136, 244–257; morality of, 74–79,